MANAGING
THE
DIGITAL LIBRARY

MANAGING THE DIGITAL LIBRARY

Roy Tennant

Reed
PRESS

A Library Journal ® Book
Published by Reed Press ™
360 Park Avenue South
New York, NY 10010
www.reedpress.com

Library of Congress Cataloging-in-Publication Data

Tennant, Roy.
  Managing the digital library / by Roy Tennant.
    p. cm.
  Edited versions of all the author's "Digital libraries" columns
which appeared in Library journal between Nov. 1997 and Oct. 2003.
  ISBN 1-59429-020-2 (alk. paper)
  1. Digital libraries. I. Library journal. II. Title.
ZA4080 .T46 2004
025'.00285--dc22

                                            2003023949

Book design by John Reinhardt Book Design

Printed in the United States of America

10 9 8 7 6 5 4 3 2 1

ACKNOWLEDGMENTS

Among those who have informed and/or influenced my thoughts on digital libraries, whether directly or unwittingly, are Howard Besser, Stephen Chapman, Steve Coffman, Walt Crawford, Thomas Dowling, Daniel Greenstein, Brian Kelly, Anne Kenney, Anne Lipow, Clifford Lynch, Eric Lease Morgan, Andrew K. Pace, Art Rhyno, Karen Schneider, and Stephen Sloan. Anyone privileged to know these people will realize the incredible variety of influences that these individuals represent. What this says about me I will leave to your imagination.

Francine Fialkoff at *Library Journal* took a chance on me, for which I am grateful. First, Norman Oder, and then Brian Kenney, labored to make my column both informative and readable—a formidable task to which they applied themselves with dedication and grace. A good editor will always make an author sound better than he or she really is, a fact you may wish to remember as you read. Of course, any remaining slips are my own.

CONTENTS

PREFACE

You would think that after six years of writing the "Digital Libraries" column for *Library Journal* I would have nothing left to say. But although I still have moments when I wonder where the next column will come from, in general I have no trouble finding new things to write about—or topics that have changed sufficiently to warrant another look.

Such is the nature of libraries today. What we learned yesterday is not necessarily going to be what we use today, and almost certainly not what we use tomorrow. If you take anything away from reading this book, make it that the only constant is change, and that those who can foster and shape change will lead us into the future. If you are so disposed, it is you to whom I have been writing, every month for six years in *Library Journal*. In fact, it is mostly through my desire to make whatever small contribution I can to the ongoing self-education of library personnel (myself included) that keeps me writing today. Well, that and the money.

This book contains every *Library Journal* "Digital Libraries" column from its beginning in November, 1997 through October, 2003. But in creating this compilation, each column was edited, link-checked, rewritten as needed (sometimes substantially), and new content has been added. For a complete accounting of when each column ran, and in which book chapter you will find the updated version, see Appendices A and B. Note, please, that not all columns will stand the test of time well, but I thought that even those which don't would at least provide a historical perspective on digital library development, and thus may prove useful.

When I first started writing the column, I wrote with my Power-Book 145 balanced on my knees while making sure my four-year-old twins didn't drown in their bath. The following years weren't much different. Some columns were written on the road while traveling (e.g., "Reality Check: Shanghai Surprise"), while most others were cobbled together in snippets of time around other obligations. Even now, I'm writing on my PowerBook G4 while waiting in the car to pick up my kids from drama rehearsal.

I'm telling you this only as an illustration of what the life of nearly all modern professionals must surely be like. My full-time job does not provide me with enough time to keep up, to be engaged professionally, or, certainly, to write. I doubt that your job is much different. The point is that the time to do these things is never handed to you on a plate. You must get up and grasp it. You must do it because it needs doing and it's important. You must do it because you're the only one who can.

I firmly believe that to build practical, effective digital library collections and services requires more than a few technical cognoscenti. It requires more than large government grants awarded to a handful of top research universities. It takes many individual librarians—with scanners and good intentions. It takes librarians with imagination, and with the guts to do something with it. It will, in the end, take all of us. Here's hoping that six years' worth of columns will help, in some small measure, to get us all where we need to go.

Roy Tennant
Sonoma, CAL
28, September 2003

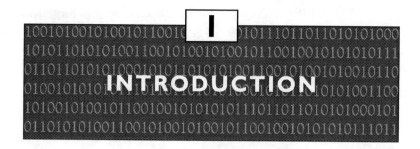

INTRODUCTION

Digital Potential and Pitfalls

The Grand Challenges

The Banal Barriers

The Digital Library Divide

The Digital Library Federation

Digital Potential and Pitfalls

With the influx of millions of dollars in grant funds and a fast-growing awareness of the potential of digital technologies to transform access to information, digital library hype has outrun reality. Scenarios of digital library futures sometimes imply that nirvana will have been reached by the early twenty-first century, wherein the whole of recorded knowledge (or at least enough for most people) will be no further away than the nearest Internet-connected computer. Therefore, I feel compelled to break my rule against predicting the future—an exercise best left to fools and geniuses—assert:

- only a very small fraction of the millions of print items currently held by the world's libraries will ever be in digital form;
- digital library collections and services enhance traditional libraries, they don't replace them; and,

- the need for services provided by real libraries and those who staff them will grow, not disappear.

Yes, we still need real libraries and skilled people to staff them. But what those staffs will be doing will be different, sometimes very different, from what they do today. This is not a prediction, but a dead certainty. How many reference librarians can completely ignore online databases, CD-ROM databases, and the web, and still do their jobs? Not many can, or should. But think back twenty years. Most reference librarians performed their jobs just fine without the very things that are now essential to adequate service. The game has changed.

How the game is changing is at the core of this book, and of the magazine column upon which it is based. Those who build digital libraries are helping to change the rules, and by so doing forge a framework that will take libraries well into this century. However, among the techniques, technologies, and draft standards that will serve as the foundation for these new libraries are research projects that will go nowhere, technologies that will never be adopted, and new paradigms that are a dime short. I will try to steer you through the mess and highlight what should be on your horizon: projects and people to watch, technologies to learn about, and how to keep current.

Defining the Digital Library

There are almost as many definitions of "digital library" as there are projects using the term, but the Association of Research Libraries (ARL), in its "Definitions and Purposes of a Digital Library," has defined a digital library as having these qualities:

- the digital library is not a single entity;
- the digital library requires technology to link the resources of many;
- the linkages between the many digital libraries and information services are transparent to the end user;
- universal access to digital libraries and information services is a goal; and,

- digital library collections are not limited to document surrogates: they extend to digital artifacts that cannot (or will not) be represented or distributed in printed formats.

ARL's broad definition of a digital library leaves a great deal of room for diversity, which is reflected in projects by the Library of Congress, the University of Virginia, the Fine Arts Museums of San Francisco, and many others.

The Digital Library Federation (DFL) defines digital libraries as "organizations that provide the resources, including the specialized staff, to select, structure, offer intellectual access to, interpret, distribute, preserve the integrity of, and ensure the persistence over time of collections of digital works so that they are readily and economically available for use by a defined community or set of communities."

Within the United States, certainly, and to some degree abroad as well, the multimillions of U.S. dollars made available, beginning in 1994, by the National Science Foundation to support research in the area of digital libraries was pivotal in bringing the spotlight to bear on this issue. Prior to the initial call for research proposals, libraries mainly discussed this issue as being one of "electronic libraries" in a typically inclusive style. That is, the term "electronic library" encompassed information available in electronic analog as well as digital form, such as early videodiscs.

However, the announcement of the NSF Digital Library Initiative was the death knell of the term "electronic library," and ever since, the term "digital library" has held sway—at least in the United States.

The initial awardees of the NSF Digital Libraries Initiative Phase 1 Awards (DLI1) were as follows:

- Carnegie Mellon, to create a multimedia library consisting of video, audio, images, and text. The research was to involve speech recognition, image understanding, and natural language support.
- The University of Illinois, to bring together disparate sources of scientific information and improve search results for federated (joined) databases.

- Stanford, to tackle the issue of interoperability, or how disparate databases can be treated as one by the user.
- The University of Michigan, to create intelligent agents to aid in locating information.

The University of California, Santa Barbara's Alexandria Digital Library, to create an interface to distribute collections of spatially referenced information (that is, anything that can be associated with a particular region of the earth). Examples include aerial photographs, seismic data, and remotely sensed digital imagery.

These projects were followed by the Digital Libraries Initiative Phase 2 Awards (DLI2) in 1999.

These projects unfortunately are not indicative of the very real progress made by line librarians in making real services available to their user communities today. For more on what I call the "digital divide" between research and production digital libraries, see "The Digital Library Divide" in this chapter.

Meanwhile, stick your neck out. Take the plunge. Leave your comfort zone and expand your horizons. Digital libraries are here to stay, and there has never been a better time to learn about what they will mean for you, your library, and your users.

Resources

ARL Digital Library Definition
    www.arl.org/arl/proceedings/126/2-defn.html
"Building Large-Scale Digital Libraries," Computer, May 1996
    computer.org/computer/dli/
Carnegie Mellon University Informedia Digital Video Library
    www.informedia.cs.cmu.edu
Digital Library Initiative Phase 1
    www.dli2.nsf.gov/dlione/
Digital Library Initiative Phase 2
    www.dli2.nsf.gov
DLF Strategic Plan
    www.diglib.org/about/strategic.htm
"The DLI Testbeds: Today and Tomorrow," D-Lib Magazine, July/August, 1996
    www.dlib.org/dlib/july96/07contents.html

Stanford University
   Interoperation Mechanisms Among Heterogeneous Services
   diglib.stanford.edu
UC Berkeley
   Environmental Planning and Geographic Information Systems
   elib.cs.berkeley.edu
UC-Santa Barbara
   Spatially referenced map information
   alexandria.sdc.ucsb.edu
University of Illinois
   Federating repositories of scientific literature
   dli.grainger.uiuc.edu
University of Michigan
   Intelligent agents for information location
   www.si.umich.edu/UMDL/

The Grand Challenges

Decades ago, our professional predecessors laid the foundation upon which so much of library technology rests. Through sheer hard work and determination, they eventually created a metadata standard for the interchange of bibliographic data between computers called Machine-Readable Cataloging (MARC).

Now we are at a similar professional crossroads, at which the particular technologies, standards, and models we choose to adopt will shape digital libraries for decades to come. But today the stakes are even higher. While MARC solved one particular problem, with digital libraries we are re-creating libraries from the bottom up, with literally no function unaffected. How digital items are selected, acquired, organized, accessed, and preserved is completely different from our familiar methods. Thus, making the wrong decisions or selecting the wrong standards or technologies can have disastrous consequences. Here are some key challenges; other parts of this book will address them in more detail...

Interoperability

A popular vision of the digital library is that a library user at one location using one interface could seamlessly search the digital collections of hundreds of libraries. To make this vision a reality, the systems we build must be able to interoperate very effectively. This will require digital library systems, nationwide and internationally, to comply with certain key standards. (In reality, we will probably see islands of noncompliance among regions of interoperability.) Interoperability on a grand scale is the digital library Holy Grail; we are doomed forever to seek it, without attainment. However, we have seen some initial successes in limited domains where draft standards are emerging. See Chapter 9 for more information.

Standards

Standards help create interoperability among different systems and a smooth migration path among technologies. One of the most important areas for standards development in digital libraries is metadata—information about information, or as librarians know it, cataloging. Metadata is the information required to manage an item, organize it among other items, make it retrievable, and in some cases, make it navigable.

There are two basic reasons why we need metadata standards. First, we need them standards for situations in which we want to record much less metadata in a much simpler fashion than full MARC cataloging. For example, many digital library collections consist of thousands (and, soon, millions) of individual items (such as photographs), many of which it would be too labor-intensive to fully catalog. These items may need to be managed as a collection instead, which calls for a different style of metadata.

Also, we need standards when we wish to record more metadata. While a book's catalog record includes the author, title, publisher, and some other key information, for the digital version we also may need to record information about how it was created (e.g., scanning resolution, bit depth, file format) and also information that allows us to create navigation systems (e.g., which is the first page?). I discuss standards more in Chapters 4 (Cataloging and Classification) and 9 (Standards and Interoperability), although they serve as an undercurrent in other chapters as well.

Rights management

Librarians are quite familiar with rights management in the print world. We buy a book, and it's ours to lend as we choose. Photocopiers only gave us a brief pause, until we posted signs by our machines warning against copyright infraction.

But in the digital environment we face some serious challenges. What comprises "fair use" in a digital environment? You will likely get very different answers from a librarian and from a publisher. Given such a confusing situation, most digital libraries avoid any copyrighted material when embarking on digitization projects. Luckily there is much material that falls into this category, largely manuscripts and archival items. For more discussion of these issues, see Chapter 11.

Preservation

You will find no digital format among the currently accepted preservation formats. Computers haven't been around long enough to determine if any digital format can be preserved effectively. Rather, when we talk about digital preservation we typically talk about a strategy, the main parts of which—as outlined in the Research Libraries Group's (RLG) "Preserving Digital Information" report—are storage, refreshment, and migration. Storage must be backed up with recovery systems should a disk drive crash or a natural disaster occur. As particular instances of storage media start to fail (e.g., a CD-ROM begins to delaminate), the information must be moved to a fresh copy of the same medium.

Migration is the most difficult problem. As entire technologies die (remember 8-track tape?), the information must be rescued in an entirely different technology, which may require entirely new or rescued access software. Much work remains to determine rescue procedures, failure prevention, and organizational structures that can manage these responsibilities. Look to the Digital Library Federation (DLF), the Research Libraries Group (RLG), the Coalition for Networked Information (CNI), and other large consortium organizations for leadership on this issue. Only by banding together will we be able to make headway on this problem. See Chapter 12 for more on this topic.

Resources

We do not create digital libraries to save money. We create them to greatly expand access, increase usability and effectiveness, and establish entirely new ways for individuals to interact with information. Rather than being cheaper to create, maintain, and preserve than print collections, the evidence so far seems to indicate the opposite. Meanwhile, we are retaining and expanding our print collections. How can we create new models for sustaining an expanded operation within a budget climate of stable or shrinking resources? How can we recruit or retrain staff for digital libraries when we're still learning what it means to build digital library collections and services? Chapters 7 and 8 touch on these issues.

User interface design

You know the problem. University students consider it a point of pride when they complete their paper solely from web resources and thus avoid entering the library. One of our most important yet most difficult tasks in creating digital libraries will be to build structures that do not leave print resources behind. We must fight our patrons' tendency to believe that everything on the Internet is now (or will be) free. See "The Convenience Catastrophe" in Chapter 5 for more discussion of this point. Also, we must design intuitive yet powerful interfaces for a wide variety of systems and resources. And the resources to be discovered will require user environments that support sophisticated operations such as selecting and charting statistics, or selecting and overlaying geographic information system coverages on a base map.

Public Services

We all know what public services we need to provide for a print collection, but what about our digital collections? Surely we still need to provide reference assistance to our virtual users as well, and luckily software is becoming available that can help us do that (see Chapter 6). But many questions remain, and only through experience will we be able to build the right mix of on-line help, live assistance, and web tools and resources to help our users find what they need.

Digital libraries are still possible without solutions to these grand challenges. But they will never achieve their potential if such solutions aren't found. When our professional descendants look back, as we now look back at the creators of MARC, it is up to us to make sure they see that the challenges were met with imagination, perseverance, and skill.

Resources

RLG's Preserving Digital Information Report
www.rlg.org/ArchTF/

The Banal Barriers

Grand challenges are all well and good, but as many a monarch has discovered, the fate of empires all too frequently turns instead on the commonplace difficulty.

Digital library development is no different. Moreover, as a new and different activity within a stable, and often staid institution, it is even more vulnerable to internal politics, individual failings, and inevitable snafus. The list below may serve as a starting point for avoiding little problems that can lead to big consequences.

Illusions of inadequacy

Ask people to name a single digital library project, and they will likely name one of the National Science Foundations (NSF), Defense Advanced Research Projects Agency (DARPA), and National Aeronautics and Space Administration (NASA) funded Digital Libraries Initiatives. These well-supported projects are indeed performing some interesting research. But the attention they draw can lead less well-funded organizations and individuals to conclude that this activity is outside their grasp.

There are, however, projects that can be done with very little funding. Many useful digital library projects are being created by reassigning existing staff and budget, or taking advantage of grant opportunities large and small. For example, Canada's University of New Brunswick is a medium-sized institution of about thirteen thousand students. At the library's web site you will find an Electronic Text Centre which hosts a number of projects—like the Maliseet-Passamaquoddy Dictionary—that would be the envy of much larger libraries. Another quite different example is the Librarians' Index to the Internet. It began as one public librarian's set of bookmarks and the desire to provide a selected, organized guide to Internet resources. Now it comprises more than twelve thousand annotated and categorized links maintained by a team of public librarians using web forms to create and update records.

If you believe your organization cannot participate because of a lack of expertise, you should know that those people currently building digital libraries are largely making it up as they go along. We're all learning here. If you want to get up to speed fast, do some background reading and arrange to visit some sites that are doing the kind of project that you are planning.

Organizational obstacles

Organizations often are not structured to encourage and facilitate change, and bureaucratic organizations are downright adversarial to it. How do you free up staff to take on a digital library project? To whom will they report? Is there an existing organizational body that can logically oversee this work and make policy decisions regarding it? Will a new organizational body need to be created, and if so, who should be the members?

All institutions have a history, and too often that history makes certain changes difficult or impossible. The people who have the most aptitude for the project may be otherwise engaged or may have a history of animosity. Problems such as these must be met with sensitivity, imagination, and patience.

Lack of commitment

One of the greatest dangers to digital library projects is the tendency to over-hype and under-support them. No one seems to have any problem envisioning a utopian future in which our users easily browse through massive collections of digital objects. But most everyone seems to have difficulty making the tough choices—like deciding what won't get done—that are required to make this vision a reality. If an organization wants to create a digital library, someone or some group of individuals must be given the time and support to do it. If the organization is unwilling to make such a commitment, then fine. But don't promise what you can't deliver.

Lack of vision

Librarians have been trained, both in school and in work, to build and manage libraries and library services in particular ways. To help ourselves break out of that mold, we need to talk with experts in other professions, read non-library journals, and query users. We need to think imaginatively, by first throwing out our common assumptions and frames of reference and then by brainstorming possible solutions. Only then should we eliminate possibilities by acknowledging our limits in funds and resources.

The perfection prison

Librarians are fond of disparaging the Internet as a jumbled mess of useful information buried in a sea of trivia. We talk smugly about how our skills and knowledge are needed to help make sense of it. We propose solutions that are too often overly complex or based only on past practices that may fail when dealing with the vast Internet environment. Meanwhile, computer scientists and graduate students created the only widely recognized solutions to the problem (e.g., Google and Yahoo!).

We need to break out of the prison we erected for ourselves which dictates that our solutions must be professionally perfect. "Good enough" is often the right solution. But by discounting such solutions in favor of perfection, we too often leave ourselves out in the cold, whining to ourselves that people should be paying attention to us.

Resources

Google
   google.com
Librarians' Index to the Internet
   lii.org
University of New Brunswick Electronic Text Centre
   www.lib.unb.ca/Texts/
Yahoo!
   yahoo.com

The Digital Library Divide

All digital library projects are not created equal. Some projects attract millions of dollars of research funding, while others create useful collections without a dime of outside support. Some projects serve only research purposes, while others produce specific online collections or services. Knowing the difference should help you to determine which projects may help you today and which may help you tomorrow.

Research projects

Digital library research projects are usually conducted by university computer science faculty. The aim is to expand our collective knowledge. A research project can be termed successful even if the only outcome is a description of the research results and a call for further research. Some research projects may also have goals that approach those of production projects (to create a useful collection or service), but they need not do so—which is often the case.

Most projects in the National Science Foundation's (NSF) Digital Libraries Initiative fall into this category. After multi-millions of dollars in federal funding was spent over nearly a decade, there is very little available that could be considered a production library collection or service. Whether any of the technologies explored in these projects will ever result in real production digital library services is anyone's guess.

Also, ostensible digital library projects may not even have

much to do with libraries as they are today, nor with how we might envision them in the near future. For example, see the research by the University of California, Berkeley (UCB), computer science department that went into "Blobworld," retrieving images by querying shapes and colors. I find it difficult to imagine a circumstance in which such an interface would be useful in a typical library setting. If you don't believe me, go there and try it out for yourself.

Production projects

Production digital library projects aim at meeting actual user needs today with existing technologies—and should be more helpful to peer libraries. For example, the Colorado Digitization Project has specific production goals for digitizing content and making it available to the citizens of Colorado and beyond. Other clear examples of production digital library projects include the Library of Congress' (LC) American Memory Project and the New York Public Library Digital Library Collection, among many others.

Although these types of projects do not tend to be truly cutting edge, they often must set up new methods and procedures from which other libraries can learn. LC has been particularly good at sharing its methods with others. (See the Building Digital Collections site.)

Librarians vs. computer scientists

There is a professional aspect to the digital library divide as well. Librarians as a whole will tend to find production projects more instructive for everyday library needs—at least in the short term—than research projects. The relatively small number of library schools in the United States means that the profession lacks a solid core of library-focused research efforts in digital libraries. Since much of the digital library research dollars are awarded to computer scientists, computer scientists set the research agenda. Generally, they lack the in-depth knowledge of library and user needs that librarians possess. Since this situation is unlikely to change dramatically, librarians should team up with computer scientists on research projects whenever possible. Funding sources for production-oriented digital library projects are also available.

Bridges across the divide

Thankfully, the divide is not without bridges. The following are examples of projects that bring together librarians and computer scientists to create functioning services that also push the knowledge envelope. These projects demonstrate that research and production can go hand in hand, and when they do they can be both groundbreaking and effective.

One of the first digital library projects that actually created a production digital library collection was the Networked Computer Science Technical Reports Library (NCSTRL, pronounced "ancestral"). NCSTRL is a worldwide network of computer science technical report repositories. All collections are searchable from any one repository, although when a particular paper is selected it is retrieved from a remote location. As a production service, this project has library participation on a number of levels. A Stanford librarian helped create a record format for the bibliographic information, and several libraries (UC Berkeley, for one) are now supporting the NCSTRL project on their campuses.

The Open Archives initiative (OAI) (see "Open Archives: A Key Convergence," in Chapter 9) has had library participation from the outset since it promises to provide a key piece of interoperability infrastructure. To some degree, it builds on the NCSTRL work in this area. Key library organizations involved in this effort include the Digital Library Federation and the Association of Research Libraries.

Since the purpose of the Dublin Core metadata initiative is to create a low-barrier syntax for encoding metadata about digital objects, it should come as no surprise that the library community led the way (via OCLC staff). But the effort now includes a number of computer science professionals and organizations worldwide, as well as participants from other disciplines. This emerging metadata standard is being used today to describe a wide variety of electronic resources in a number of different technical environments.

Building more bridges

The digital library divide is real, and it can present a barrier to communication and cooperation. But overcoming this barrier is important to both librarians and computer scientists. Librarians can learn much about new possibilities from current computer science research; computer scientists can understand better what people want, and how they expect to be able to use it, by working with librarians. Working to bridge the digital library divide is not just for large research libraries. Some projects, like OAI, have fairly low barriers to participation. Free software such as the University of Southampton "eprints" package, can give any library an Open Archives—compliant e-print repository if it has a staff member with a modicum of technical skill. We all must work to expand our horizons about what is possible and good for our users.

Resources

Blobworld
    elib.cs.berkeley.edu/photos/blobworld
Building Digital Collections
    memory.loc.gov/ammem/ftpfiles.html
Collaboration Through the Colorado Digitization Project
    www.firstmonday.org/issues/issue5_6/allen/
Dublin Core
    dublincore.org
eprints Software
    www.eprints.org
NSF Digital Libraries Initiative Phase I
    www.dli2.nsf.gov/dlione/
NSF Digital Libraries Initiative Phase II
    www.dli2.nsf.gov
NCSTRL
    www.ncstrl.org
NYPL Digital Library Collection
    digital.nypl.org
Open Archives Initiative
    www.openarchives.org

The Digital Library Federation

Note: Although dated (Daniel Greenstein now heads the California Digital Library, and David Seaman heads up the Digital Library Federation (DLF), this column is included for its historical perspective.

It was the beginning of February, 2000, and although Daniel Greenstein had been traveling for weeks, he was only halfway through his itinerary. As the new Executive Director of the Digital Library Federation (DLF), Greenstein was on a whistle-stop tour of all of the federation's twenty-three organizational members, from one U.S. coast to the other. One would expect someone with such an arduous travel schedule to be tired, but he exhibited no such symptoms as he animatedly discussed the DLF and how it may be able to help its members solve digital library problems.

His British accent hearkens back to his recent position as director of the Arts and Humanities Data Service in the U.K., where he demonstrated a clear grasp of pressing digital library issues and the ability and energy to do something about them. For example, the AHDS publication that he coauthored, "Managing Digital Collections: AHDS Policies, Standards and Practices," exhibits a well developed sense of what it means to create and manage digital collections over time.

In undertaking his whirlwind tour of the U.S., Greenstein had also demonstrated that he understands the essential purpose of the DLF—to serve its membership by helping to solve pressing digital library problems. In his presentation to members he identified four key objectives:

1. Identify tomorrow's opportunities today.
2. Leverage shared investment in research and development on the leading edge.
3. Disseminate information, raise awareness about, and propagate the use of policies, standards, practices, and tools that will govern the American national digital library.
4. Incubate innovative information services.

One purpose of his tour was to confirm those key objectives with the membership. Also, he was gathering input regarding which program areas the DLF should be active in, how well communication occurs between the DLF and its members, and whether it is organized appropriately to achieve its aims.

Among the DLF membership are twenty-three "partners," which are mostly large research libraries such as Harvard and University of California at Berkeley, as well as organizations like the Council on Library and Information Resources (CLIR) and governmental entities like the Library of Congress (LC). Participating institutions each contribute $19,000 annually toward the operating costs and $25,000 over five years to a capital fund. Each participating organization has a seat—usually filled by its executive officer—on the steering committee. In addition, the DLF includes "allies" such as OCLC and the Coalition for Networked Information (CNI) that sit on the steering committee but lack a vote (and don't pay dues). Membership dues help support the two full-time paid staff members (including Greenstein). CLIR provides a home (both digital and actual) for the federation.

A brief history

The DLF was formed as the National Digital Library Federation on May 1, 1995, by a group of sixteen large research libraries, organizations, and governmental agencies. The stated purpose was to "bring together—from across the nation and beyond—digitized materials that will be made accessible to students, scholars, and citizens everywhere and that document the building and dynamics of America's heritage and cultures." Recently "National" was dropped from the title, but the DLF remains U.S.-centric in membership and focus.

The DLF Planning Task Force Final Report in June, 1996 advised the creation of an organizational infrastructure and described several areas of activity. The areas defined as being the "business" of the federation at that point included discovery and retrieval, intellectual property rights and economic models, and archiving of digital information. In 1999, the DLF launched a publication series, with two titles now published in print and on the web.

Present initiatives

The DLF is now brokering an expanded list of areas of interest classified under the headings of Discipline-based Activities, Access Management, Digital Archiving, Discovery and Retrieval (metadata), Digital Imaging, and Digital Library Architecture. A couple of key projects under these categories are the Making of America II project and the Digital Certificate Prototype.

The Making of America II project aims to develop a method and syntax for encoding complex digital objects in a standard way, so that objects from different repositories can be used transparently by the same access tool or method. For example, if two different libraries digitize a diary in their collections, it should be possible for the same access method to retrieve and display the individual page images and transcriptions from those diaries as if they were in the same collection. To do this, there must be encoding standards that can "encapsulate" the various pieces of a digital object in an intelligent (and open) way. Five DLF library members are collaborating on this project, which has spawned the Metadata Encoding and Transmission Standard, which in turn has emerged as a key digital library standard (see discussions of METS elsewhere in this book).

The Digital Certificate Prototype aims to develop and test a protocol that enables a commercial resource provider to verify that a user is a legitimate patron of a library that has licensed the resource. Such a protocol is required, for example, to enable library patrons to access licensed library databases from home without the problems associated with other kinds of authentication (e.g., IP filtering, proxies). Key DLF participants in this effort include the California Digital Library, Columbia University, JSTOR, and OCLC.

Future directions

Despite some success in certain specific areas, the DLF has not been known for sweeping and decisive action. As is the case with many large membership organizations, the process of reaching consensus before taking action can hinder progress. The DLF has been chartered for nearly five years, with little of demonstrable significance achieved. The interests of the various players are often too divergent—ranging from private universities to public ones to public libraries—to lead to any clear, unanimous mandate, and the institutional culture of some of the participating institutions can further hamper collaboration.

But it appears that Greenstein has a plan. Rather than trying to achieve an unattainable consensus, he may use the DLF to identify key challenges, bring together the members who wish to address those challenges, and help develop collaborative solutions. In working this way, no consensus is required, and only those organizations that wish to work on a problem need to be involved. All indications are that this go-getter from across the pond is just what the DLF needs.

Resources

Arts and Humanities Data Service
  ahds.ac.uk
The Council on Library and Information Resources
  www.clir.org
Digital Certificate Prototype
  www.diglib.org/architectures/digcert.htm
Digital Library Federation
  www.diglib.org
DLF Publications
  www.diglib.org/publications.htm
Making of America II
  sunsite.berkeley.edu/moa2/
Managing Digital Collections: AHDS Policies, Standards and Practices
  ahds.ac.uk/managing.htm
NDLF Planning Task Force Final Report
  www.ifla.org/documents/libraries/net/plntfrep.htm

2
AQUISITION AND DIGITIZATION

Beg, Buy, Borrow, License, or Steal

So Much to Digitize, So Little Time (and Money)

Selecting Collections to Digitize

Everything You Always Wanted to Know About
Digital Imaging But Were Afraid to Ask

In-House Digitizing Options

OutsourcingDigitization

The Purpose of Digital Capture:
Artifact or Intellectual Content?

Beg, Buy, Borrow, License, or Steal

Acquiring intellectual content on behalf of a particular group of
users isn't always as simple as buying it outright. Librarians have
long used a blend of techniques to acquire content, but with the
advent of digital content yet another technique (licensing) has
been added to the mix. Meanwhile, we must adjust our tried-and-
true acquisition methods.

Although most libraries will use several techniques over time,
these days licensing is by far the most popular strategy (mostly

because that's what vendors offer). This may change, though, as we become more comfortable with "borrowing" content from other libraries and begin to change license agreements from leases to purchases. If that is your goal, than as Beverlee French of the California Digital Library advises, "The time to advocate change is before you sign."

Licensing and consortia

Licensing access to digital material is a new and difficult technique for library acquisition. As Leslie Harris says in an article that explains common licensing terms ("Getting What You Bargained For," *Library Journal netConnect*, Spring 2000, pp. 20-22), "Licensing, rather than ownership, raises a whole series of issues not previously experienced by librarians." These include how to integrate licensed resources with existing collections, how to catalog them or otherwise provide access, how to provide assistance, and how to negotiate contracts.

Given the complexity of negotiating licensing agreements, it is often best to accomplish it through a licensing consortium. This allows one experienced person to handle the chore; or, at the very least, the responsibility can be spread among consortium members. The International Coalition of Library Consortia (ICOLC) is a good source for information. See the document "Statement of Current Perspective and Preferred Practices" (in Resources section) for guidelines.

Consortium licensing raises new challenges, however. If the group negotiator lacks the authority to commit all the libraries to purchasing a particular product, then the negotiator won't get the best price. Prices are based on a specific number of users or libraries, so if some libraries opt out after the agreement is reached, then the contract must be renegotiated at a less favorable cost.

Whether you license content in consortia or individually, a team approach is likely to be a good idea. Library departments including collections, acquisitions, public services, and systems should be involved, since licensing digital databases or full-text content affects them all. (For more on consortium licensing, see "Where's the Fiscal Sense?," *Library Journal*, June 15, 2000, pp. 48, 50).

Key resources for licensing information and assistance include LibLicense, a site hosted by Yale University that includes a "Standard Licensing Agreement," "Principles for Licensing Electronic Resources" from the Association of Research Libraries (ARL), and the International Coalition of Library Consortia's (ICOLC) "Guidelines for Technical Issues in Request for Proposal (RFP) Requirements and Contract Negotiations." Also, the California Digital Library of the University of California offers a Licensing Tool Kit that contains licensing guidelines, selection criteria, a model license, and more.

Buying is hard

Purchasing digital content is simple in principle but difficult in practice. One difficulty is determining cost effectiveness. Digital collections offer increased functionality over print resources (full-text searching, 24/7 access, etc.) but are often more expensive. How do you decide if the price of the material is worth it to your clientele?

Unfortunately, levels of enhanced service are difficult to quantify, and so you must often make a value judgment based on little evidence. Also, in the print world you were fairly certain that the material would stick around for the foreseeable future (unless it was lost or stolen). Not so with digital material, since we only have an inkling of what it might take to preserve it over the long haul (see Chapter 12).

Borrowing could grow

The Internet allows you to provide access to the content of other libraries. Even the tiniest of libraries can point users to the massive digital collections of the Library of Congress. Still, we are far from doing this seamlessly.

But what if the Library of Congress (or other libraries with digital collections) offered MARC records for digital resources that could be loaded into your local catalog? Users often don't care where the physical item is located if they can get to it online. So "borrowing" the online collections of other libraries may become commonplace.

Any barrier to such arrangements is most likely to be political or organizational rather than technical. If even the most basic record exists for a digital item, a MARC record could be output from most systems with, at most, a simple translation script. Therefore, if we begin adding items to our catalogs on the basis of patron need rather than our need to have an inventory control system, we may see more "borrowing" of other libraries' collections.

Two places that are making this easy are the California Digital Library and the Indiana University Digital Library Program. Both locations offer significant collections of freely-accessible electronic books, and the MARC records to match. CDL's offerings are made available as "eScholarship Editions," mainly in partnership with the University of California Press, while Indiana University has focused primarily on nineteenth-century American fiction in the public domain (in their Wright American Fiction Collection). Both freely offer MARC records for their open e-books for libraries to load into their local catalogs.

Begging for value

Library development staff may quibble with the term "beg," but certainly gifts and grants can provide virtually any library with the opportunity to acquire previously unaffordable digital content. Before asking for donations, it helps to have a wish list in various topic areas, so potential donors can match their interests and funds with your needs.

"Stealing" is easy

The Internet offers a great deal of freely available content. For example, Project Gutenberg offers thousands of electronic texts—most being in the public domain and popular (albeit older) literature. The project allows any library to offer copies of these texts from its own server, or simply to offer a link.

As time goes on, this kind of public domain content will become more significant to libraries. Not only will more of it become available, but it also should improve in quality. Plain-text files (as in Gutenberg) are OK for the typical novel in English, but just about anything else requires more sophisticated presentation. As better methods become widely available for presenting non-roman text, scientific formulas, and other characters not easily represented in plain text, the breadth and quality of public domain texts will increase.

The proper mix

The appropriate mix of acquisition techniques for any particular library will vary according to local opportunities and needs. What is certain, however, is that no library can be content with only one method.

Resources

CDL Licensing Tool Kit
    www.cdlib.org/inside/collect/toolkit/
eScholarship Editions
    texts.cdlib.org/escholarship/
Guidelines for Technical Issues
    www.library.yale.edu/consortia/techreq.html
ICOLC
    www.library.yale.edu/consortia
ICOLC Statement
    www.library.yale.edu/consortia/statement.html
LibLicense
    www.library.yale.edu/~llicense/
Principles for Licensing Electronic Resources
    www.arl.org/scomm/licensing/principles.html
Project Gutenberg
    www.gutenberg.net
Standard License Agreement
    www.library.yale.edu/~llicense/standlicagree.html
Statement of Current Perspective and Preferred Practices
    www.library.yale.edu/consortia/statement.html
Wright American Fiction
    www.letrs.indiana.edu/web/w/wright2/

So Much To Digitize,
So Little Time (and oney)

So, you want to build a digital library. You have some money or some staff to throw at the project—ideally, both. Now what? More specifically, on what do you choose to spend that money and staff time to digitize? It's a good question, mostly because there is no single best answer. Rather, there are a number of issues librarians at any level must consider.

Publication rights

A primary consideration concerns what you have the right to digitize. For published material, it depends on the publication date. Generally, anything published at least seventy-five years ago is now in the public domain. For most published material less than seventy-five years old, and for unpublished material, you must receive publication permission from the rights holder. That rights holder may be the person who created it, an estate, or some other entity. Generally speaking, it's less costly to get permission to digitize unpublished or out-of-print material, but costs vary widely. For more information about copyright, see links (in Resources) to "Copyright Basics" and "How To Investigate the Copyright Status of a Work." For more information on how to research the rights holder of unpublished material, see "Locating U.S. Copyright Holders."

Choosing material

Critical mass. There should be enough related material available in one place to make the collection worthwhile to search or browse. No one wants to find only a few photographs, a couple of books, or a handful of manuscripts devoted to a topic. Therefore, you should overlook your collection of three rare published volumes and focus on, for example, your large collection of historical photographs.

Diversity of material type. It's also good to have a variety of material types united by topic. For example, an author's archive, along with published works, could include correspondence, photographs, manuscripts, and critical work. Such richness of material in one place attracts scholars and interested amateurs alike, since they can explore a person's work or a topic in a variety of ways.

Uniqueness. If you are going to spend a lot of staff time or money—and you'll do at least one, maybe both—then you don't want to stumble across a rival who beat you to your topic. So, focus on material that is unique to your library or that is highly unlikely to be digitized by others.

Reputation. If your library has already established a reputation for a strong collection in one area, build on it digitally. Your reputation as the prime source on a topic will only be enhanced by your digital collection. On the other hand, try to avoid areas in which other libraries have better-known collections, unless you are fairly certain you can establish a substantial digital presence before they do. Never underestimate the power of a committed individual with a scanner.

Money and technical questions

Preservation. Digitizing print material to preserve it is a questionable proposition at best. Nothing created or stored on a computer has lasted as long as a cheap paperback, if only because it hasn't yet had the chance. Computers have only been around for several decades; acid-free paper will last for centuries, even millennia. When you talk about digital preservation, you must consider migration, preservation strategies, and long-term institutional commitment. If you don't throw away the original after digitizing it, then you have a good chance at increasing the odds that the material won't disappear after creating a digital copy.

Audience and potential use. It's hard and, expensive work to create digital library collections and services. Before embarking on a project, you should be sure you know the target audience and what they want. Overwise, if you build it, they might not come. And if they do, the materials must be presented in ways that encourage and support exploration and use.

Available support and revenue opportunity. In the end, one of the most influential factors is funding. While this may sound crassly opportunistic, it is also realistic. Any library will have only limited (if any) funds to devote to digitizing activity. But you would do a grave disservice if you ignored the opportunity to obtain grant support. Such may not be your first choice, but something is better than nothing.

Ease/difficulty/expense. There are many different ways to digitize material. Virtually none are easy and inexpensive. Therefore, relative cost, or difficulty, may provoke you to alter your decisions. For example, the cost and expense of reproducing newsreels digitally may lead you to focus on the transcriptions instead.

Looking ahead

Access. Digitizing rare and fragile material can greatly increase access to it without harming the original. Thanks to the digital efforts of libraries around the world, anyone with access to the Internet can now view such fragile treasures as ancient papyri (see the Duke Papyrus Archive) and the Lindisfarne Gospels. (By the way, you haven't lived until you've seen this treasure using the British Library's "page turning" system.) While some believe that such digital facsimiles decrease "foot traffic," anecdotal evidence so far indicates just the opposite. Once facsimiles are easily accessible, people want to view the originals.

Experimentation. Consider picking materials to digitize that allow you to experiment with different kinds of materials and formats. One Library of Congress digital collection consists of panoramic photographs, another contains old movies, and another features large-format maps. The best situation may be to mix material types that share a common theme. For example, the Everglades Digital Library includes published works, technical reports, photographs, university course materials, brochures, and other materials.

The bottom line

When choosing a group of items or a collection to digitize, keep in mind a few very general (and seemingly conflicting) considerations. First, you may not soon get another chance. Therefore, think carefully about which digitization effort will provide the largest and most lasting impact for your users. However, you may soon get many chances, either through grant opportunities, cost recovery options, or greater institutional support. Therefore, think about how you can logically build on your digitization efforts to create critical mass and synergies from related collections. And finally, as long as you stay away from your personal bottle cap collection, it's really hard to go too far wrong. You are, after all, a librarian. You know about selection.

Resources

Copyright Basics
   www.loc.gov/copyright/circs/circ1.htm
Duke Papyrus Archive
   scriptorium.lib.duke.edu/papyrus/
Everglades Digital Library
   everglades.fiu.edu/library/
How to Investigate the Copyright Status of a Work
   www.loc.gov/copyright/circs/circ22.html
Lindisfarne Gospels
   www.bl.uk/collections/treasures/digitisation.html
Locating U.S. Copyright Holders
   tyler.hrc.utexas.edu/us.cfm

Selecting Collections To Digitize

In "So Much to Digitize, So Little Time (and Money)," I looked at the issues to be considered when selecting items or collections to digitize. There are also a number of resources available to help in making often tough decisions, aimed mostly at university and research libraries, but helpful to others as well.

One of the most important works in this area is "Selecting Research Collections for Digitization," by Dan Hazen, Jeffrey Horrell and Jan Merrill-Oldham, published by the Council on Library and Information Resources. It begins correctly with the issue of copyright, since no digitization project can get off the ground without permission to make it available (see "Before Digitizing" in Chapter

11). The paper considers issues relating to the intellectual nature of source materials; to current and potential users; to anticipated use; to the format and nature of the digital product; to describing, delivering and retaining the digital product; to relationships to other efforts; and to costs and benefits.

Do not overlook the decision-making matrix provided at the end, since it distills into one useful flowchart a process for determining if a given collection is suitable for digitization.

The British view

The Research Libraries Group (RLG) and the National Preservation Office of the United Kingdom have cosponsored a "Guidelines for Digital Imaging" conference. "Selection Guidelines for Digital Preservation" by Janet Gertz of Columbia University, and "Guidance for Selecting Materials for Digitization" by Paul Ayris of University College, London, addressed selection issues. Gertz considers selecting for preservation of the physical item, selection for access, the value of the content, the demand for the materials, intellectual property rights, the required infrastructure, the cost of digitization and its sources of funding, and the preservation of the digitized files. Ayris begins with considering the context of the digitization process and continues with categories of questions that should be considered in several areas. A U.K.-based case study is included, and Ayris concludes the paper with a decision matrix.

Moving Theory into Practice, a book by Anne R. Kenney and Oya Y. Rieger, offers the chapter "Selection for Digital Conversion" by Paula de Stefano of New York University Libraries (RLG, 2000). Noting that there are different purposes for digitization, she highlights the types of selection to match those purposes: selection to enhance access, selection based on content, and selection for preservation. Case study sidebars augment the chapter by providing additional perspectives. A fine tutorial based on this book is available online.

An outgrowth of the popular School for Scanning offered annually by the Northeast Document Conservation Center is the just-published "Handbook for Digital Projects: A Management

Tool for Preservation and Access" (NEDCC, 2000). In the chapter "Selection of Materials for Scanning," Diane Vogt-O'Connor of the National Park Service outlines a strategy for soliciting suggestions of collections to digitize from staff and stakeholders and scoring and ranking those collections for selection. Both books can also help in other stages of a digitization project.

Institutional criteria

Selection guidelines produced by individual institutions understandably are focused on the particular needs of that institution and its clientele but may inspire you. Columbia University, in "Selection Criteria for Digital Imaging," considers the issues of technical feasibility, intellectual property rights, institutional support, and the value of the materials. The University of California Preservation Program describes similar guidelines in its "Selection Criteria for Digitization."

A report by Canada's Federal Task Force on Digitization contains a section "Selection of Materials for Digitization." It provides advice to government agencies beginning such projects as well as for those seeking federal grants.

The decision

Most guidelines basically agree on some key issues, no matter what your institutional environment or clientele. Do you have the legal right? Does the material have intrinsic value that will make it popular to the target clientele? Is there potential for adding value to the material by increasing access to it, associating it with related materials, etc.? Is it unique? Is it possible per adequate institutional support, technical feasibility, etc.? If the answers are yes, then you're good to go.

Resources

Columbia University Library Selection Criteria for Digital Imaging
   www.columbia.edu/cu/lweb/projects/digital/criteria.html
Guidance for Selecting Materials for Digitization
   www.rlg.org/preserv/joint/ayris.html
Moving Theory into Practice Digital Imaging Tutorial: Selection
   www.library.cornell.edu/preservation/tutorial/selection/selection-01.html

Selecting Research Collections for Digitization
   www.clir.org/pubs/abstract/pub74.html
Selection Criteria for Preservation Digital Reformatting
   www.loc.gov/preserv/prd/presdig/presselection.html
Selection Guidelines for Preservation
   www.rlg.org/preserv/joint/gertz.html
Selection of Materials for Digitization
   www.nlc-bnc.ca/8/3/r3-409-e.html
UC Selection Criteria for Digitization
   www.library.ucsb.edu/ucpag/digselec.html

Everything You Always Wanted To Know About Digital Imaging But Were Afraid To Ask

If you are faced with managing a digital imaging project for the first time, you are probably one scared individual. There are so many variables, and few clear, unequivocal answers. Ask digital imaging experts their opinions and often the answers begin with, "It depends..." It does indeed depend... on a number of factors unique to a project and the purposes behind it.

Fortunately, there are resources to help you understand what questions must be answered and also to suggest possible answers based on "best practices." And if you want to know more, there are technical treatments available to help you build a foundation of digital imaging knowledge. Most of this assistance is just a click away.

The key questions

A key resource for those just starting identifies the main questions that need to be answered for a given project. As Howard Besser outlines in "Procedures and Practices for Scanning" (commissioned by the Canadian Heritage Information Network), these are some questions you will need to answer in the course of a scanning project:

- Do you have copyright permission? Or are these materials in the public domain?
- How are these images going to be viewed?
- How many images are going to be digitized?
- What kind of file size do you want?
- What dimensions are your thumbnail images going to be?
- How and where are you going to record information about images?
- What kind of standard information are you going to record?
- How will you maintain your work flow?
- What kind of material are you scanning?
- What kind of equipment do you have?
- How are you going to store the images?
- What file format are you going to store the images in?
- What size and quality of images do you need?
- What kind of imaging software do you need?

Lest you throw up your hands at this point, Besser provides advice on all of these. This, plus the "best practices" documents, below, should give you a good start.

Best practices information

The Library of Congress (LC) is an excellent source for "best practices" information relating to digital libraries. The document "Digital Formats for Content Reproductions" by Carl Fleischhauer, is one of the clearest resources for how to capture digital representations of different types of materials. This and other documents were created in support of the National Digital Library Program, a program in which LC works with libraries throughout the United States to make their collections available digitally. Other papers available at the "Library of Congress Background Papers and Technical Information" site provide additional background on processes related to building digital collections.

A similar document to LC's, but from the perspective of the National Archives and Records Administration (NARA), is "NARA

Guidelines for Digitizing Archival Materials for Electronic Access" (January 1998). While these guidelines were developed for internal use for a specific pilot project, they are nonetheless useful to others. Some of the guidelines are quite specific, while others are more general, or state a range of acceptable values.

If you are seeking a briefer treatment of important key issues (e.g., digitization methods for various materials, how much information to capture, what versions to provide online), then "Technical Recommendations for Digital Imaging Projects," a Columbia University project, may be all you need. In particular, a handy table provides a summary of key issues and guidelines.

By using the guidelines in these documents, you may soon be digitizing like a professional. But you should also keep in mind that these guidelines will likely change, over time, as the cost of storage continues to decrease and network speed increases. So check back now and then with the big digitization projects to make sure your own practices are current with the state of the art.

Technical background papers

While information on best practices can be helpful, sometimes you need a more complete understanding of the underlying technical issues. A number of good papers provide deeper background on technical terminology and on issues relating to digitization.

"Recommendations for the Evaluation of Digital Images" provides a thorough technical grounding in imaging as well as specific information on the evaluation of digital image quality. The report was produced by the Image Permanence Institute under contract to LC and is available in Adobe Acrobat format, which preserves its many diagrams and technical illustrations. The principal investigators were James Reilly and Franziska Frey, both experts in the field of digital imaging. This resource includes such informative discussions as "What Is Digital Resolution?"

For those who decide to digitize their material onto Kodak Photo CDs, "Using Kodak Photo CD Technology for Preservation and Access" is essential. It covers a great deal of evaluative information regarding digitizing to this format. Even those who decide to use another digitization method may find some useful advice (such as general guidelines on scanning) that can apply to their projects.

"Digital Image Collections: Issues and Practice" by Michael Ester, available from the Council on Library Information and Resources, can serve as a good introduction to digital imaging. In this 36-page paperback, Ester addresses such topics as color matching, access issues, and fidelity to the original. "Digital Imaging for Libraries and Archives" (1996) by Anne R. Kenney and Stephen Chapman was an early, and very thorough and useful resource for digital imaging projects. But now it's probably better to consult "Moving Theory Into Practice: Digital Imaging Tutorial," also from Anne Kenney. A guide that Stephen Chapman probably had a hand in creating is Harvard's "Guide to Image Digitization." This is particularly useful in showing how a specific institution has incorporated general digitization advice with guidance specific to a particular situation.

After fear, relief

Once you've looked at some of these materials, you probably won't be so frightened of the prospect of managing a digital imaging project. You are not the first one to do it. Others have not only gone before, but have made note of their decisions along the way, too.

Resources

Digital Formats for Content Reproductions
   memory.loc.gov/ammem/formats.html
Digital Image Collections: Issues and Practice
   www.clir.org/pubs/abstract/pub67.html
Moving Theory Into Practice: Digital Imaging Tutorial
   www.library.cornell.edu/preservation/tutorial/
Guide to Image Digitization
   hul.harvard.edu/ois/systems/guide_images.html
Image Scanning Helpsheet
   etext.lib.virginia.edu/helpsheets/scanimage.html
Introduction to Imaging
   www.getty.edu/research/institute/standards/introimages/

Library of Congress Background Papers and Technical Information
memory.loc.gov/ammem/ftpfiles.html
NARA Guidelines for Digitizing Archival Materials for Electronic Access
www.archives.gov/research_room/arc/arc_info/guidelines_for_digitizing_archival_materials.pdf
Procedures and Practices for Scanning
sunsite.berkeley.edu/Imaging/Databases/Scanning/
Recommendations for the Evaluation of Digital Images
memory.loc.gov/ammem/ipirpt.html
Technical Recommendations for Digital Imaging Projects
www.columbia.edu/acis/dl/imagespec.html
Using Kodak Photo CD Technology for Preservation and Access
www.library.cornell.edu/preservation/kodak/kodak-htm.htm

In-House Digitizing Options

Once you've selected the material you want to digitize, you must decide how to capture the digital surrogate. One option is to find a commercial digitization company (see "Outsourcing Digitization" in this chapter for more information). But you may decide to do it yourself, and if so you should consider the following methods.

All of these options concern "capturing" individual dots, or "pixels," of information that can then form a digital surrogate for the original item. In almost all cases, the captured file will be further processed before it is made available on a web site or in a database. The quality of the derivative file likely will never be as good as the original scan, due to the loss of information through file compression or file editing (sharpening the image, for example). Therefore, aim to create the highest quality original scan. For good, basic information on digital imaging concepts and techniques, see Kodak's Digital Learning Center.

Flatbed scanners

Probably the single best known digitization technology is the flatbed scanner. As an example of this, people often talk about "scanning" a work rather than digitizing it. Scanners vary widely in price, from less-than-$100 low-end consumer devices to professional machines that cost $3000 or more. You must consider a variety of factors, including budget, the quality of the result, the durability of the device, scanning speed and customer support.

For most general digital library purposes, a scanner costing in the $500—$800 range will generally be fine. For high-volume scanning of individual sheets (either unbound material or bound material that has had the binding sliced off), an automatic sheet-feeder is a must. Note: except for the case when a binding is slashed, most materials—except truly fragile ones—can be scanned without damage.

When shopping for a flatbed scanner, the two main quality specifications are optical resolution and bit depth. The former describes the number of pixels (or "dots") per inch (dpi) that the scanner can physically capture. These days, you shouldn't settle for less than1200 x 2400 dpi optical resolution. Bit depth refers to the number of gray or color shades the scanner can capture. Most flatbed scanners can capture 42 to 48 bits of information per pixel. Also consider the bed size (will you be scanning material larger than 8 1/2" x 14"?) and whether the scanner will complete the scan in a single "pass" of the internal scanning device, thereby allowing for faster scans. If you are digitizing to capture the text via optical character recognition (the transformation of scanned text from a picture into editable text), grayscale scanning (rather than color) is sufficient, but you won't find a scanner that just does gray these days, and in any case a color scanner can do grayscale scanning just fine.

Slide/film scanners

Although some flatbed scanners offer a "transparency adapter" option or add-on, flatbed scanners normally aren't as good as special-purpose devices for negatives or slides. Slide scanners are optimized to capture a high-pixel density from small format slides and negatives. These scanners generally cost $400—$2000. The optical resolution of these devices generally runs in the 3600 dpi range, which is not as impressive as it might sound considering that the "master" scanned is generally much smaller than the page of a book or a photographic print.

Digital cameras

The digital camera market contains two basic categories: inexpensive consumer devices ($100—$1500, with most costing under $500) and very expensive production devices ($15,000—$35,000). Inexpensive cameras can be found at camera stores, in computer mail-order catalogs, and even in general retail stores. They generally can't produce high-quality masters of documents and photographic prints, but they may work if you don't need a high-resolution master. For a ton of information on digital camera equipment and photography aimed at the consumer, see ShortCourses.com. To compare various products, try the Digital Photography Review site.

Most digital library projects will require the resolution and production capacity of the high-end cameras. These are largely digital camera backs that are attached to a normal 35mm single-lens reflex camera or 3x5 camera. They are most often attached to a copy stand that allows the camera to be moved up or down over a table upon which the item being photographed is placed (often under a sheet of glass to force the original flat).

Kodak PhotoCD

Alternatively, any roll of film from a standard camera can be "developed" onto a Kodak PhotoCD, which provides high-resolution digital files. No special equipment is required, just special processing. (Any photo finishing service should be able to send this out.) The images are stored on the CD in the Kodak ImagePac format (also known as PCD), which can then be read, edited, and saved in a different format (e.g., JPEG, for delivery on the web) using image-editing software such as Adobe Photoshop. For more information, see "Using Kodak PhotoCD Technology for Preservation and Access."

General Assistance

For good overall information and guidance on planning and executing an in-house digitization project, see "Guides to Quality in Visual Resource Imaging" from RLG and the Digital Library Federation. Also, books like NEDCC's "Handbook for Digital Projects" and "Moving Theory Into Practice" are very helpful as well.

Resources

Digital Photography Review
   www.dpreview.com
Guides to Quality in Visual Resource Imaging
   www.rlg.org/visguides/
Handbook for Digital Projects
   www.nedcc.org/digital/dighome.htm
Kodak Digital Learning Center
   www.kodak.com/US/en/digital/dlc/book3/
Moving Theory Into Practice
   www.rlg.org/preserv/mtip2000.html
ShortCourses.com
   www.shortcourses.com
Using Kodak PhotoCD Technology for Preservation and Access
   www.library.cornell.edu/preservation/kodak/cover.htm

Outsourcing Digitization

Digitizing in-house may be the right path for some projects (see "In-House Digitizing Options," above) but for other projects it may be better to outsource the digitization to a commercial company.

Why outsource?

There are several reasons why you should consider letting someone else digitize your material:

Expense. Unless you already have a digitization infrastructure established, you must make significant investments in both technical capability and staff expertise to digitize in-house.

Expertise. If you don't anticipate a regular schedule of digitization, or if certain projects are unique, you may not want to invest in such expertise.

Time. It's time-consuming to train in-house staff or to hire experienced help.

For more on the pros and cons of outsourcing, see "Digital Imaging for Libraries and Archives", in which experts Anne R. Kenney and Stephen Chapman outline advantages and disadvantages of both approaches. The decision depends on a variety of factors unique to each project, e.g., how much control you wish to have over the entire process, whether you know your requirements in advance or not, what kind of throughput you need to achieve, and if you have fragile or rare materials.

Kodak PhotoCD

In "In-House Digitization Options," I discussed using Kodak PhotoCD as an option. In reality, when using Kodak PhotoCD, the image capture part of the process is accomplished in-house, but the digitization of the images is outsourced. This combination allows libraries to retain control over the material, which may be fragile or rare, while using the expertise, capability, and efficiency of vendors to digitize the images. With this option, you photograph the material using a standard 35mm camera and copy stand, then send the film out to be "developed" onto a Kodak PhotoCD. The images are returned on one or more CDs in five different resolutions (including thumbnails), from which you can create viewing versions for the web. For more information on this format, see "Using Kodak PhotoCD Technology for Preservation and Access," by Anne R. Kenney and Oya Y. Rieger. For a description of how a particular project used this method, see "Digitizing the California Heritage Collection: Image Capture."

A digitization vendor

A digitization project is typically outsourced by contracting for the services of a digitization vendor, a commercial firm that specializes in digitizing. Even the Library of Congress (LC) has found this method to be fruitful, particularly when dealing with odd-sized originals that may require expensive specialized equipment. The article "Imaging Pictorial Collections at the Library of Congress" is a useful description of one such project.

Metadata questions

No matter who does the digitization, it's essential to capture information that describs the item being digitized as well as the digitization process used. If you outsource the process you must be sure you can link up your descriptive metadata information that describes the item, mostly for discovery and retrieval purposes—with the appropriate digital object when it is returned from the vendor. Also, if you need metadata about the digitization process—administrative metadata such as the scanning hardware used, etc.—you must be explicit with the vendor about what is required.

If all you require is information that is likely to be the same for all or most of the materials (such as the scanning hardware used), then the capture of metadata is unlikely to be problematic or costly. But if you require metadata specific to each image, then the increased cost to acquire and record that metadata may be significant. Also, it will require work on your part to provide detailed specifications for metadata capture.

Outsourcing resources

When outsourcing a project, most government-supported institutions must put a project out for competitive bidding. The main tool for this is a Request for Proposal (RFP). According to the Research Libraries Group (RLG), the RFP aims to "convey the terms and conditions of an institution's digital imaging project to potential service providers." It also provides a documentary foundation that will be used in creating the digital imaging service contract.

An essential guide to creating such an RFP is the "RLG Guidelines for Creating a Request for Proposal for Digital Imaging Services." This and other helpful documents can be found at the RLG Tools for Digital Imaging web site. LC has made several of its RFPs for digital imaging available at the American Memory Background Papers and Technical Information site. Although the papers date back to 1996 and 1997, a lot of the text still applies.

Once you have the RFP written, you must send it to potential bidders. One good source for such vendors is the Digital Imaging Vendors list at the Colorado Digitization Project. The best overall resource for learning about outsourcing a digitization project remains "Digital Imaging for Libraries and Archives," which covers services that vendors can be expected to perform, how to locate and evaluate potential vendors, and the entire RFP process, from proposal development to contract preparation. A library school student paper ("Outsourcing Digitization" by Kara Malenfant and Jennifer McCarty) takes a look at this topic as well, and points to some additional resources on outsourcing library services (although some resources are aimed at traditional library activities such as cataloging, and be aware that the paper is becoming dated).

Looking to the future

As digitizing materials becomes more commonplace, and as hardware and software increase in capability while falling in price (a common trend), it should become less expensive to digitize library materials. Also, as more libraries take on digitizing projects, vendors will gain more experience at meeting our needs. Still, even now, outsourcing digitization can be a savvy decision.

Resources

American Memory Technical Information & Background Papers
    memory.loc.gov/ammem/ftpfiles.html
Digital Imaging Vendors
    www.cdpheritage.org/resource/scanning/rsrc_vendors.html
Digitizing the California Heritage Collection: Image Capture
    sunsite.berkeley.edu/CalHeritage/image.html
Imaging Pictorial Collections at the Library of Congress
    www.rlg.org/preserv/diginews/diginews3-2.html
Moving Theory Into Practice
    www.library.cornell.edu/preservation/tutorial/
"Outsourcing Digitization"
    leep.lis.uiuc.edu/seworkspace/malenfan/437/
RGL Tools for Digital Imaging
    www.rlg.org/preserv/RLGtools.html
Using Kodak Photo CD Technology for Preservation and Access
    www.library.cornell.edu/preservation/kodak/cover.htm

The Purpose of Digital Capture: Artifact or Intellectual Content?

It's a visceral, deeply affecting feeling to hold a very old book in your hands, gently turning the brown and fragile pages, experiencing the unique smell of aged paper, and having a physical link to history. Others who lived before you have touched and read these same pages. We tend to look differently at old books merely because of their age. A school primer that wouldn't get a second glance today may someday be cherished. That's also what makes digitization of such materials so darn hard.

Reproducing old books

If all we wanted to do were to capture the intellectual value of a book, it would be relatively easy. We could digitize many books in shades of gray ranging from white to black. (Who needs to know the paper has deteriorated to a warm, yellowish patina?) Since the file size would be much smaller than that required by a full-color scan, we could afford to capture a much higher resolution file with more detail. We could even use software to recognize only the letters in the resulting image and toss the image entirely, saving just the electronic text. After all, the intellectual value of a book is in what it says, right? Not in the graphic depiction of the text, its layout on the page, or the embellishment of leading capitals. Well...maybe, maybe not.

As any historian, rare book dealer, or archivist would be happy to tell you, it isn't quite that simple. Very old books can be valuable for reasons other than their content. How the book has been printed, illustrated, and bound can be of great interest to scholars. Thus, some digital publishers strive to reproduce old volumes as closely as possible to their original physical manifestations using digital technology. One such digital publisher is Octavo, Inc., which specializes in reproducing very old and rare books in digital editions. It partners with several libraries, including the Library of Congress (LC) and the New York Public Library. Octavo makes no attempt to clean up the warped pages and water stains that have accumulated over the centuries, preferring instead to ensure that what the camera sees is what the customer gets. The purpose of such fidelity to the original is to give readers an experience with the text that is as close to reality as possible.

Improving old photos

Old photographic prints often appear brownish, faded, and cracked. However, most of this is reparable using image-editing software, such as Adobe Photoshop. But what do you want to accomplish? Do you want the user to experience the artifact, in all its faded glory, or a close approximation of the original? This is a tough question, partly because you do not want your users to be disappointed if they discover the actual print. Take, for example, a photograph of Teddy Roosevelt and John Muir at Yosemite. The version available at the California Heritage collection at the University of California looks different from that at LC. Either the former has deteriorated more over time, or LC has digitally enhanced its version for clearer viewing, or they digitized from the negative rather than the print.

But digitizing the negative instead of the print carries its own peril. Negatives are only the raw material for prints. Photographers such as Ansel Adams spent a good deal of time and effort in the printing process to achieve a specific photograph. What, then, is the "real" version of a photograph?

Masters and derivatives

Digital librarians find it useful to make a distinction between a master file and its derivatives. The purpose of a master file is to capture as much information as is possible or practical regarding an item exactly as it currently appears and save it with no information loss from compression or editing. Due to the large sizes of such master files, smaller derivative images are then created for online viewing. Creating viewable images presents the opportunity to sharpen them, increase the contrast, or perform any number of other manipulations or enhancements to offer versions which are better than the original scan.

Making the tough decisions

As I've said about access, the bottom line is: more is better. In the case of photographs, this means offering both versions to the user—a copy of the item "as is" and a copy that has been enhanced or transformed to provide additional legibility, usability, or clarity. With books it's not quite so simple. Because of the large number of files involved and their sizes when scanned, you will want to choose between reproducing the "look" of the book as well as the content, or simply capturing the content. As always, before making a decision, consider carefully the needs of the diverse audiences you wish to serve.

Resources

California Heritage Photograph
   sunsite.berkeley.edu/FindingAids/dynaweb/calher/corners/figures/
   z052.jpg
Library of Congress Photograph
   memory.loc.gov/pnp/amrvp/3c07389r.jpg
Octavo
   www.octavo.com

3

BUILDING COLLECTIONS

The Emerging Role of E-Books

The Other E-Books

Institutional Repositories

Electronic Theses and Dissertations: Progress?

Open Access Journals

The Emerging Role of E-Books

In my very first "Digital Libraries" column in *Library Journal*, I asserted that print books were going to be around for quite some time ("Digital Potentials and Pitfalls," *Library Journal*, vol. 122, no. 19, November 15, 1997, pp: 21-22.). Shortly thereafter, I advocated that we should get better at providing combined access to both digital and print material ("The Print Perplex: Building the Future Catalog," *Library Journal*, vol. 123, no.19, November 15, 1998, pp.224). My opinion has not weakened over time but rather has strengthened.

That column came out before all the hype about e-book companies, services, and devices, so I simply focused on the retrospective conversion problem. The dilemma remains intractable (cost, copyright, etc.) and suffices to point to a hybrid environment for the foreseeable future. But what about new material? What about e-books and e-book readers? How will they fit into our mix of collections and services?

E-book hype notwithstanding, there are still many purposes for which they are not the right solution. From board books for toddlers to coffee-table books for adults, e-books are unlikely to unseat print completely as the format of choice. But clearly there are also clearly places where they do fit and in which they are increasingly likely to replace print books.

E-book niches

Any book aimed at students is prime territory for an e-book. When I was a student, I lugged dozens of pounds of textbooks from class to class. (Who needed P.E.?) For students, e-books are clear winners. One slim device is all that's required to put dozens of titles at the fingertips, along with annotation capabilities, easy dictionary look-ups, etc. E-books seem made-to-order for students. The problem is that libraries typically don't purchase textbooks. Nonetheless, just about any nonfiction title, particularly those that are used in reference or quick look-up fashion, seem appropriate as e-books.

Another niche that seems ready for e-books is the one occupied by technical books. Software programmers, web managers, systems administrators and others in technical fields must constantly refer to manuals, how-to books, and other documentation in the course of their work. The search capabilities of e-books, as well as the benefit of having dozens of books in one small device, make e-books an excellent solution for these professionals.

One technical book publisher that seems to understand this is O'Reilly & Associates. They offer something called Safari Bookshelf, which goes beyond simply mounting its books online. Subscribers are able to search and browse the books to which they subscribe through a unified interface that lets them pull content together at a level deeper than chapters.

A potential audience for e-books (identified by Roberta Burk in "Don't Be Afraid of E-Books," *Library Journal,* vol. 125, no. 7, April 15, 2000, pp. 42-45) are people who enjoy series books, or books in a particular genre (e.g., mysteries). Libraries can provide an e-book reader with all of an author's titles, and the borrower can happily plow through the collection.

E-books and libraries

E-books come in device-dependent formats made specifically for a particular reading device such as the Rocket eBook or SoftBook Reader (neither of which are still on the market) or device-independent formats delivered either as Adobe Acrobat files, Microsoft Reader files, or online directly to a web browser (e.g., as does netLibrary).

Device-dependent e-books bring with them particular challenges for libraries, since the device—not just the content—must be managed. Imagine, for example, if we still had to check out VCRs along with the videotapes we offer for loan. Add to that the difficulty of each VCR being preloaded with a certain set of titles, none of which could be used by someone who checked out a different VCR. Perhaps some day we can expect people to own the readers themselves, as they now do with VCRs, but not yet. As Burk reports, it is necessary to not only catalog the individual e-book titles but also on which reader they are loaded. When a user checks out that particular e-book, all the titles on that reader must also be checked out. Therefore, the selection of books loaded on the readers requires much thought.

For a while it appeared that the Rocket eBook and SoftBook Reader might be gaining some market traction, but not enough consumers were ready to pay hundreds of dollars for these special-purpose devices, so they are both now defunct (after first being bought up by Gemstar International Group).

The new kids

E-books that are independent of a particular reading device are usually web-based, but they can also be published on CD-ROMs, DVDs, or other formats. One major e-book vendor of device-independent e-books is netLibrary, now a part of OCLC, which directly courts the library market as one of its core clientele. netLibrary has been successful at signing on a number of university presses, thereby making its offerings particularly enticing for colleges and universities. Since the user is not required to have a particular reading device to use the e-books, libraries need not stock nor manage any special hardware. Similar companies that provide web-based e-books include Books24x7 (which at this point is primarily focused on technical books related to computers), and ebrary.

Not to be left out, Microsoft has waded into the pool with the Microsoft Reader software that it says makes online reading easier. The software is designed to be used on devices ranging from pocket PCs to desktops and will be able to read books coded using the Open eBook markup standard. An application is available that converts text and HTML into Microsoft's proprietary reader format.

One final note: don't buy anything as an e-book that you hope to keep around for a long time. Digital preservation is still a problem in search of a solution, and proprietary digital formats are particularly troublesome.

Making a difference

One of the best sites for those wanting to explore e-book issues is the Open eBook Forum, an "international trade and standards organization for the electronic publishing industries.Ó Although most participants come from the publishing industry, there are also some librarians involved, particularly in the Library Special Interest Group (SIG). This is our chance to make our needs heard within the e-book publishing community, beyond publishing e-books ourselves. See ÒThe Other E-BooksÓ in this chapter.

Resources

Books24x7
   www.books24x7.com
Books of the Future
   www.tk421.net/essays/ebooks.pdf
ebrary
   www.ebrary.com
Microsoft Reader
   www.microsoft.com/reader/

netLibrary
    www.netlibrary.com
Open eBook Forum
    www.openebook.org
Open eBook Forum Library SIG
    www.openebook.org/oebf_groups/library.htm
O'Reilly's Safari Bookshelf
    safari.oreilly.com

The Other E-Books

When people refer to e-books, they typically mean device-depen-dent e-books such as those formerly marketed by Gemstar. These are also what most people probably think of when hearing the term "e-book"—a device that is similar in size and shape to a hardback book but is in fact a special-purpose computer. If not, then they usually mean those marketed by netLibrary or others that deliver e-books for a fee on the Internet to standard web browsers. The term only infrequently seems to encompass efforts by libraries, universities or others to publish e-books on the net for free. That's too bad, since these efforts are significant and are likely to last longer than those of commercial companies using unproven economic models. In particular, I believe that device-dependent e-books (what the Coalition for Networked Informa-tion's Clifford Lynch has called e-book reading "appliances") are particularly vulnerable to common sense. See "Bringing Out the Dead (Technologies)" in Chapter 8.

Niche needs

Device-dependent e-books are likely to be important for niche audiences (such as students who must lug around fifty pounds of print books), but they are unlikely to take the world by storm. This has apparently occurred to Gemstar, which discovered that hardly anyone wanted to spend $400 for a device that will only allow them to read e-books—and only Gemstar-formatted e-books at that—and which in turn forced the company to retreat to publishing *TV Guide,* leaving the e-book market to those with deeper pockets or better intentions. Meanwhile, universities, libraries, and other not-for-profit publishers will still be around, publishing e-books in open, nonproprietary formats in ways that promote and enhance preservation and access.

National Academy Press

The National Academy Press (NAP) has been putting the complete texts of books online for free for years. NAP is somewhat famous for doing so, and for stating that it has actually increased sales of the hard copy versions, despite the contrary fears of commercial publishers. As an early adopter of web publication, NAP forged its own path to web production by creating a software infrastructure called "Open Book" (not to be confused with the Open e-Book markup standard). As a not-for-profit publisher, NAP intends to make much of its in-house-developed software available free as open source.

NAP's Open Book infrastructure provides a full-featured environment for using the books on the web. The book is displayed as one graphic image at a time, but a robust user interface provides just about any desired option. Browsing options include forward and back navigation, a jump to the table of contents, and the selection of a particular page or chapter. The user can search one chapter, one book, or the entire corpus from any page display. If the image is too small, one can click a button to provide a larger version. Clicking the print button will fetch that page as an Adobe Acrobat file for printing (rather than the page image that is the default display).

eScholarship Editions

Using a very different publication model, eScholarship (an initiative of the California Digital Library) has created an online publishing imprint, "eScholarship Editions," and partnered with the University of California Press to offer over one thousand of its titles online. By making some of these books available for free on the web (at least 400 at last count), the press hopes to spur additional print sales by attracting customers who were previously ignorant of the existence of the titles. It is still too early to tell if this will prove true. Soon other presses may join UC Press under the eScholarship Editions imprint.

The books are all marked up in XML (see "XML: The Digital Library Hammer" in Chapter 8) to provide an open, nonproprietary storage format. Each book is stored as one file of the full text and any associated graphic images. When the user requests to view a particular chapter of the book from the table of contents, that chapter is extracted from the XML-encoded book and translated into HTML with an accompanying Cascading Style Sheet (CSS).

Since the book is translated on the fly before being presented to the user, various interesting possibilities arise. For example, a large-print version can be easily offered simply by creating a different CSS style sheet. To go even further, users may eventually be able to create their own PDF version of the book for downloading. Options to search or buy the book in print are available in the table of contents and individual chapters. Since many of the books are publicly available, it is easy to see how the University of California approaches e-book publishing. By being stored in a standard way that is both human-readable and easily interpreted by software, these books are much more likely to be migrated into whatever future formats are required for long-term preservation.

Back at the ranch

Despite what happens to the e-book market in general, there will be a growing legacy of free online content that libraries can make available to their clientele. At least for the forseeable future, books will be published online in various ways and with varying user interfaces. This means that should a library want to publish content online, there will be examples of how to do it as well as tools and software that have proven track records in handling these kinds of publications.

But let's not kid ourselves—online books are intended for online use. Printing entire copies of online books is neither cost-effective nor particularly pleasing. A bound volume is much more useful than a pile of unbound pages printed on one side. So at least for a while, online books of any stripe will be used online, and "offline" books (or "p-books," for print books) will continue to be used offline. The projects noted above as well as others such as the University of Virginia's Electronic Text Center are built on the assumption that the books will be used online and only parts will be printed or copied for insertion into papers. The advantage of such online books comes via options that are not possible with print books—automated searching, linkages to additional content, and alternative displays for particular needs (e.g., large print).

It's also worth noting that one of the most robust storage formats for text is plain ASCII text. It can't be made to look very pretty, as more enriched formats like XML can support, but it is nonetheless unlikely to ever become unreadable. And as far as free, plain-text e-books are concerned, Project Gutenberg has virtually cornered the market.

So, the next time you hear the term "e-book," remember that the term encompasses many more options than those typically highlighted by the popular press. Projects like those cited may not make it into stories about e-books and the latest e-book appliances, but they are e-books nonetheless, and they likely will outlast their flashier cousins.

Resources

California Digital Library
   www.cdlib.org
eScholarship Editions
   texts.cdlib.org/escholarship/
National Academy Press (NAP)
   www.nap.edu
NAP Open Book
   www.nap.edu/info/site.html
netLibrary
   www.netlibrary.com
Project Gutenberg
   www.gutenberg.org
University of Virginia Electronic Text Center
   etext.lib.virginia.edu

Institutional Repositories

Faculty and researchers at universities worldwide gather and interpret data, advocate new ideas, and extend human knowledge. This work is sometimes shared with other scholars and researchers as working papers, technical reports, and other forms of prepublication work. Although such scholarship may eventually show up in a peer-reviewed journal or book, some may not. This "preprint culture" is strongest in scientific and technical disciplines, but social scientists share similar materials. This "grey literature" is often difficult to find and even more difficult for librarians to collect systematically, manage, and preserve (see "What Is Grey Literature?" in the *Resources* list). But the web and other digital technologies are changing all that. A variety of web-based systems is becoming available for accepting deposits of papers. These systems make the research output of institutions easier to discover and to manage and preserve. They also make it possible to share information globally through compliance with a standard metadata harvesting protocol.

For an institution wishing to implement a repository, there are now implementation models to consider and software decisions to make. Although you will need to know more to set up a repository, here is a beginning road map. If you want further information, your next move should be to read the recently released "The Case for Institutional Repositories: SPARC Position Paper."

Software

Some systems are open source, while others are commercial. The first open source solution to become available was ePrints, a project from the U.K.'s University of Southampton. The ePrints solution is squarely focused on faculty working papers (also called preprint or e-print). The ePrints model assumes that faculty will directly upload their own prepublication scholarship for open access via an institutional or subject-based repository. A number of institutions are now using this software, including CalTech and the Digital Library of the Commons at Indiana University.

Another open source system is DSpace, developed through a partnership between the MIT Libraries and Hewlett-Packard. DSpace is designed to be a more flexible solution than ePrints. It makes fewer assumptions regarding what type of object is being uploaded. Since the programmer who developed ePrints is now a key developer with the DSpace project, DSpace has roots in ePrints but has clearly surpassed it. MIT is not the only user of the system, and they have formed the DSpace Federation as a DSpace user support system.

The Berkeley Electronic Press (bepress) offers a commercial solution. Bepress provided a sophisticated solution for peer-reviewed journals when the University of California entered into a co-development agreement with the press to add key features for institutional repository support. Now the bepress software is both compliant with key standards and simpler to use for those who do not need the peer-review capabilities.

Implementation models

The software platform is but one essential step to creating an institutional repository. Perhaps more important is identifying an appropriate implementation model. There are nearly as many models as there are institutional repositories, but focusing on a few examples may highlight some important differences.

MIT uses a distributed model, championed by Southampton's Stevan Harnad and others as "self-archiving," whereby individual faculty upload and manage their own scholarly output. DSpace has the widest focus of any repository described here; it explicitly welcomes any scholarly object. "Educational material in digital formats (e.g., online lecture notes, visualizations, simulations, original graphics) are some of the most valuable assets produced by colleges and universities today and are extremely important to the faculty that create them," says Mackenzie Smith, DSpace's project director. "Much of this material is really like a new kind of publication and clearly needs to be captured, managed, and often preserved... what better place to take responsibility for this than the library?"

The University of California's eScholarship uses a semi-distributed model that assigns management responsibility to organizational units (research units, departments) that then assist faculty with uploading their papers. CalTech uses a semi-centralized model, wherein repository sites can be set up for any university unit, but the library uploads the papers on the faculty's behalf. Its digital collections range from computer science technical reports to theses and dissertations.

It is too early to tell what benefits will accrue to each model, but it is highly unlikely that any single model will work for all institutions. Each institution should consider alternative models in light of its particular circumstances.

Federation for free

Any institution implementing a repository using one of the software solutions described above will automatically expose its metadata to harvesting through the Open Archives Initiative Protocol for Metadata Harvesting (OAI-PMH). This protocol establishes a standard way for metadata about digital objects to be harvested (retrieved by software) from any repository that complies with the protocol. This metadata can then be indexed along with other harvested metadata to provide one-stop searching for papers on a particular topic.

For example, just days after the eScholarship Repository opened in April, 2002, records for papers in that repository were showing up in locations such as the EconPapers site. Meanwhile, a project of the University of Michigan called OAIster (say 'oyster') has harvested over half a million records for digital resources using the Open Archives protocol. A significant number of these records come from institutional repositories.

Economic models

All of the repositories highlighted here began with support from their libraries. How each of these institutional repositories will be sustained over time may vary as much as the implementation models, but in all cases the long-term economic model is unclear. Will each academic institution decide to fund the repository as part of the basic infrastructure? Or will it require the library to charge participating departments for their use of the infrastructure? Although many active in the field expect institutions to fund these services as part of the underlying support for the academic enterprise, it is not yet clear that university administrations will agree.

Subject terminologies

One of the thorniest issues is the lack of a single, controlled vocabulary for fields of scholarly pursuit. For example, "medicine" may be a perfectly legitimate subject heading for one university, while it would be ridiculously broad for a medical school. When searching or browsing a specific repository, this may not be much of a problem. But as access to institutional repositories becomes federated in central portals, it becomes more problematic. How can a user profitably browse papers from a variety of repositories that use very different subject terminologies?

Publication and removal

Since at least some of what is being deposited in institutional repositories is "prepublication," at least a few will be published in a journal. In some cases, faculty may request that their papers be removed from the institutional repository. eScholarship allows removal of papers, although a citation must always remain. CalTech is more conservative in that it disallows removal. If the journal publisher does not require the removal of the prepublication version, it may still be useful for a reader to discover that a preprint was subsequently published by a journal. Putting such information into the record in the institutional repository is typically the responsibility of whoever deposited the paper originally.

From grey to black and white

Although the software and implementation model that an institution chooses to employ is still anyone's guess, the likelihood that universities and research institutions will implement something is increasing. Institutional repositories fill an important void and are likely to remain a part of our information landscape. They provide much better access to a given body of literature than has ever previously been possible and should be a no-brainer for most academic institutions.

Resources

bepress
  bepress.com
Caltech Collection of Open Digital Archives
  library.caltech.edu/digital
The Case for Institutional Repositories: a SPARC Position Paper
  www.arl.org/sparc/IR/ir.html
Digital Library of the Commons
  dlc.dlib.indiana.edu
DSpace
  www.dspace.org
EconPapers
  econpapers.hhs.se
ePrints
  www.eprints.org
eScholarship
  www.cdlib.org/programs/escholarship.html
eScholarship Repository
  repositories.cdlib.org/escholarship
Institutional Repositories at SPARC
  www.arl.org/sparc/core/index.asp?page=m0
OAIster
  www.oaister.org
Open Archives Initiative
  www.openarchives.org
SPARC Institutional Repository Checklist & Resource Guide
  www.arl.org/sparc/IR/IR_Guide.html
SPARC-IR Discussion List
  mx2.arl.org/Lists/SPARC-IR/
What Is Grey Literature?
  www.nyam.org/library/greylit/whatis.shtml

Electronic Theses and Dissertations Progress?

Somehow the art of Salvador Dalí seems to be an appropriate accompaniment to an eclectic group of people interested in electronic theses and dissertations (ETDs). In March, 2000 an international group of librarians, computer scientists, university administrators and graduate students were sipping wine and munching hors d'oeuvres at the Salvador Dali Museum in St. Petersburg, Florida, at the reception for the Third International Symposium on Electronic Theses and Dissertations (TISETD).

The art is surreal, but the participants were in earnest. Some attendees—such as those in the Networked Library of Theses and Dissertations (NDLTD)—had been working in the field for a decade or more, while others were there only because a university dean or provost told them to attend. But they all shared an interest in accepting and providing access to theses and dissertations submitted electronically.

There are several ways by which universities provide access to their ETDs, as well as various permutations and combinations of these methods. How this will shake out remains, unfortunately, an open question.

UMI, XML, and other formats

The easiest way for a library to make its theses and dissertations available online is to let a commercial company do it. UMI Dissertation Services (part of Bell and Howell Information and Learning) can provide copies of over one million theses and dissertations, with more than 100,000 available online as Adobe Acrobat files.

After the ETD has been accepted, it is simply forwarded to UMI, which then creates an Adobe Acrobat version of the file and provides access free to the originating university. Other users must pay a fee that ranges from the lowest charge for online download of the Adobe Acrobat version to the most expensive version printed on paper between hard covers (roughly twice the cost of online delivery). The benefit of this strategy is that it requires little or no infrastructure development or support on your part. However, the responsibility for providing access and long-term preservation for the material resides with a commercial company that may not last forever.

While UMI may epitomize the easy way out, conference speakers seemed to be unanimous in their depiction of XML as the "right way" to do ETDs. The problem is that implementing an XML work flow for ETDs is unlikely to be either easy or clear at this time. Right now, various universities are using nearly half a dozen different structural descriptions (document type definitions, or DTDs) for ETDs. Thus, it is unlikely that various ETD projects will be able to interoperate very well without first converting their ETDs to a common DTD.

Yet another strategy is to accept ETDs in other formats, such as Microsoft Word and/or Adobe Acrobat. This will be much easier than requiring XML markup for the material, but it also means a less assured migration path as MS Word and/or Adobe Acrobat change or are replaced by other, competing applications.

Key players home and away

The home of the ETD effort is Virginia Tech University, and the person at the center is Edward Fox, a professor in the Department of Computer Science. He began the NDLTD, and Virginia Tech now has over two thousand of its students' ETDs online.

Another leader is the Massachusetts Institute of Technology (MIT), which has put more than four thousand dissertations online. MIT has taken a very pragmatic approach. Since it was already duplicating dissertations to sell to those requesting them, MIT decided simply to digitize them, based on demand, for online access as part of the process. Now, about fifty percent of the dissertations requested have been digitized.

Outside the United States, the Australian Digital Theses Program is very ambitious, with seven Australian universities involved in a pilot project, eventually to include all forty Australian universities, once they have fully developed and tested the infrastructure. (Twenty-two were participating at last count.) They are using a modified version of the submission software developed at Virginia Tech.

Several people from the Humboldt University of Berlin were present, and discussed their project to mark up ETDs in XML. As they noted, one key issue is the diversity of DTDs being used by various projects to mark up what are essentially the same kinds of documents. To address this problem, they are attempting to bring together the competing DTDs into one standardized DTD. By having ETDs marked up with the same structural tags, the user will be able more easily to search for and use ETDs from around the world. Since the underlying structure of the documents will be the same, search and display systems will be able to provide access to ETDs, from a variety of sources.

Finding ETDs

There are now two main methods for locating ETDs. The primary method is to use UMI's ProQuest Digital Dissertations site, which allows searches by a number of fields (keyword, author, title, school and subject). You can also browse by broad subjects, but in most cases there are too many results to make such browsing very productive—for example, there are no narrower subject categories to select within "language and literature." Once a subject category has been selected, however, additional search terms can be added to further narrow the set. ProQuest provides a twenty-four-page "preview" of the ETD for free as individual page images.

To find ETDs that are part of the NDLTD, you either must go to each institution's web site individually or try out the experimental "federated" search (which was not working as of this writing). Clearly the NDLTD has some distance to go to compete with UMI in both ease of searching and the sheer number of ETDs. But at least you don't have to pay for them if you access them through an NDLTD site.

Speeding ahead?

Standing on the pier in St. Petersburg, I couldn't help thinking about Dalí's dripping clock. To my untrained eye he seems to be saying that time is elastic, which somehow seems all the more appropriate regarding ETDs. People like Fox have been laboring for years, and yet the number of ETDs available online through NDLTD institutions still remains rather unimpressive. There clearly are issues that need to be addressed if ETDs are to become a major source of free content for digital libraries. But it's also clear that there will be many more people working to solve those issues, since this conference drew several times the number of attendees as either of the previous two symposia.

Time may have been moving slowly in the ETD universe before, but now it appears that things are speeding up.

Resources

Australian Digital Theses Program
adt.caul.edu.au
Humboldt University Ditigal Dissertations Project
dochost.rz.hu-berlin.de/epdiss/index_en.html
NDLTD
www.ndltd.org
NDLTD Federated Search
www.ndltd.org/browse.html
ProQuest Digital Dissertations
www.lib.umi.com/dissertations/gateway
Salvador Dalí Museum
www.salvadordalimuseum.org
UMI Dissertation Services
www.il.proquest.com/hp/Support/DServices/

Open Access Journals

It doesn't take a rocket scientist to figure out that the current system of scholarly communication is in need of major changes. Journal price increases have been so dramatic and devastating that faculty who typically don't know or care about library expenditures are now front-and-center in the battle to change the dominant paradigm.

The dominant paradigm is this: faculty and researchers at universities, many of which are public institutions, create most scientific and academic journal literature. These faculty typically publish their articles with commercial publishers for no compensation (and in many cases even pay to publish). Once published, university libraries license from the commercial publishers, often at top dollar, the research and scholarship of their own faculty. For example, UC collectively libraries spend 50¢ per second on journals from the top four science, technology, and medical journal publishers, or $79 per student per year. Did the commercial publisher add value? Sure, in most cases. Is that value worth the cost? Increasingly, faculty, librarians, and others say no. And here's what they're doing about it...

The movement

In May, 2000, a large group of high-level university administrators and librarians met in Tempe, Arizona, and agreed to a set of "Principles for Emerging Systems of Scholarly Publishing." It was a line in the sand drawn by those determined to change a "system of scholarly publishing [that] has become too costly for the academic community to sustain."

Every revolution must have its leaders, and this one is no different. One dominant figure is Stevan Harnad, who has written prolifically on this topic for years. His discussion list, in the September, 1998 American Scientist Forum, is his main vehicle for his strongly held views on open access to scholarly literature. Another key personality is Peter Suber, who manages the SPARC Open Access Newsletter and previously ran a Free Online Scholarship bulletin board. Others include Dr. Harold Varmus and Michael Eisen of the Public Library of Science (PLoS).

Models and exemplars

One of the earliest (1995) and most well-developed e-journal platforms is HighWire Press at Stanford University. HighWire has a large stable of mostly scientific and medical peer-reviewed journals, which it supports with a robust and full-featured publishing platform called Bench>Press. The HighWire model is one of fee-for-service, with many of the journals using the HighWire service charging subscription fees. However, there are some open access e-journals at HighWire, which also offer a "moving wall" for most journals wherein older issues become open access.

The Berkeley Electronic Press ("bepress") offers another commercial system for open journals. Their EdiKit system also takes papers from the submission stage through the peer review process, but the end products are usually articles in Adobe Acrobat, although they can accommodate HTML. Again, the model here is fee-for-service, with a number of the journals charging subscription fees.

The PLoS, also aimed at creating a production-grade online publishing system, has a very different model. With a $9 million grant from the Gordon and Betty Moore Foundation, the PLoS aims to make the full content of all its journals freely available. The economic model is based on charging authors for publication, although an author's inability to pay "will never be a consideration in the decision whether to publish."

The University of California's eScholarship Repository has launched its new journals as well, supported by the same bepress EdiKit system that's behind the non-peer-reviewed content of the eScholarship Repository. In this model, the institution supports the infrastructure that makes online publication possible, with faculty and researchers from UC institutions and elsewhere providing the supervision and professional expertise. For those wanting to go it alone, the Open Journal System (OJS) offers a free, open source solution for journal publication. A full-featured online peer-review system from the Public Knowledge Project at the University of

British Columbia, OJS seeks to dramatically lower the barrier for those wishing to start new publications.

Further information

More descriptions of journal management systems are available at "Bibliography and Summary: Electronic Peer Review Management," "Journal Management Systems," "Tools and Resources for Online Journal Editing and Publishing," and "Web-Based Journal Manuscript Management and Peer-Review Software and Systems." Just be aware that some of the systems listed may not still be active.

Some ways of keeping up with what is happening with open access e-journals include the aforementioned SPARC Open Access Newsletter: the September 1998 American Scientist Forum, the SPARC web site, and the Open Access Now site by BioMed

Central. To find out what open access journals are available, see the Directory of Open Access Journals.

Will the paradigm shift?

It's too early to tell what impact, if any, the open access revolution will have on the dominant paradigm. But the breadth and depth of the movement is impressive, and seems to indicate that although the revolution has not yet been successful in all of its aims, it nonetheless is gaining enough ground that one at least can now envision the toppling of the current regime—something that was hard to picture even just a few years ago.

Resources

Bench>Press
   benchpress.highwire.org
bepress
   bepress.com
Bibliography and Summary: Electronic Peer Review Management
   spo.umdl.umich.edu/monthly/peerreview.html
Directory of Open Access Journals
   www.doaj.org
eScholarship Repository Peer-Reviewed Content
   repositories.cdlib.org/escholarship/peer_review_list.html
highWire
   highwire.stanford.edu
Journal Management Systems
   www.arl.org/sparc/core/index.asp?page=h16#journals
Open Access Now
   www.biomedcentral.com/openaccess/
Open Journal Systems
   www.pkp.ubc.ca/ojs/
Public Library of Science
   plos.org
American Scientist Open Access Forum
   amsci-forum.amsci.org/archives/september98-forum.html
SPARC
   www.arl.org/sparc/
SPARC Open Access Newsletter
   www.earlham.edu/~peters/fos/

Tempe Principles
www.arl.org/scomm/tempe.html
Tools and Resources for Online Journal Editing and Publishing
www.library.unr.edu/ejournals/editors.html
Web-Based Journal Manuscript Management and Peer-Review Software
and Systems
konstanza.emeraldinsight.com/vl=5128433/cl=21/fm=html/nw=1/rpsv/
cw/mcb/07419058/v19n7/s7003/p3l

4
CATALOGING AND CLASSIFICATION

Twenty-first Century Cataloging

21st Century Cataloging

Cataloging has basically remained unchanged for decades. Despite the development of Machine-Readable Cataloging (MARC) and the "Anglo-American Cataloging Rules", Second Edition (AACR2), much of what is recorded about a library item is the same as it was when we used handwritten catalog cards. Today, many library catalogs simply duplicate the catalog card on a computer screen.

Now, the game has changed. In the digital library, we no longer deal with the typical printed book or serial. We may need to describe a collection of digitized photographs, or a series of pages that must somehow be navigable as a logical whole like the printed book from which they are derived. And we must keep track of such things as how the digital representation was captured and manipulated. Librarians have historically called this "cataloging." We in digital library work call it "metadata."

Metadata, simply put, is structured information about an object or collection of objects. The key is "structured." In metadata, as in cataloging, a free-text description usually won't suffice. Rather, in order to limit a search to a particular field, the information must be structured, often highly so. That is why MARC has tag and subfield markers, which allow software to understand exactly how to treat each descriptive element.

Does MARC translate?

So why don't digital library projects use MARC? Some do, such as when records for digital objects are merged with a library catalog and loaded into the catalog as with the record for a print book. The State Library of Victoria Multimedia Catalogue has over one hundred-twenty thousand records for digital objects. However, for many purposes, MARC is a poor fit. In some cases it is too complex, requiring highly trained staff and specialized input systems; in others, it is too focused on print material and can't be extended for digital collections. Digital librarians have identified several categories of metadata information about digital resources: descriptive, structural, administrative, and information required to preserve the item or collection of items. Of these categories, MARC really only deals well with descriptive metadata.

- *Descriptive metadata* includes the creator of the resource, its title, appropriate subject headings—basically the kinds of elements that will be used to search for and locate the item.
- *Structural metadata* describes how the item is structured. In a book, pages follow another. But as a digital object, if each page is scanned as an image, metadata must "bind" hun-

dreds of separate computer files together into a logical whole and provide ways to navigate the digital "book."

- *Administrative metadata* may include such things as how the digital file was produced, and its ownership.
- *Preservation metadata* consists of information that may be required to preserve the item over time.

All of this potential metadata needs containers. However, most of the metadata described above has no standard container waiting to receive it, as MARC receives the information specified by AACR2. There are, however, some emerging standards that may be to digital libraries what MARC was to print-based libraries.

Dublin Core emerges

The best general-purpose metadata standard is the Dublin Core. The Dublin Core represents a multiyear (and ongoing) effort by librarians, computer scientists, museum professionals, and others to devise a simple yet extensible standard that could be used to describe a wide variety of objects within a wide variety of subject disciplines and systems. The Dublin Core consists of fifteen elements such as title, subject, and so on. The element names and basic purposes are fixed, but most details regarding them remain unresolved problems. Meanwhile, dozens of projects around the world are now using it. A few are:

The Nordic Metadata Project. A consortium of Nordic countries working to create a metadata production and use system has created a utility for translating Dublin Core records into MARC, and vice versa.

DSTC Resource Discovery Unit. This Australian organization uses the Dublin Core in a variety of projects.

UK Office of Library Networking (UKOLN). UKOLN provides a wealth of software for metadata production and utilization, focusing on the Dublin Core.

Outside the Core

While the Dublin Core specifies certain elements to describe an item, it does not specify a specific transfer syntax or a MARC equivalent. Rather, the Dublin Core effort has identified a number of transfer syntaxes that can be used to encode DC elements. For example, at the time of this writing, the "Encoding Guidelines" page at the Dublin Core web site lists the following ways DC elements can be encoded: HTML, RDF, XML, and HTML/XHTML Meta Elements.

XML represents an advance over HTML, which offers very little structural or intellectual information about a document. XML, whether it is only behind the scenes or not, is the future of the web. Keep your eye on the World Wide Web Consortium (W3C) and the XML.com site.

While the Dublin Core is useful for describing individual objects, there is another draft standard that is useful for describing collections of objects, specifically archival materials. The Encoded Archival Description (EAD) is the standard for creating machine-readable archival finding aids. EAD specifies how archival finding aids should be tagged using the Standard Generalized Markup Language (SGML) in the past, or now using XML. Although the standards effort began at UC Berkeley, it is now managed by the Library of Congress. See examples at EAD Sites on the web.

These emerging standards all attempt to provide a highly structured way to describe various digital objects and make them easy to locate and use. That, after all, is what cataloging is all about.

Resources

DSTC Resource Discovery Unit
    www.dstc.edu.au/RDU/
Dublin Core
    dublincore.org
Dublin Core Encoding Guidelines
    dublincore.org/resources/expressions/
EAD sites on the web
    www.loc.gov/ead/eadsites.html
Encoded Archival Description (EAD)
    www.loc.gov/ead/
IFLA Metadata Resources
    www.ifla.org/II/metadata.htm
MARC
    www.loc.gov/marc/

Nordic Metadata Project
   www.lib.helsinki.fi/meta/
Resource Description Framework (RFD)
   www.w3.org/RDF/
State Library of Victoria Multimedia Catalog
   catalogue.slv.vic.gov.au
U.K. Office of Library Networking (UKOLN) Metadata
   www.ukoln.ac.uk/metadata/
XML at the W3C
   www.w3.org/XML/
XML.com site
   www.xml.com

Metadata As If Libraries Depended On It

In digital library work, we often talk about metadata, what I jokingly call "cataloging by those paid better than librarians." A more serious definition would be "a structured description of an object or collection of objects." A MARC record for a book is clearly metadata, but so too is an archival finding aid encoded in EAD, or even descriptive information embedded in META tags at the top of a web page. Metadata is increasingly everywhere—sometimes hidden, sometimes apparent. But, as any cataloger will tell you, not all metadata is created equal. Excellent metadata is constructed in layers. First you must settle on what is important to you or to those you serve. You create containers (defined and codifed by schemata) to squirrel away the tidbits that will, taken as a whole, describe something well enough for your purposes.

Qualities of containers

Metadata containers are a tricky business. A new metadata schema or definition requires the correct mix of power, flexibility, and complexity for a given user community and that community's readiness for it. Do it well—as with MARC when it was created in the 1960s—and you'll prosper. Do it poorly, and you're toast.

A good container must solve a problem that people care about, but it must do so in a method that allows and encourages adoption (e.g., by being readily understandable). It should be extensible without breaking systems that will come to rely upon it. It also should be interoperable with systems that may have other metadata requirements. Also, a metadata container can succeed or fail depending on how well it deals with granularity issues—how finely you chop your metadata. This is a critical issue (see "The Importance of Being Granular" in this chapter). To create a new metadata container, you must imagine all required uses and provide the right hooks to make those uses possible. If you have done your work really well, you will have enabled uses that you never imagined.

A variety of containers

When it comes to metadata containers, we live in interesting and fruitful times. Besides such longstanding workhorses as MARC, we also have the Dublin Core, the Metadata Encoding and Transmission Standard (METS), and the Metadata Object Description Schema (MODS).

The Dublin Core has been in development for several years and is meant to be a common meeting ground among richer descriptive metadata standards. METS is relatively new and aims to encapsulate a digital object or set of objects in a standard wrapper. Descriptive metadata can either be embedded directly in the METS object, or the METS record can point to an external description using another metadata standard such as MODS or MARC. MODS, the newest draft standard, is much richer and more granular than Dublin Core but without some of the baggage of MARC.

Consider the following scenario: a book is digitized, and METS is used to organize all its files. The METS record points to (or embeds within it) a descriptive record using MODS. A simplified version of the MODS record is made available for harvesting in Dublin Core format so that service providers can build cross-collection search services.

More standards are not necessarily a problem, as long as they can fruitfully interoperate and exchange data when required. As libraries digitize collections, metadata is required to organize and provide access to this content outside of, or in association with, the library catalog. Also, some libraries are developing such things as working paper repositories, which have different metadata requirements. With such diversity of uses, a diversity of metadata containers likely is essential.

Qualifying information

A good metadata container must provide for a method of qualifying the information held within a particular element, e.g., a subject heading. It may be useful to know that the text found within a subject field comes from a controlled vocabulary. If so, you can then qualify that information with a reference to the controlled vocabulary from which it comes. Using Dublin Core within an HTML META tag, this could be expressed as:

<meta name='DC.subject' scheme='LCSH' content='Vietnamese Conflict, 1961-1975'>

Another classic case that may require user qualification is the role that a person has in relation to the item. Dublin Core specifies a "creator" field, but what does that mean? In one case, the person identified may be an author; in another, a painter. There should be some method of providing this information.

Usage guidelines and information

A standard container and a means to qualify the information contained therein is only a start. Without guidelines on how the container is to be used, errors in interpretation and usage could render the metadata less useful. A classic example of usage guidelines is the *Anglo-American Cataloging Rules (AACR)*, which defined how and with what information a cataloger was to fill the MARC metadata container. Such guidelines are still a dream away for some recent entries into the metadata container field. But these issues are understood by the librarians involved, so it is only a matter of time before they are codified. Also, usage of these emerging metadata standards will inform and enhance the process of codifying their use.

Finally, we arrive at the ingredient that is at the very center of this enterprise—the information itself. What we know about that information both informs our intellect and limits our imagination as we develop new schemata. In the 1960s, when MARC was created, who would have thought that it would help to have a place to put such things as book reviews and not so helpful to have a physical description?

What this means to you

Catalogers must learn new things, certainly, but also must apply much of their longstanding knowledge and many skills in new and interesting ways. Reference librarians must understand both the possibilities for user services presented by these new schemata and the consequences to their mission should they not be used. Check the great list of metadata resources compiled by the International Federation of Library Associations and Institutions (IFLA).

Library administrators, pay close attention. Your library has the potential to serve your clientele in ways you never dreamed of. Your library also might be increasingly marginalized until your clientele never supports a bond issue again. Not everything libraries need to collect or provide access to can be usefully described using MARC, or accessed via a database vendor for a fee. We're in a brave new world, in which MARC must make room for METS and MODS and whatever else becomes necessary to do our work better. Stand by your staff, give those who are eager what they need to learn and grow, and provide incentives to those who are reluctant.

Resources

Dublin Core
   dublincore.org
EAD
   www.loc.gov/ead/
IFLA Metadata Resources
   www.ifla.org/II/metadata.htm
MARC
   www.loc.gov/marc/
METS
   www.loc.gov/standards/mets/
MODS
   www.loc.gov/standards/mods/

The Importance of Being Granular

Our libraries are increasingly dependent on metadata. Besides the obvious (our catalogs), other uses are becoming more commonplace. Virtually any content we digitize and make available to our clientele requires metadata for discovery and access. Every interlibrary loan transaction is a slug of metadata that helps libraries get a book or journal article to a user. Libraries now license so many databases and collections of online content that they increasingly offer a way for users to search for a resource based on their topic. Such a service requires metadata.

In "Metadata as if Libraries Depended on It," I discussed metadata and its various components: a standard container, qualification, usage guidelines, and the information being captured. In that overview I set aside one topic as being worthy of special focus: metadata granularity.

How you chop it

Granularity refers to how finely you chop your metadata. For example, in the standard for encoding the full text of books using the Text Encoding Initiative (TEI) schema, a book author may be recorded as: <docAuthor>William Shakespeare</docAuthor>. That's all well and good, except if you never need to know which string of text comprises the author's last name and which the first. If you do—and most library catalogs should have this capability—you're not going to get very far with information extracted from a book encoded using the TEI tag set.

Although TEI has been around in one form or another for fifteen years, its focus is mainly on the recording of aspects of a work for humanities scholars. As such, it is not particularly well suited for library-style bibliographic description. Nonetheless, as more texts are digitized in their entireties, libraries increasingly will be using either some form of TEI or another similar schema (e.g., ISO 12083). Therefore, it behooves us to know how well or how poorly standards such as TEI and MARC can interoperate.

How granularity helps

Granularity is good. It makes it possible to distinguish one bit of metadata from another and can lead to all kinds of additional user services. For example, you can't sort records on author names if you can't tell the last name.

Generally speaking, most of the information in a MARC record is sufficiently granular for the purposes for which it was designed. But it becomes less than adequately granular should you wish to start loading up the MARC record with such things as book reviews. Then you are reduced to such questionable tactics as smashing it into a note field. As time goes on, in other words, we may begin to find that MARC isn't quite as extensible or granular as it will need to be (see "MARC Must Die" and "MARC Exit Strategies" in this chapter for more on this).

External compliance

The issue of granularity becomes critical in the apparently slavish devotion we tend to have toward standards. Don't get me wrong. Standards are vital to sharing data with others. They are important to any situation in which you must interoperate with other systems. They are important to providing a method to layer services easily on top of a collection of metadata. But we sometimes confuse internal compliance with external compliance.

External compliance with standards means that you can export your data into whatever metadata standard applies to a given situation. For example, some libraries are involved with the Open Archives Initiative (OAI), which aims to share metadata among repositories. Although internally a given archive may have a richer and more granular collection of metadata, OAI specifies that at minimum the archive should be able to make its metadata available for "harvesting" (collecting via software) using the Dublin Core metadata specification. Therefore, an OAI-compliant archive will likely "dumb down" its metadata (in some cases making granular metadata more homogenous) to meet this minimum specification.

Internal compliance

Internal compliance means storing the metadata in a particular standard even when it makes little sense to do so. Some standards are meant to provide interoperability among systems (such as the Dublin Core), while others are designed to provide a base level of standardization upon which software systems can be built (such as MARC).

Not all metadata are equal

Therefore, not all metadata standards are created equal. They are sometimes inadequate for your internal needs or would prevent you from complying with a different standard. In the case of the OAI-compliant archive above, for example, being internally compliant with the Dublin Core would make no sense in and of itself. So long as it could "speak" Dublin Core when required, a richer set of internal metadata may allow many other additional uses of the same information (such as MARC records for a library catalog).

Granularity questions

Nearly all metadata standards raise granularity issues. In the TEI example, for greater flexibility the author's name should be chopped up at least into the part of the name upon which sorting can take place (usually the last name). Therefore, should I decide to encode a digitized book using the TEI set of XML tags, I will have metadata that is only adequate for TEI compliance.

On the other hand, should I create my own set of tags—perhaps the TEI tag set plus additional tags, for example, to identify the author's first and last name—to provide more granularity, then a standard such as TEI can be covered like a blanket. And a number of other metadata standards that may be important (such as MARC) can be supported as well. Once you have your metadata stored in a standard, machine-parsable container, whether in a database or an XML data stream, it's easy to spit out the information in various configurations and formats.

Remember: select (or create) and use metadata containers that are granular enough for any purpose to which you can imagine putting them. If you do this, not only can you serve your own purposes, but you can also share your metadata with anyone you wish. If this is not practical, then you must decide which needs will remain unfulfilled. Highly granular metadata doesn't come cheap. There is a trade-off between all possible uses that you may wish to support and the staff time required to capture the metadata required to do so. In some cases, the benefit will not warrant the cost; in others, it will be worth it.

Another path to granularity

Good granularity doesn't necessarily mean that any single metadata standard or container must chop up every field into the smallest reduceable part. For example, the emerging standard for digital object description, METS, is designed to take advantage of other, more granular metadata containers.

As a wrapper, it is meant to enclose some things and link to others. It can refer to a metadata record for the item being described. Therefore, a digital object described using the METS schema may, in fact, refer to a MARC record for descriptive metadata.

Granularity of metadata is hard-won and easily lost. Identifying and appropriately encoding metadata elements usually requires a person with training. Once granularity has been achieved, it should not be permanently surrendered through internal compliance with an external standard, unless the benefits clearly outweigh the drawbacks and no alternatives are possible.

The time of cataloging staff is valuable, and once granularity is lost it may not be practical to recover it. Our libraries depend on metadata. They are becoming even more dependent as we move into the realm of creating, managing, and preserving collections in digital form. Doing so well requires us to understand thoroughly what is at stake and the consequences of our actions.

Resources

Dublin Core
   dublincore.org
ISO 12083
   www.xmlxperts.com/12083.htm

MARC
   www.loc.gov/marc/
METS
   www.loc.gov/standards/mets/
Open Archives Initiative
   www.openarchives.org
Text Encoding Initiative
   www.tei-c.org

The Art and Science
of Digital Bibliography

For decades, librarians have been cataloging books and journals for their libraries' collections. So it's only natural that some who embrace the Internet talk about "cataloging the net." They envision creating MARC records for each Internet resource, complete with Library of Congress Subject Headings (LCSH) or Dewey Decimal Classification, and merging them into their catalogs of library holdings. Norman Oder, in "Cataloging the Net: Can We Do It?" (*Library Journal,* Vol. 123, No.16, October 1, 1998, pp. 47-51), describes one such project from OCLC called InterCat. But let's take a look at the cataloging process for a moment. Modern library cataloging is characterized by the following:

- A proprietary (nonweb) automated system for creating and editing complex records in MARC format;
- A highly trained individual (one of a small subset of librarians) who knows cataloging practices in general and AACR2 specifically; and,
- A significant amount of time to create each record.

The above requirements can be met when, as with printed materials, there are relatively few items to be originally cataloged. With the Internet, however, we're faced with not a few thousand but literally millions of possible information sources from hundreds of thousands of access points (web servers). Then, add the following requirements:

- A set of guidelines specific to Internet resources that help catalogers to do such things as locate information which in print is normally on the title page verso;
- A way to automatically check links; and,
- Catalogers who know Internet resources and are capable with the web.

Soon it becomes clear that we have a complex, time-consuming system that only a few can help build. There aren't that many catalogers to begin with, much less those with enough time and Internet savvy.

We also have trouble in tailoring such a system, either by providing narrative descriptions of the resources or expanding access by offering uncontrolled keywords. Catalogers already find it tough to locate LCSH that are both appropriate to the topic and what a searcher might use. When Yahoo is your competition, relying on LCSH for topic access is ludicrous. Then we also must face how to proceed with the records. Should we load them into our library catalogs, merged with records for items on our shelves? Or do we keep them in a separate database?

The problem is that we have the wrong metaphor

In contrast, instead of cataloging the net, a number of organizations are practicing digital bibliography. Bibliography is the art of finding, reviewing, selecting, and annotating important information resources on a particular topic, often for a particular audience. The resulting collections have in the past been published in article or book form, while others were distributed more informally (e.g., handouts). But no one would question the utility of this service, or that it is central to libraries.

Some librarians are now using their tried-and-true bibliographic skills in new and interesting ways, many of which are chronicled in Oder's article. Sometimes these bibliographies are called "indexes" and/or "subject gateways." But they all share some characteristics that distinguish them from cataloging projects:

- Although adeptness in evaluating resources is important, no specialized cataloging skill is required;
- Annotations, either descriptive or evaluative, can be added;
- Periodic link checking is a standard part of the system;
- Such projects can be tailored for a particular audience or purpose; and,
- Records can be enhanced with additional vocabularies or uncontrolled keywords.

While there are any number of such projects, are were some early efforts in this area...

All ROADS lead to Bath

The largest, most organized, and most technically sophisticated effort was ROADS, the Resource Organisation and Discovery in Subject-based Service project of the eLib Programme of the U.K. Office of Library and Information Networking (UKOLN, located at the University of Bath). The project aimed to build standards-based software for creating subject indexes or gateways to Internet resources, to investigate methods of interoperability between gateways, and to participate in the development of standards for the indexing, cataloging (in a simplified, non-MARC/AACR2 fashion), and searching of subject-specific resources. ROADS used templates (record formats) for different resource types, such as documents, datasets, images, etc. These templates specified the appropriate fields for recording information about a resource and thereby ensure interoperability between separate subject gateways. These templates formed the foundation record standard that enables searches across gateways to function the same way. A set of modules written in Perl provided web-based interfaces, which allowed individuals anywhere to participate in creating and editing records, if they had the proper authorization.

At least sixteen subject gateways—mostly in the UK—used the ROADS infrastructure, covering such diverse subject areas as art and architecture, engineering, literature, and medicine. Most had fewer than three thousand records, and since most are independent operation, their depth and quality likely differed.

Although funding for this project is at an end, the ROADS software is still available via SourceForge, and a number of projects still use it.

The Internet Scout scouts out new territory

The Internet Scout Project has for several years produced the Internet Scout Report, a high-quality current awareness service and database of Internet resources. From that effort grew a couple of projects to create a subject directory infrastructure.

Project Isaac was their first effort to federate subject gateways. Internet Scout staff looked at ROADS as a way to implement Isaac but decided instead to build an infrastructure based on the Lightweight Directory Access Protocol (LDAP) for searching and indexing and the Common Indexing Protocol (CIP) to distribute queries, return results, and exchange index information. They asserted that this offered a more flexible and extensible data model as well as better industry support for the base protocol. For more information, see "A Distributed Architecture for Resource Discovery Using Metadata" (D-Lib Magazine).

Mining the Internet

INFOMINE began at the University of California, Riverside, several years ago and now lists well over one hundred thousand resources of interest to an academic audience. Although it has broader participation among UC librarians, it began as a project of just a few UC Riverside Library staffers, and most manual contributions still come from those key implementers.

INFOMINE also has automated processes for identifying and adding records.

INFOMINE records are Dublin Core compliant: the records can be output using Dublin Core elements, which makes interoperability with other indexes easier. For subject terms, INFOMINE uses "modified" LCSH and uncontrolled keywords.

INFOMINE has received grants both to further develop the INFOMINE service as well as make available software tools for others to create similar services. These software tools are now available as the iVia open source Internet subject portal, or virtual library system.

Bringing it all together

In our well-intentioned effort to create one interface to all information resources appropriate to our various clienteles, librarians have a strong tendency to cram everything into their library catalogs. Again, we have the wrong model. For example, a user may wish to search a library catalog, a subject index of Internet resources, and descriptions of local CD-ROM databases to explore a particular subject area. With the appropriate interface, all these could be searched simultaneously and the results presented in a manner that allows further investigation. For a more complete description of this model, see Terry Hanson's "The Access Catalogue Gateway to Resources." This model would allow designers of each component to build on its strengths individually and tailor its service to particular needs but also support combined searching and display.

As another example, consider the federated search portal model. Someone seeking information about AIDS might want to search not only subject gateways of Internet resources, but also the medical journal literature and one or more library catalogs. The key to supporting customization for an audience or purpose and also cross-disciplinary searches is the appropriate infrastructure. And that is simply not the traditional library catalog. For more on why library catalogs are the wrong solution for one-stop shopping, and what may be the right solution instead, see the next chapter.

Resources

"The Access Catalogue Gateway to Resources"
  www.ariadne.ac.uk/issue15/main/
"A Distributed Architecture for Resource Discovery Using Metadata"
  www.dlib.org/dlib/june98/scout/06roszkowski.html
Dublin Core
  dublincore.org
INFOMINE
  infomine.ucr.edu
Internet Scout Project
  scout.cs.wisc.edu/scout/

IMesh ToolKit
  scout.cs.wisc.edu/research/imeshtk/
iVia Software
  infomine.ucr.edu/iVia/
ROADS
  www.ukoln.ac.uk/metadata/roads/
ROADS at SourceForge
  roads.sourceforge.net

The Print Perplex:
Building the Future Catalog

While seated at my desk (in 1998), I can look out over nearly two million volumes. Well, to be precise, I can see the grass that covers them. Beneath the grass is a four-story underground building that holds the main library collection of the University of California, Berkeley Library. (Another six million volumes are in branch libraries or storage.)

Most of these books, I'm fond of telling anyone who will listen, will never exist in digital form. Not just in my lifetime—or that of my children—but never.

There are several reasons for my certainty. Recently published items are protected under copyright law, and obtaining permission to digitize them is likely to be time-consuming, and often impossible. For many older items we have neither the time nor the money; the potential usage simply does not warrant it. And, even if an item is important enough, it takes many resources to digitize a book, to produce usable versions of it, and to place it within the appropriate context so that people can find and use it.

So there's the rub. We must deal with a future of mixed print and digital material not only for now but for the foreseeable future as well. We need to get used to it. More than that, we must get good at it. By getting good at it I mean that we must get better at guiding users to the information they need in whatever format it is to be found or, if something is available in different formats, at guiding them to the format they need at the time. Here are a few possible strategies that libraries are using, or can use, to try to provide integrated access to both print and digital collections...

"One catalog fits all"

Most libraries have invested a great deal of time, energy, and money in constructing a database of their resources. Therefore, librarians often will want to include digital resources—from records for online databases to those for individual digitized photographs—directly in their library catalog.

Some benefits of this model include:

· one (tried-and-true) location for library holdings information;
· a familiar interface for users and maintainers; and,
· complete integration of print and digital information resources.

Some drawbacks of this model include:

• records can only be created by a small, highly trained subset of library staff (those with experience creating MARC records using AACR2);
• record creation and maintenance can be time-consuming;
• the "granularity" problem (for example, does it make sense to have both a record for a collection of items and records for each individual item in the same location?); and,
• digital items often need metadata elements that are not part of MARC in order to support such things as appropriate navigation methods.

So far this model is most evident when libraries link catalog records for print resources to their digital equivalent using the MARC 856 field. Most of the largest digital library projects have not loaded records for digital items directly into a library catalog.

The "side-by-side" model

Another method is to create two parallel systems, sometimes using the same infrastructure (e.g., integrated library system software). The user must select one or the other before searching. If both systems are presented together, the user will be aware of both systems and can at least go back and select the other database to search at a later time. An example of this is the catalog of the State Library of Victoria, Australia.

Some benefits of this model include:

- the same infrastructure and search interface can be used to access both types of records;
- the differences between the collections can be made more apparent; and,
- the database can be tailored to the special needs or challenges of the items being cataloged.

Some drawbacks of this model include:

- no unified interface—the collections must be searched separately;
- records can only be created by a small, highly trained subset of library staff (those with experience creating MARC records using AACR2);
- record creation and maintenance can be time-consuming; and,
- digital items may require metadata elements that are not native to MARC.

The gateway, or union, catalog

With the gateway model, some of the benefits and strengths of the other models can be retained while minimizing some of their drawbacks. There are two basic ways to implement this model. In one, you add to the side-by-side model a user interface that offers simultaneous searching of both databases. The gateway sends the search to both and presents the integrated results either merged or in groups that can be easily selected. A variation on this model is to load records from one or more systems into a union catalog. In both of these methods, individual catalogs for print holdings and digital items can be used to provide services tailored to those collections while presenting a unified interface to the user for resource discovery. This is particularly important in relation to the kinds of digital bibliography activities discussed in "The Art and Science of Digital Bibliography" (in this chapter), which may benefit from an entirely different infrastructure for records creation and maintenance than that provided by a library catalog.

In the "one catalog fits all" model, we lose the capacity to tailor the system to the unique needs of digital resources. Therefore, the gateway or union catalog model holds the greatest promise for providing unified searching of print and digital materials. The article "The Access Catalogue Gateway to Resources," describes this model in more detail.

Some benefits of this model include:

- true "one-stop shopping" for the user; and,
- separate systems let you tailor the database structure to the needs of print or digital materials.

Some drawbacks of this model include:

- the need for another system to join one or more existing systems together, or to serve as a union catalog; and,
- the cost to create and maintain another system interface.

Print, digital, or both

While striving to build systems that will allow users to discover print materials alongside digital ones, we shouldn't forget that sometimes users will want to see only one type of material. Just because we present users with a merged interface doesn't mean we can't let them limit the results to items of a particular format. The point is to build systems that are flexible enough to meet the various needs of our users, whether they want to locate a digitized photograph or one of eight million volumes that will never be digitized.

Resources

"The Access Catalogue Gateway to Resources"
   www.ariadne.ac.uk/issue15/main/

State Library of Victoria
  catalogue.slv.vic.gov.au

The Consequences of Cataloging

As our usage statistics decline (on average), owing to the perceived promise of the Internet, we must think imaginatively. More and more, I believe this means establishing ever-wider cooperative relationships with other libraries. After all, there is no cheaper way to expand your collections than to make it possible (and easy) to request and receive materials from other institutions.

The Westchester Library System in Ardsley, New York is a great example (see "Technology and Teamwork," *Library Journal*, September 1, 2000, pp. 77-80). The 38 cooperating libraries made it easy for patrons to receive any book within the system by using the Integrated Interlibrary Loan (ILL) software of their Dynix system and by backing it up with a robust delivery service. In a challenge to conventional wisdom, older, long-ignored books began flying off the shelves.

However, underlying this increased cooperation and its benefits are some niggling details that may prove to be significant stumbling blocks. Look no further than the icon and foundation of libraries: the catalog. Though it may be painstakingly constructed using respected standards such as MARC and AACR2, the catalog may be less standard, and therefore less interoperable than we think.

Too many records

Such became dramatically apparent as I prepared a talk for some ILL librarians. I decided to search the region's union catalog system for one of my books. The numerous records returned in part reflected multiple editions and printings. I decided to winnow down the results to only those records that seemed to describe the exact same book. I reduced the number to seven—seven independent records for the same book, in one region.

It appeared that two or three base records had been embellished or altered in various, mostly trivial ways. One misspelled the place of publication and added 'maps' to the physical description. Another quibbled with the copyright date (1993, though it was published at the end of 1992) and measured the book one centimeter smaller than the other records. One record said 'leaves' instead of 'pp.' for the pagination notation.   For subject headings, the records grouped around two main clusters. The differences seemed to revolve around plain mistakes of various kinds (misspellings mostly), added information, and disagreements. Except for the differences in subject headings, all the differences were completely and utterly inconsequential to the user.

Since these variations were so trivial, why hadn't these records been merged? Because the system being searched is a "virtual" union catalog. The records don't come from the same system but are merged on the fly after searching separate catalog systems.

Karen Coyle, in "The Virtual Union Catalog," cautions that, with systems that retrieve large sets of results, merging records on the fly will be extremely difficult. With "real"' union catalogs, where records are contributed to one central database, there is more opportunity to merge duplicate records successfully, as well as to iron out trivial differences over time.

There is no question that merging such records is vital to effective user services in a cooperative environment. It's not clear, though, how we should handle records that vary, however slightly. For example, do most users care whether they get a hardback or a paperback? Some may, some may not. We must make it easy for them to select the correct title, and then the appropriate copy, without inundating them.

How to merge records

We consider it more important to know that we have a specific item in our collections rather than that several printings of a work hold the same content. Jeremy Hylton, in "Identifying and Merging Related Bibliographic Records," advocates Michael Buckland's idea of an "information dossier" approach to merging relating records. This goes beyond the standard library practice of duplicate record detection and merging (see "Record Matching:

An Expert Algorithm") to merge records that describe different physical items but are algorithmically perceived to be the same intellectual object.

Although Hylton's algorithm may be inadequate when faced with some of the ambiguous records that can be found in large library catalog systems, it nonetheless highlights an important issue: Do users initially want to see that there are many different physical copies of a book, or do they want that this information initially hidden until they select a specific book to retrieve? How should our catalog systems mask information in displays where it isn't important but still make it displayable when users want to see it?

Thankfully we are beginning to see the fruit of some projects that tackle this problem head-on. Both OCLC and RLG are working on ways that they can use the principles laid out in IFLA's Functional Requirements of Bibliographic Records to bring together catalog records that refer to the same intellectual item into one virtual record. (For more on this, see "Not Your Mother's Union Catalog" in Chapter 5.) As we move toward providing access to ever-larger pools of library content, these are questions we will need to answer, and answer well. It is clear that our cataloging practices can have unintended—and detrimental—consequences.

Resources

Functional Requirements of Bibliographic Records (FRBR)
    www.ifla.org/VII/s13/frbr/frbr.pdf
"Identifying and Merging Related Bibliographic Records"
    ltt-www.lcs.mit.edu/ltt-www/People/jeremy/thesis/main.html
"Record Matching: An Expert Algorithm" *ASIS Proceedings*, 22 (1985),
    pp. 77–80
"Technology and Teamwork," *Library Journal* (Vol. 125, No. 18, September 1, 200), p. 160–163
"The Virtual Union Catalog"
    www.dlib.org/dlib/march00/coyle/03coyle.html

MARC Must Die

When MARC was created, the Beatles were a hot new group and those of us alive at the time wore really embarrassing clothes and hairstyles. Computers were so large, complex and expensive that it was ludicrous to think that you would one day have one in your home, let alone hold one in the palm of your hand. Although age by itself is not necessarily a sign of technological obsolescence⁻how much has the wooden pencil improved in the last 40 years?⁻ when it comes to computer standards it is generally not a good thing.

The very nature of the MARC (Machine-Readable Cataloging) record is to some degree an anachronism. It was developed in an age when memory, storage and processing power were all rare and expensive commodities. Now they are ubiquitous and cheap.

MARCing time

Just look at a raw MARC record to see what I mean. But don't get too much of a headache. There are only two kinds of people who believe themselves able to read a MARC record without referring to a stack of manuals: a handful of our top catalogers and those on serious drugs. In MARC, fields are not explicitly labeled but coded with a numbering scheme that cannot be read by someone unfamiliar with the complicated syntax. But needless obfuscation, as annoying as it may be, is not the real nature of our emerging difficulty with MARC.

The problems with MARC are serious and extensive, which is why a number of us are increasingly convinced that MARC has outlived its usefulness. See, for example, Dick Miller's slides, "XML and MARC: A Choice or Replacement?" "The rigidity and internal irregularities of MARC are beginning to create problems for catalogers and users," says David Flanders in the article "Applying XML to the Bibliographic Description" (*Cataloging & Classification*, vol.33 mo.2, 2001, p. 17-28). He continues, "MARC is beginning to lag behind current research into bibliographic description standards."

When I refer to MARC, I am actually conflating a few inter-related things. There are the MARC syntax, the MARC data elements, and the *Anglo-American Cataloging Rules* (AACR). These pieces are so intertwined that teasing out which must be jettisoned and which can be kept will be at least as difficult as starting from scratch. In MARC Exit Strategies" I take a closer look at this issue by addressing. Meanwhile, let's examine some specific problems with this confluence of standards that I'm calling MARC.

Granularity

Although MARC is a complex standard, it lacks essential checks and balances to assure that appropriate granularity—how finely the individual elements are chopped—is achieved when coding a record. For example, the editor of a book should be encoded in a 700 field, with a $e subfield that identifies the person as editor. But the $e subfield is frequently not encoded, thus leaving one to guess the role of the person encoded in the 700 field. In many cases, it is only by reference to the title field, of all things, that one can discover the identity of the editor. This can happen because MARC and *AACR2* are largely focused on capturing the paper catalog card in computer form. In the title field you would think you would find only the title of the book. But there are strange appendages, such as "edited and with an introduction by Peter Green" stuffed into one of a series of subfields. Peter Green's having edited the book should not be buried in a text string in a subfield of the title field. A more egregious example is the ambiguous encoding of respective parts of a personal name (last name, first name, etc.).

Extensibility and language

Migrating our catalogs from printed cards to computers was a massive job, now largely completed. A number of libraries are now enriching those records with additional information, such as the table of contents. Although it is possible to smash the table of contents into a MARC record (see Blackwell's description of its Tables of Contents Enrichment Service for the gory details), it's not pretty. By its very nature, MARC is flat, whereas a table of contents is hierarchical. This would be a breeze in XML. (For more information on translating MARC into XML, see the XMLMARC web site.) I cannot even imagine where in the MARC record we would put a book cover graphic (or book jacket information, or reviews) in a way that would make this sort of information both easily available to those who need it and easily ignored by those who don't. While MARC offers at least some facility for dealing with multiple scripts—such as a book title in Chinese and a translated or transliterated title—it handles them in such a way that it can be difficult for them to be properly processed by software. For example, relationships among related titles are problematic in MARC. More information about these problems can be found at the Moving from MARC to XML web site.

Technical marginalization

MARC has always been an arcane standard. No other profession uses MARC or anything like it. When we shop around for software to handle such records, we are limited to the niche market of library vendors. For their part, vendors must design systems that can both take in and output records in MARC format.

Meanwhile, the wider information technology industry is moving wholesale to XML as a means to encode and transfer information. Such a movement doesn't mean we abandon our existing systems for any XML-aware search tool. But if we redesign our bibliographic record standard to use XML, the vendors will likely find it both easier and cheaper to produce the products we require.

The real reason

Libraries exist to serve the present and future needs of a community of users. To do this well, they need to use the very best that technology has to offer. With the advent of the web, XML, portable computing, and other technological advances, libraries can become flexible, responsive organizations that serve their users in exciting new ways. Or not. If libraries cling to outdated standards, they will find it increasingly difficult to serve their clients as they expect and deserve.

To create standards that are both adequate for present needs and flexible enough to offer new opportunities, we should begin with the requirements of bibliographic description (see Functional Requirements for Bibliographic Records, for example) and devise an encoding standard that provides power and flexibility. This is clearly a huge undertaking, and one that will take commitment from organizations such as the Library of Congress and OCLC. We did it once, over thirty years ago, and we can do it again. MARC may have been born in the Beatles era, but it is time to show it the long and winding road.

Resources

Applying XML to the Bibliographic Description
     Cataloging & Classification, vol 33, no 2, 2001
Functional Requirements for Bibliographic Records
     www.ifla.org/VII/s13/frbr/frbr.htm
MARC Standards
     www.loc.gov/marc/
Moving from MARC to XML
     ihome.ust.hk/~lblkt/xml/marc2xml.html
Tables of Contents Enrichment Service
     www.blackwell.com/pdf/TOCEnrichment.pdf
XML and MARC: A Choice or Replacement?
     elane.stanford.edu/laneauth/ALAChicago2000.html
XMLMARC
     xmlmarc.stanford.edu

MARC Exit Strategies

In "MARC Must Die," I briefly outlined why it is time for us to rethink our most basic bibliographic standards: MARC elements, MARC syntax, and *AACR2* (the rules for populating them). Here, I'll be looking at various ways in which we can build on our strengths without allowing the past to limit our future.

Saving what's good

Librarians have more than thirty years of experience encoding bibliographic information in computer-readable form. Along the way we've learned a few things. As physicians are instructed to "first, do no harm," so we should make sure that a new biblio-graphic standard does not harm what we value.

We've learned that granularity is good (see "The Importance of Being Granular" earlier in this chapter). Granularity is the degree to which metadata elements are chopped up into constituent parts. For example, unambiguously recording the various parts of a personal name is good because sometimes you want to display a name as someone would refer to a person (e.g., Mark Twain) and sometimes you want to display a name in reverse order (e.g., Twain, Mark). If a name is not recorded as individual parts, computers are unable to manipulate the name accurately.

Language and hierarchy

We know that not all words are created equal. Recording the title of a book (e.g., *The Adventures of Tom Sawyer*) is fine for most purposes. But when you need to create an alphabetical list of book titles, the word *The* becomes an impediment. In MARC we have a method of identifying how many "nonfiling" characters are at the beginning of a title string.

Names we understand to be tricky things. When users search for "Mark Twain," do they want to find all of the works by Mark Twain, or do they want to find all the works by Samuel Clemens, whether he used his pseudonym or not? Authority control provides a way to uniquely identify particular individuals and all the different names or name forms they may have used in their lifetimes.

Some information is hierarchical in nature, while some is not. Most bibliographic information has no hierarchical relationship. That is, a book will or may have one or more authors, a title, some subject headings, etc. Yet none of that information could logically be nested within any other information. The table of contents for the same book, on the other hand, may be quite hi-erarchical in nature—a section may have one or more chapters nested within it.

Dumping what's bad

Our current standards are focused on the book as a physical object. Indeed, the physical object is paramount. Second editions of a book require a completely separate record. Therefore, when users search for a book, they are often presented with several separate records for different editions, or sometimes even for different printings. Sorting out the one that is wanted is not always easy when much of the same information is duplicated for each record.

This problem is significantly exacerbated with union catalogs—particularly virtual union catalogs that attempt to merge duplicate records at the moment a user performs a search (called "on-the-fly"). We need to separate the base bibliographic description (author, title, subjects, etc.) from the manifestations of that item. There should be one bibliographic record and one or more holdings records, with the details of a given holding recorded with that holding. A print copy may have a physical description (e.g., the number of pages, etc.) while an electronic copy will need to record other details (e.g., the URL and format).

Adding new features

We need easy extensibility. As any cataloger knows, changing MARC is a painstaking and lengthy process. But the XML community has shown us how to specify a well-codified basic set of tags while allowing for further enhancement with any arbitrary set of tags.

Being hierarchical in nature, XML would allow a bibliographic record to have a MARC-like container for basic bibliographic information, as well as related but separate containers, or other sets, of metadata elements.

One such enhancement might be an accurate encoding of the table of contents, which would significantly enhance our bibliographic records. Smashing a table of contents into MARC is like forcing a square peg into a round hole—it's difficult, and the peg usually gets damaged in the process. Being a flat structure, MARC doesn't easily accommodate hierarchy.

Improve merging and authority control

There should be hooks for record merging. As libraries share their bibliographic information with other entities—such as in building a union catalog—merging records for the same intellectual item is presenting significant difficulties. This problem is particularly acute for systems that attempt to merge records on-the-fly. Why not create a field specifically for the purposes of record merging?

I'm not yet sure of the best method to create a unique ID for each bibliographically distinct item, but I'm certain it can be done, whether by software or catalogers. An ISBN is not sufficient, since a unique ISBN is assigned to the cloth and paper copies of the same bibliographic entity. If such a code could be created or assigned, merging records for the same book would be a piece of cake. Information that is specific to a particular physical item would be carried along.

Authority control should be robust. Our current catalogs and the standards upon which they are based have never provided us with truly effective authority control. With a new standard, we have the opportunity to treat names in an entirely different way. For example, we could record the author's name as it appears on a book, and also record the unique ID of that person's record in a central name authority database. At the time of indexing, such a database could be consulted to pull in the name variants for that individual.

Start from scratch

I'm not certain that I did an adequate job in "MARC Must Die" of drawing distinctions among the problems with MARC element sets (e.g., title statement, subject heading, etc.), the MARC syntax (e.g., the numeric fields, subfield indicators, etc.), and *AACR2*. Unfortunately, the length of the "Digital Libraries" column in *Library Journal* does not always permit such nuances. But I'm also not sure if nuance is needed to make my case. You can move the deck chairs around the *Titanic* all you want, but the ship is still going down. While we are not (yet) in such a dramatic situation, the analogy has a kernel of truth. If we do not consider what we can achieve by starting anew, we will never know what possible solutions there are beyond our present set of standards.

So, for the sake of argument, let's assume that in the fullness of time we have indeed created a new set of standards for bibliographic description. What do we do with our millions of existing MARC records? I can suggest a some possibilities...

Some exit strategies

One method is entombment. My least favorite option is to stop creating new MARC records and begin building a parallel system based on the new standard. With cross-database search tools becoming a reality (see Chapter 6), it may be possible to create a portal that stitches the two systems together for the user while you work over time to migrate the old records.

Another option is encapsulation. The Library of Congress is already hard at work defining an XML standard for bibliographic information that breaks some of the bonds of MARC. This developing standard, the Metadata Object Description Schema (MODS), is sufficient for capturing most of what is presently in our MARC records, although it is not possible to "round-trip" (go from MARC to MODS and back to MARC again) with MARC records using MODS.

For a project at the California Digital Library, we extracted MARC records from our catalog, translated them into MODS, and embedded the records in an XML wrapper via the Metadata Encoding and Transmission Standard (METS). We also demonstrated how we could take metadata from the publisher and embed that as well in its own section of the METS record. We were then able to index and display fields selectively from both metadata sources for user searching and display.

Or maybe migration

Then there is migration. A complete transition to a new set of bibliographic standards would require migrating our existing record base into whatever we devise.

Before you object to the scale of such an undertaking, consider how only a few years ago there were no records at all in digital form. And migrating digital information from one format to another will be easier, since some parts (but likely not all) can be automated. The point here is to do this migration once and to a standard that is flexible enough to allow future extensions and changes without requiring another migration.

So, am I out of my mind? Possibly. Am I stirring up trouble? Likely. Have I stated facts and outlined possibilities that are worth considering? Ours to judge, but we have nothing to lose by considering what our future could be, even if it means questioning our most basic professional assumptions.

Resources

MARC
    www.loc.gov/marc/
METS
    www.loc.gov/standards/mets/
MODS
    www.loc.gov/standards/mods/

5

ACCESS

Where the Rubber Meets the Road

User Interface Design: Some Guiding Principles

Personalizing the Digital Library

Library Catalogs: The Wrong Solution

Cross-Database Search: One-Stop Shopping

The Right Solution: Federated Search Tools

Not Your Mother's Union Catalog

The Convenience Catastrophe

Where the Rubber Meets the Road

Rubber spinning in opposition to pavement makes a car move. Without such traction, a car would make a better boat anchor than a means of transportation. Likewise, a digital collection without effective means of access is nothing but a pile of bits awaiting a purpose. Access is where the digital library rubber meets the road. Questions of access are often overshadowed by other digital library dilemmas, so it's hard to not lose sight of your goal. For many projects, that goal is to create a collection of digital materials—books, journals, manuscripts, photographs, etc.—with a particular audience or audiences in mind. Important questions include:

- Whose needs are you hoping to serve?
- How will users naturally tend to approach such a collection or system?
- What kinds of activities will they want to perform?
- How sophisticated might they be in terms of using interface controls, searching syntaxes, or manipulation options?
- Do they want to bring together individual items from a variety of collections, or would they prefer to view items within the context of a collection?

Remember: *More is better.* With often just a little forethought and work, a collection can be made available through a variety of methods or interfaces. Items may be browsed by topic, or located through searching, or by visiting an online exhibit of highlights. Each of these methods will be useful to different users, or for different purposes. If you spend a lot of time, effort and money to create a digital collection, don't be stingy when it comes to making it usable.

Making it functional

Some key access decisions concern how users will be able to interact with the digital collection. A common access method is searching, but in what ways will searching be supported? Is the capacity to construct complex search queries—e.g., using Boolean operators—important? If a database is involved, which fields should be searchable? How should the search results be displayed?

For browsing, another common access method, you must organize a collection by topic, provenance (the origin of a collection), or some other scheme. You also must decide whether the entire collection—or only a subset, as in an online exhibition—will be "browseable."

Once items of interest are located, will the user wish to see them together, manipulate them in some way, or download them?

If so, your access methods and interface should support these activities. For example, if you want users to be able to bring together onto one screen a set of items, you must provide a way to select them.

Questions of cataloging

A key access issue, particularly for archival and museum collections, is whether to catalog digital items individually or as a collection. The emerging text markup standard for archival finding aids, Encoded Archival Description (EAD), is being used as a container for digitized items from the collection (see "Twenty-first Century Cataloging" in Chapter 4).

Therefore, access is largely restricted to the context of the collection, such as in the California Heritage Digital Image Access Project, which encompasses approximately thirty thousand photographs relating to California history. The California Heritage collection is part of a larger collection of archival finding aids called the Online Archive of California.

There are advantages to organizing digital objects completely within the collection description. Individual item-level records are not required. In fact, items require little or no description if the collection itself is described sufficiently. Also, the collection provides the individual items with both context and provenance.

The downside

But there are disadvantages as well. Without item-level descriptions of digital objects, it will be difficult or impossible to achieve different modes of access to the items. For example, a user of the California Heritage site will find it very difficult to pull together a set of related images that come from different collections.

A search on "Chinese" turns up a few dozen individual collections holding a varying number of photographs that match the search. But navigating among those "hits" is a nightmare because the individual images must be browsed within the context of each collection.

Meanwhile, a site created to highlight such digitized items by the California Digital Library (aptly named californiadigitallibrary.org) displays search results as individual thumbnail images from different collections on one page. Item-level records for each image make this second interface possible. Each record includes at least the caption of the photograph and a link to the finding aid of the collection of which it is a part.

Avoid technology overkill

Cutting-edge technologies are likely to hinder access rather than enhance it. Requiring the user to have client-side technologies like specific plug-ins or browsers is a potential source of problems. Such requirements may be commonplace at commercial web sites but should be rare at a library site. Such cutting-edge technologies are often employed for trivial reasons (e.g., needless animations) or better accomplished on the server (for example, by software that runs behind the scenes and only sends standard HTML to the client).

Improving accessibility

I've seen web pages with print so small that I'm tempted to use a magnifying glass. But even standard-sized print can be too small for some. And the software that reads the contents of web pages to the blind will be stymied by most graphics-heavy web sites. So designers should take steps to ensure that those with disabilities have at least a chance at access. One good way to determine how your web documents check out is to use "Bobby," produced by the Center for Applied Special Technology, which will grab a copy of your page and check it for accessibility problems. The resulting report can also sensitize you to issues you should consider when designing digital library collections and services for all users.

Customizing access

Not all users are the same. Your collection likely will be approached by a wide variety of people with an equally varied set of needs and experiences. The more you can align your user interface to the way they think, the better they will understand how to use your site.

At the Library of Congress, the American Memory collection offers the "Learning Page," designed specifically for educators, in addition to its default interface. Such audience-specific views of a site can be very effective. Libraries are also beginning to allow users to create their own views of library resources. A couple of projects worth watching in this regard are North Carolina State University's MyLibrary, which allows you to create a portable web page listing available library information resources, and the University of Washington's My Gateway, which lets you organize frequently-used web resources in a way similar to bookmarking.

As with the other issues above, the goal is to bring our users to the information they need quickly, easily and effectively. If we do that well enough, they will be able to go zooming off down the information highway with all the traction they need.

Resources

American Memory
  memory.loc.gov
Bobby
  www.cast.org/bobby/
California Heritage Digital Image Access Project
  sunsite.berkeley.edu/CalHeritage/
California Digital Library
  californiadigitallibrary.org
Encoded Archival Description
  www.loc.gov/ead/
My Gateway
  https://www.lib.washington.edu/Resource/Login.asp?Start=Custom
MyLibrary
  my.lib.ncsu.edu
Online Archive of California
  www.oac.cdlib.org

User Interface Design:
Some Guiding Principles

Until the last few decades, the user interface to the library had long remained relatively unchanged. For decades, the only changes in the card catalog were minor tweaks in production techniques (from cards written in "library hand" to ones produced by computer). From grade school, library users became accustomed to the interface, and it changed not at all or very little (say, from Dewey Decimal to Library of Congress Classification) for the rest of their lives.

Now user interfaces vary significantly from library to library, and even within a library, from library holdings to CD-ROM databases to web resources. Why such variation? Of course, there are different kinds of resources or different types of information. But good user interface design remains more art than science. The few "rules" can be successfully broken at various times and in various ways, although most rule breakers are unsuccessful. Also, designers honestly disagree about how best to make systems user-friendly. In the end, one person's great interface may be, unfortunately, another person's nightmare. System designers cannot use such difficulties to ignore their responsibility to design usable systems. Nor should they think that once a design is created, their work is done. A good user interface will evolve over time, as an organization learns about its shortcomings or becomes aware of new techniques or technologies.

Guiding principles

Without formal rules, guiding principles should always be considered, but need not be slavishly followed for all audiences or purposes. The ones below are not the only principles to consider, just some basic ones from my own experience and that of others. The resources identified below offer more suggestions.

To every element, a purpose. Alternatively: be thankful for everything you can throw away. Because there is no more valuable "real estate" than space on a computer monitor, do not needlessly waste space or allot it to items of little or no importance. If something is on screen, it must serve a useful purpose. This doesn't mean you can't use images or other embellishments; just avoid gratuitous ones.

Avoid inconsistency. Few things will frustrate users as quickly as an inconsistent user interface. Do not move things around on the screen from page to page. Do not change what you label the same thing. And religiously follow whatever navigation scheme you devise.

Strive for efficiency. In a web interface, users must follow particular "click trails" to accomplish certain tasks. Make that trail as short and as productive as possible, given other important considerations and constraints. Make every click count, and every screen appreciated.

Support multiple users and multiple purposes. One truism concerning user interface design is that there is no single user. Therefore, any design must account for the diversity of users and their diversity of purposes, which may change over time.

Talk to your users. The best way to discover how users like your system is to ask them. That "asking" can include focus groups, surveys, polls and informal conversations. Methods that are always available (such as links from web pages) will encourage ongoing user feedback.

Get help. Few individuals can ably handle all elements of a user interface design project. Be aware of your strengths, but acknowledge your shortcomings. Fill in for your lack of knowledge or experience by signing on additional talent. If you can't hire help, use internship, community service programs or local volunteers.

Choose labels wisely. Jargon should be avoided in most user interfaces (unless obfuscation is your goal). Beyond that, make sure labels are readily understandable to your user groups. And, as said above, avoid inconsistency.

Do not introduce a new way of working when a familiar one will do. For example, programs for playing music on a computer often borrow features from a stereo system, with similar readouts, buttons and functionality. Keep such real-life examples in mind.

Introduce a new way of working when it is clearly better. The familiar way is not always the most efficient or effective. If a new metaphor is clearly better, don't shrink from it simply because it requires users to learn it. You may be establishing a new model.

Good examples

One of the best ways to learn about good design is to look at other web sites. You can get some recommendations of web-savvy librarians of web sites they like by posting such a question to Web4Lib. If you want to browse around on your own, use Libweb, a directory of library web sites.

Additional Information

User interface expert Jakob Nielsen, formerly with Sun Micro-systems, now consults, speaks and writes on web usability issues. His online periodical, "The Alertbox," archived back to 1995, is a must-read. For a brief and useful review of user design considerations (albeit aimed mainly at software developers), see "User Interface Design Tips and Techniques."

The "User Interface Design Bibliography" will point you to a rich selection of print resources, with a list of web sites at the end. The "Human-Computer Interaction Bibliography" is a huge resource of about twenty-five thousand entries.

A good overall book on effective web design (increasingly the interface of choice to library resources of all types) is "Information Architecture for the World Wide Web" by Louis Rosenfeld and Peter Morville, both librarians and consultants.

Few things are as important to a digital library project as effective user interface design. Unfortunately, it is often a secondary consideration. To avoid the pitfalls of a bad design, do your homework, look at what others have done, get help, and talk to your users.

Resources

The Alertbox: Current Issues in Web Usability
 www.useit.com/alertbox/
Human-Computer Interaction Bibliography
 www.hcibib.org
Information Architecture for the World Wide Web
 www.oreilly.com/catalog/infotecture2/
Libweb
 sunsite.berkeley.edu/Libweb/
User Interface Design Tips and Techniques
 www.ambysoft.com/userInterfaceDesign.html
User Interface Design Bibliography
 world.std.com/~uieweb/biblio.htm
Web4Lib
 sunsite.Berkeley.edu/Web4Lib/

Personalizing the Digital Library

Within a decade, many libraries have gone from having virtually no online presence to offering an incredible variety of online information resources. No wonder our users are confused. When they are faced with a plethora of choices, many users become frustrated. One solution is to create finding tools (such as directories of databases) and ways to guide users to the appropriate resource (such as bibliographies and pathfinders). Another is to allow users to create personalized sites—their own library interfaces.

Commercial web sites have already begun personalization, as in Yahoo's "My Yahoo," which gathers headlines, stock prices, TV listings and weather, among other features, not to mention advertising. Now some innovative librarians are working to offer similar functionality as a library service. The following projects exemplify this trend, offering different solutions to the same problem. Although the projects are all based at academic institutions, any library with a clientele who regularly visits the library web site to use online databases should consider offering this service.

VCU, Cal Poly, and UW efforts

The MyLibrary system at Virginia Commonwealth University is fairly simple both in presentation and infrastructure. Users select items for display from an initial setup screen listing possible resources (including choice of URLs) and then can adjust them later by clicking on the "edit" button on the personalized page. Guests can try out the system by going to a test site (see the Resources list below). Behind the scenes is a Perl program and a text file for each user. The text file stores information about each user's selections in an easily processed format. VCU's Perl script is yours for the asking (see the About link in "Resources" below) but will require local customizating to use your graphics and web pages.

The California Polytechnic State University MyLibrary system leads new users through a configuration process during which they can select items to display within the following categories: articles, monographs, web sites, research databases, and personal web links. Once the page is set up, each category can be easily changed by hitting the "Change" button for that category. More information about each item can be found by clicking on an icon next to the item title, which appears in a new window created by a Javascript. Unfortunately, there is no easy way for guest users to test-drive the system.

The My Gateway service at the University of Washington offers a large array of resources. Using a "Category Manager," users can add or delete entire categories of resources from personal pages but have difficulty adding or removing specific resources. Thus, if you choose a category such as Music Databases, you get all ten resources in that category even if you aren't interested in all of them. To help make up for this, users can create their own categories and enter URLs of their choice, as well as pick from resources within the system.

Each resource has a much more detailed record (only a click away) than those at rival systems since the resources are downloaded from the library's INNOPAC system into a Microsoft SQL database. The catalog record includes subject headings and clickable keywords that will pull up additional, related resources. The INNOPAC system is also used for patron authentication and information (name, address, etc.). The system uses Microsoft's Active Server Pages (.asp) technology to provide web page templates that can be filled with information extracted from the SQL database. Any change to the template is immediately reflected in pages sent to the user.

Eric Morgan's MyLibrary

The MyLibrary project that began with Eric Lease Morgan at North Carolina State University is the best-documented of such projects, and has a well-developed and fairly intuitive interface for both users and administrators. When Eric moved to Notre Dame, he took the MyLibrary development project with him, so now his MyLibrary Development Site at Notre Dame is the place to go for up-to-date software and documentation. To try out the system, you can login as a guest to the North Carolina State system, but be aware that you will be seeing the screen the way the last guest left it.

MyLibrary offers a highly configurable entry point to library services and collections, while allowing users to control even the background and banner colors of the page.

Screen areas not configurable by the user include a global message (a library "message of the day"), a message from the librarian (a free-text field), and "your librarians"—a place to put names, contact hours, phone numbers and e-mail addresses of professional staff in a particular discipline.

Users can customize the following areas of the page: Library Links (for example, a link to the library catalog), University Links, Current Awareness, Personal Links (URLs of user's choice), Quick Searches (a search box for searching databases), Reference Shelf (links to online reference resources), Bibliographic Databases, and Electronic Journals. Next to the header text for each of these areas is a customization link that allows users to select or deselect items to be displayed in that area. The menu of items is selected by librarians. If users want to track links not available on one of these lists of resources, they must use the "Personal Links" section. Once users have completed an initial process to set up their pages, they need not login to the system unless they use a different computer—thanks to web "cookies" that store information on each user's computer.

The administrative interface is also fairly straightforward. There are several categories of functions available: functions for webmasters, functions for content providers, and reports. These three administrative functions allow any authorized individual to change just about any content element of the system: the list of academic disciplines, links and descriptions of databases and web sites, names and contact information for librarians, and help text.

Behind the scenes is an SQL database (MySQL), Perl programs, and a web server running on a Unix platform. Any library with a Unix machine (a PC running Linux qualifies) can therefore have the basic infrastructure in place at no additional cost.

Bringing MyLibrary home

If you want to provide personalized access to library resources and services, you no longer need to create a system from scratch. Several of these projects are willing to share their code (VCU, UW, and Eric

Morgan's MyLibrary), although technical infrastructure needs and local configuration requirements vary. Of all the projects, the most sophisticated systems—and the ones that are likely to scale well—are those from the University of Washington and the MyLibrary development project. If you are using MS Internet Information Server (IIS) as your web platform, then the UW system may be best—particularly if you have an INNOPAC catalog. If you are using the Apache web server on Unix, take a look at Eric's system. If you can go either way, then Eric's open source system is your best bet. The server requirements to support any of these systems are negligible. Any decent web server platform can handle the load, and little disk space is needed to store information, settings and data from which the screen displays are constructed. While staff time for setup and configuration will vary, the hard work is already done.

It's simply good public service to allow your users to customize their own interface to library resources. And since they are increasingly faced with a bewildering array of digital resources from which to choose, it is also merciful public service.

Resources

My Gateway at University of Washington
   https://www.lib.washington.edu/Resource/Login.asp?Start=Custom
MyLibrary: Personalized Electronic Services in the Cornell University Library
   www.dlib.org/dlib/april00/mistlebauer/04mistlebauer.html
MyLibrary at Cal Poly
   discover.lib.calpoly.edu/mylib/
MyLibrary at Cornell
   mylibrary.cornell.edu
MyLibrary at NCSU
   my.lib.ncsu.edu
My Library at Virginia Commonwealth University
   www.library.vcu.edu/mylibrary/test.html
   www.library.vcu.edu/mylibrary/about.html
   www.dlib.org/dlib/july02/ghaphery/07ghaphery.html
MyLibrary Development Site
   dewey.library.nd.edu/mylibrary/
My Yahoo
   my.yahoo.com

Library Catalogs: The Wrong Solution

Most integrated library systems, as they are currently configured and used, should be removed from public view. Before I say why, let me be clear that I think the integrated library system serves a very important, albeit limited, role.

An integrated library system should serve as a key piece of the infrastructure of a library, handling such tasks as materials acquisition, cataloging (including holdings, of course), and circulation. The integrated library system should be a complete and accurate recording of a local library's holdings. It should not be presented to users as the primary system for locating information. It fails badly at that important job.

Lack of content

The central problem of almost any library catalog system is that it typically includes only information about the books and journals held by a particular library. Most do not provide access to journal article indexes, web search engines, or even selective web directories like the Librarians' Index to the Internet. If they do offer such access, it is only via links to these services.

The library catalog is far from one-stop shopping for information. Although we acknowledge that fact to each other, we still treat it as if it were the best place in the universe to begin a search. Most of us give the catalog a place of great prominence on our web pages. But information for each book is limited to the author, title, and a few subject headings. Seldom can book reviews, jacket summaries, recommendations, or tables of contents be found—or anything at all to help users determine if they want the material.

Lack of coverage

Most catalogs do not allow patrons even to discover all the books that are available to them. If you're lucky, your catalog may cover the collections of those libraries with which you have close ties—such as in a regional network. But that leaves out all those items that could be requested via interlibrary loan. As Steve Coffman pointed out in his "Building Earth's Largest Library" article, we must show our users the universe that is open to them, highlight the items most accessible, and provide an estimate of how long it would take to obtain other items.

Inability to increase coverage

Despite some well-meaning attempts to smash everything of interest into the library catalog, the fact remains that most integrated library systems expect MARC records, and MARC records only, meaning that whatever we want to put into the catalog must be described using MARC and *AACR2* (see "Marc Must Die" in Chapter 4).

This is a barrier to dramatically increasing the scope of a catalog system, even if we decided to do it. How would you, for example, use the Open Archives Initiative Protocol for Metadata Harvesting (OAI-PMH) to crawl the bibliographic records of remote repositories and make them searchable within your library catalog? It can't be done, and it shouldn't. The library catalog should be a record of a given library's holdings. Period.

User interface hostility

Recently I used the library catalogs of two public libraries, new products from two major library vendors. A link on one catalog said "Knowledge Portal," whatever that was supposed to mean. Clicking on it brought you to two choices: Z39.50 Bibliographic Sites and the World Wide Web. No public library user will have the faintest clue what Z39.50 is. The other catalog launched a Java applet that before long froze my web browser so badly I was forced to shut the program down.

Pick a popular book and pretend you are a library patron. Choose three to five libraries at random from the lib-web-cats site (picking catalogs that are not using your system), and attempt to find your book. Try as much as possible to see the system through the eyes of your patrons—a teenager, a retiree, an older faculty member. You may not always like what you see. Now go back to your own system and try the same thing.

What should the public see?

Our users deserve an information system that helps them find all different kinds of resources—books, articles, web pages, working papers in institutional repositories—and gives them the tools to focus in on what they want. This is not, and should not be, the library catalog. It must communicate with the catalog, but it will also need to interface with other information systems, such as vendor databases and web search engines.

What will such a tool look like? We are seeing the beginnings of such in the current offerings of cross-database search tools from a few vendors (see "Cross-Database Search: One-Stop Shopping" and "The Right Solution: Federated Search Tools"). We are in the early stages of developing the kind of robust, user-friendly tool that will be required before we can pull our catalogs from public view. Meanwhile, we can begin by making what we already have easier to understand and use.

Resources

Building Earth's Largest Library
    www.infotoday.com/searcher/mar99/coffman.htm
Lib-web-cats
    www.librarytechnology.org/libwebcats/
Open Archives Initiative Harvesting Protocol
    www.openarchives.org/OAI/2.0/openarchivesprotocol.htm

Cross-Database Search: One-Stop Shopping

You know you want it. Or you know someone who does. One search box and a button to search a variety of sources, with results collated for easy review. Go ahead, give in—after all, only librarians like to search—everyone else likes to *find*.

Why should we make our users hunt down the best resource for a given information need and learn how to use its particular options for searching? Why not provide them with a simple way to get started? In the past, we might argue that such a wide-ranging search service was too difficult or impossible to build. It remains difficult, certainly, but such a service can no longer be called impossible, as these examples show...

Cross-database search services

Some early adopters of this type of technology use commercial applications, while others have built their systems from scratch. Unfortunately, because most search commercial databases, the curious are often locked out. However, in a message to the Web4Lib electronic discussion ("Cross-Database Search Tools Summary"), I listed some staff contacts for some of these services. Also, some are publicly searchable.

SearchLight. The California Digital Library (CDL) has offered its SearchLight tool since January, 2000. Based on the Database Advisor service of the University of California, San Diego, SearchLight offers one-stop searching of abstracting and indexing databases, library catalogs, web sites, and other types of resources. After selecting which "flavor" of Searchlight they wish to search (either "Sciences and Engineering" or "Social Sciences and Humanities"), users type in the search. An intermediary screen describes what is happening and also counts down the minutes that it will take by default before results are returned (which can be adjusted by the user).

The user's search words are sent to a wide variety of databases (well over a hundred), with the results organized by resource type (books, journal indexes, electronic journals, e-texts and documents, reference resources, and web directories). The number of hits is noted beside each resource, and clicking on that number will automatically take users to the results in that particular database, when possible. Alternatively, they can click on a link to go to the resource and search it directly. Anyone can try it out, but those not part of the UC community won't see results for licensed databases.

NLM Gateway. This cross-database search operates in a variety of databases from the National Library of Medicine (NLM). A web page describing the service states, "One target audience for the Gateway is the Internet user who is new to NLM's online resources and does not know what information is available there or how best to search for it."

Flashpoint. The Research Library of the Los Alamos National Laboratory wrote an in-house Perl program to search a set of databases simultaneously. In the article "Flashpoint @ LANL.gov: A Simple Smart Search Interface," the authors describe how their system underwent several design iterations in response to user feedback, testing, and analysis of failed searches. It presently searches nine bibliographic databases and one full-text database.

Multi-SEARCH. The University of Arizona Library uses OCLC's SiteSearch software to search multiple databases. SiteSearch uses the Z39.50 protocol to search databases that are compliant with that standard—in this case, three state catalogs and the OCLC FirstSearch databases.

Software for cross-database searching

Several sites use the WebFeat product to search multiple databases. Other products that offer similar capabilities include Fretwell-Downing's Zportal, MetaLib from Ex Libris, Endeavor ENCompass, and OCLC's SiteSearch (and see "The Right Solution: Federated Search Tools" for more information on vendor options). Several other site developers have written their own software but then must maintain it as resources (search targets) change.

More libraries than those noted above are developing their own cross-database search services, including OhioLink and the National University of Mexico (UNAM). It's clear that there is a widely perceived need for one-stop searching of bibliographic databases, though it is also too early yet have much data yet on what features are essential.

One key challenge for software of this type is how to package up the search and process the results. Unless the database supports the Z39.50 search protocol it can be daunting to deal with the particular needs of a proprietary database. Even if sending the search is straightforward, the results may emerge via a somewhat primitive technique called "screen scraping." Screen scraping is the process of collecting needed information by clues such as the location of the information on the screen. The problem is that the slightest change in screen displays can break the process. Some applications are limited to Z39.50 databases, while others (such as SearchLight) encompass other databases as well. In general, the more databases a search service covers, the more challenges it will face.

Some early experience indicates that simply broadcasting the search and getting back results from separate databases is a start, but not what most users really want or expect. Most users likely want such features as de-duping (dropping duplicate records from different databases), merging and ranking (instead of keeping the results separated by the source), and methods for trimming down or sorting the results set.Unfortunately, most of these features are likely to be somewhat difficult to achieve and probably extremely difficult to achieve with much accuracy. But increasingly, librarians serving user groups from the general public to academic researchers are realizing that it is a goal well worth pursuing.

Resources

Cross-Database Search Tools Summary
   sunsite.berkeley.edu/Web4Lib/archive/0109/0021.html
Endeavor ENCompass
   encompass.endinfosys.com
Ex Libris MetaLib
   www.exlibris-usa.com/Metalib/overview.html
Flashpoint
   lib-www.lanl.gov/lww/flashpoint.htm
"Flashpoint @ LANL.gov: A Simple Smart Search Interface"
   www.library.ucsb.edu/istl/01-summer/article2.html
Fretwell-Downing's Zportal
   www.fdgroup.com/fdi/products/zportal4.html
Multi-SEARCH
   www.library.arizona.edu/indexes/links/multisearch.shtml
NLM Gateway
   gateway.nlm.nih.gov/gw/Cmd
OCLC SiteSearch
   www.sitesearch.oclc.org
SearchLight
   searchlight.cdlib.org/cgi-bin/searchlight
WebFeat
   www.webfeat.org

The Right Solution:
Federated Search Tools

In "Library Catalogs: The Wrong Solution," (in this chapter), I took library catalogs to task for being the wrong solution for the right problem—general information discovery. But I believe that federated or cross-database search tools now available on the market are the correct solution for unifying access to a variety of information resources. These tools can search not only library catalogs but also commercial abstracting and indexing databases, web search engines and a variety of other databases, while often merging and de-duplicating (a.k.a. de-duping) results.

Although these software solutions are still in an early stage of development, they already offer key functionality, both proving the benefits of federated search tools and pointing to their potential. A number of libraries are already using such tools to serve their clientele better.

The players

Representative players in this market space are MuseGlobal, Endeavor, Ex Libris, Innovative Interfaces, WebFeat, and Fretwell-Downing. All have products that unify the searching of a variety of databases (known as "targets"). They also provide additional services such as authentication, merging, and de-duping. The market is still in an early stage of development, with products varying quite a bit in features, stability, and ease of implementation. This means if you're purchasing a system, you should use due diligence in comparing features, talking with current customers, and making sure that the product will deliver on its promises. It also means that implementation may not be a breeze.

Not just point and shoot

While some libraries may be perfectly happy doing a minimum amount of configuration to the "out-of-the-box" interfaces of these products, a significant number of libraries will not. They may also need to add extra targets not in the repertoire of the given application, or reconfigure the user interface. Or they may need to go deeper by getting involved with target creation or enhancement. For example, some targets may not provide exactly the searching and results options that you would like (e.g., an option to output results in XML). In cases where you exert some control over the target (e.g., your library catalog), you may be able to make changes to the system. This kind of work can be considered a type of target enhancement.

Hitting the right targets

In other cases, you may find that you must get involved in creating targets to be searched. In the case of a large academic library, an effective discovery service may require searching a number of institutional repositories (see "Institutional Repositories" in Chapter 3). While most such repositories support a standard that allows metadata to be harvested, it is not a searching protocol like Z39.50. In order to point a federated search tool at repositories such as these a library would first need to harvest the metadata from repositories of interest and make that metadata available to the federated search tool as a searchable target. In such a case, the library would be engaged in target creation.

Another example of target creation would be focused web crawling and indexing of web sites related to a particular topic area. For example, rather than relying on Google or other general-purpose web search tools, it might make more sense to do a focused crawl of web sites important to a particular discipline.

The de-duping challenge

In a market still in its infancy, there are a number of unmet challenges. Some are being addressed in varying degrees by the vendors (e.g., de-duplication). Others are likely to remain fairly intractable for some time (e.g., identifying what's online).

A key challenge is the ability to de-duplicate search results reliably. Multiple records for the same item are inevitable with cross-database searching, something users don't want. If the de-duping algorithms are too strict (i.e., records must match on multiple criteria to be merged), duplicates may get through; if they are too loose, items that are not really duplicates may be merged. Most products allow the library to set the de-duplication protocol or protocols that should be applied, but some limit the total number of records that can be de-duped per search.

Making sense of results

A tougher problem is relevance ranking. It's one thing to return search results from a variety of sources, but it's another thing entirely to list them in order of relevance. To compute relevance, a system must assume some things related to user needs (e.g., Would an overview be more appropriate than an in-depth piece?). It must also try to determine which items will best match the user's need—often with very little information to go on. Take library catalog records, for example. How would you go about ranking MARC records? If the records come from a union database, you may be able to use the number of holding libraries as an important ranking variable. But what do you use if that is not available?

A possibly intractable problem is reliably identifying what is online in full text. If you know that all of the records in a particular database have full text available, then the problem is solved for that particular target. But with libraries increasingly using OpenURL-based systems (such as Ex Libris's SFX product), it is difficult or impossible to know up front if a given search result can be accessed online.

Unfortunately, this problem is likely to get worse before it gets better. So what is a panicked undergraduate to do?

California's SearchLight

The California Digital Library launched a federated search service in 2000, called SearchLight. It prompted users to pick between sciences and engineering, or between social sciences and humanities. From there, it took this simple user query and searched dozens of resources simultaneously. Since it was an early prototype, it did not attempt to merge or de-dupe results but rather depicted the number of hits in each database, with the databases organized in categories by type of resource.

We learned that, in many cases, thousands of hits across a hundred or so resources is not always helpful, except to guide users to a particular database where they could then reenter their search using the unique options of that resource. We realized that an all-encompassing solution does not necessarily serve key user needs well.

Through the SearchLight project, we came to realize that on one end of the scale is the undergraduate, who typically needs only "a few good things" to cite in a paper; but on the other end of the scale is the graduate student or faculty member who wants a much more thorough coverage of a subject discipline. One-size-fits-all serves neither well.

Tailored portals

For a large university, tailored portals may be a better solution, where librarians can pull together resources specific to a topic area or purpose (such as a "core collection" for undergraduates).

Meanwhile, smaller libraries or public libraries may wish to use federated search tools to provide one-stop shopping to a select group of databases. Luckily, it appears that these needs can be met by the federated search tools now on the market.

To help you sort through what this type of software application offers, and which features are mandatory and which are optional, use the document "List of Portal Application Functionalities for the Library of Congress" from the Library of Congress Portals Applications Issues Group.

Resources

Endeavor ENCompass
   encompass.endinfosys.com
ExLibris MetaLib
   www.aleph.co.il/metalib/
Ex Libris SFX
   www.sfxit.com
Fretwell-Downing Zportal
   www.fdusa.com/products/zportal.html
Innovative Interfaces
   www.iii.com

List of Portal Application Functionalities for the Library of Congress
   www.loc.gov/catdir/lcpaig/
MuseGlobal MuseSearch
   www.museglobal.com/Products/MuseSearch/
OpenURL
   www.niso.org/committees/committee_ax.html
SearchLight
   Searchlight.cdlib.org/cgi-bin/searchlight
WebFeat
   www.webfeat.org

Not Your Mother's Union Catalog

For years the largest bibliographic databases in the world, OCLC's WorldCat and RLG's Eureka, have remained nearly unchanged from the user's perspective—except for new records. That will change, dramatically altering how librarians think about their catalogs. OCLC is reengineering WorldCat so thoroughly that nothing remains unquestioned, including the MARC record. Meanwhile, RLG's RedLightGreen project shares many of the same aims. As RLG's James Michalko puts it, "This is the library community's chance to reinvent what a catalog is."

FRBR-izing

In 1998, the International Federation of Library Associations and Institutions (IFLA) published a report, "Functional Requirements of Bibliographic Records" (FRBR)—a revolutionary recasting of the bibliographic record on behalf of library users. It defined such principles as the hierarchical dimensions of a creative product: work (distinct creation), expression (realization of a work), manifestation (physical embodiment), and item (a single exemplar). The revolutionary aspect is best understood as it is being applied by OCLC and RLG to their catalogs. When a user searches for a book in a catalog, they are faced with the variations of that work as multiple, separate records. Which one to choose? With FRBR, all manifestations can be collapsed into one virtual record, and methods for users to narrow in on specific items (e.g., language, form, etc.). Using RLG's RedLight-Green system provides compelling evidence for "FRBR-izing." Entering a few words in the one search box offered on the main page quickly pulls up a summary list of search results. Under the title and author of an item you may find a notation like "2 editions published between 2002 and 2003 in English." The next screen for that item provides additional information, including related hits from Google segregated in a box below the item record under the heading "Related Links." Additional features include having the bibliographic information reformatted into one of several citation styles (e.g., MLA, APA, Chicago), and finding out if your local library has a copy.

Blowing open the catalog

But OCLC is unlikely to be left behind. OCLC is well along in a project to completely recreate the WorldCat database. WorldCat is no longer based on MARC, but on an internal XML metadata schema (dubbed "XWC" for Extended WorldCat) devised by OCLC to accept nearly any type of metadata. It can also associate all kinds of related information with a book record, such as reviews and cover art, without squeezing it into an ill-suited format (i.e., MARC). Since RLG has similarly recast its MARC records in XML, it is likely that it will pursue opportunities to merge other kinds of metadata also.

Data mining

Gathering metadata is a wonderful start, but even better is studying what you've got. Data mining is analyzing a database to discover information and linkages that are not immediately apparent. For example, the same book may have different subject headings at different libraries. By comparing the subjects, data mining software can imply relationships between those terms. Doing this across a large bibliographic database creates a web of related terms that can be profitably exploited for users.

Here's RLG's description of how its data mining, provided by software from Recommind, Inc., works: "A student might enter a search for the keywords 'Civil War' without specifying the

American, Spanish, or other civil wars. Using Recommind, Red-LightGreen can organize the results in clusters of related items, letting the student pick which civil war interests her." OCLC is conducting similar experiments.

Slices, skins, and grails

When searching the present-day WorldCat or RLG's Eureka, the user is faced with two issues: everything is seen (even items that can't easily be accessed) and the screen offers no localized information. But a project from OCLC addresses this. A Midwestern state is slated to offer a "slice" of WorldCat to its citizens—holdings from libraries in the state. Although users will first receive local holdings, they can also search the broader WorldCat database. In addition, what users see will be tailored by the state, allowing links to local services. This ability to layer on a different "skin," or user interface, is crucial to providing local services, such as reference.

Taken together, this is revolutionary. Should library catalogs be allowed out of the back room that I relegated them to "Library Catalogs: The Wrong Solution?" earlier in this chapter? Not quite, since these impressive systems are still not the unified information-finding tool I envision. But with WorldCat becoming so flexible that it can ingest virtually any metadata, along with the other features that OCLC and RLG are working on, we may be on the road to finding the Holy Grail of librarianship: one-stop search service for information, wherever it may be.

Resources

FRBR
   www.ifla.org/VII/s13/frbr/frbr.pdf
OAI
   www.openarchives.org
OCLC's Research Activities
   www.oclc.org/research/projects/
ONIX
   www.editeur.org/onix.html
Recommind
   www.recommind.com

RedLightGreen
   www.redlightgreen.com
RedLightGreen Project Site
   www.rlg.org/redlightgreen

The Convenience Catastrophe

Anyone who has worked a reference desk has seen users pleased with a quick and mediocre answer when, with a bit more time and effort, they could get a better one. It's called "satisficing." It's human nature to seek that which is "good enough" rather than the best. For many, it's a simple equation of effort vs. payback. At a "good enough" point that can only be determined by a specific individual with a given need, it becomes too much trouble to reach the optimum for the perceived gain. Nobel prize-winning economist Herbert A. Simon came up with the concept of "satisficing" in 1957. Although he was attempting to explain the behavior of firms, the concept appears to apply to individuals as well, and perhaps even more aptly. Such behavior by and of itself is neither surprising nor necessarily detrimental. But when this aspect of human nature intersects with digital libraries, we have all the makings of what I call the "convenience catastrophe."

This catastrophe is nothing more or less than the disappearance of our print collections in the face of more easily obtained digital content. Collections that are easy to access by using a networked computer will very frequently win out over print collections—no matter how much better and more inclusive our print collections may be. Once our clients begin to see the Internet as the answer to all or most of their questions, our sources of support will be in jeopardy.

So how do we fight this tendency? We must provide more information online about what our print collections hold so that potential users of our holdings can more easily discover the treasures they contain. Converting our card catalogs into digital form is merely the beginning. A title, an author, and a few subject headings are often inadequate to determine if a particular book will be useful or not. We need to work cooperatively to provide much more information about our books, particularly nonfiction works.

Tables of contents

For nonfiction works, the best first step is to provide a table of contents. Can you imagine a student's face lighting up when a book with an entire chapter on his or her topic is discovered? How could a student find this from the comfort of a dorm room unless we have made such information available online?

Luckily, we don't even have to do it ourselves. Blackwell's Book Services has sold digital tables of contents of books since the early 1990s. The company web site has a great deal of information on the topic, including an argument for the added expense and an explanation of how such information can be integrated into a MARC record.

MARC record enhancement is already happening. OCLC bolsters WorldCat records with tables of contents provided by Ingram Library Services.

At Cornell, a 1997 report made the case for adding tables of contents to the catalog, and summarized the state of such enhancement services at the time. Although that report focused on books, Cornell is now developing a MyContents component for its MyLibrary system that will enable users to select journals they wish to track, and have the tables of contents of those issues e-mailed to them. The tables of contents are provided by vendors. The system is being constructed using open-source components, and the university plans to make the code available as open source.

Online book indexes

Providing book indexes online is less important, overall, than providing tables of contents, but it can be a useful service if done appropriately. To be most effective, the indexes must be searchable. This can be done very simply by using optical character recognition software to turn scanned images into text and not bothering to correct any mistakes (which is costly in time and money). Instead, when a user discovers that a particular index has the terms searched, the page images will be displayed rather than the converted text file.

This technique is used by JSTOR and others to cut down on the expense of fully correcting the scanned text, while still providing a search function. A few years ago I proposed for such a project at the UC Berkeley Library, and the proposal and demonstration site are still available. (The project wasn't funded.)

Making reviews available

Librarians write a lot of reviews. By and large, these reviews appear in professional journals such as *Library Journal* and *Choice* and are never seen by most library users. Admittedly, they are written for other librarians to make purchasing decisions, but such reviews could also be desirable for library users. Some libraries are already offering library reviews to their users.

(Many books never get reviewed by the standard review media). By reviewing these books cooperatively, as we do for cataloging, we could begin providing hundreds (and soon thousands) of additional reviews that would help users select books.

Seeing covers

Part of making books desirable is creating interest and intrigue. Book covers have been designed to do this for many years, since trying to get a customer to buy a book in a bookstore isn't all that different from getting them to come down to the library to get it. So why not use the marketing savvy of the publisher? Amazon.com certainly uses book covers (and not just the cover image, but also front and back flaps) as well as book excerpts, customer reviews, and even pointers to books that others bought at the same time. Institutions like Ferguson Library, Stamford, Connecticut and some three hundred others provide similar information via companies like Syndetic Solutions, which supplies reviews, book jackets and summaries, as well as excerpts, tables of contents and more.

Integrated searching

If a business sees a fall-off in customers, it would be wise for that business to consider what it is no longer doing right. We should be no different. Our customers are increasingly leaving us for the Internet.

We need to create powerful, effective and easy-to-use search systems that integrate access to not just Internet resources but also to our rich set of online databases and print content. If libraries began providing the kind of integrated portal services that I discuss in "The Right Solution: Federated Search Tools" (in this chapter), users would beat a path to our doors. And in so doing, they would discover that print collections have something to offer as well. But to enable them to discover this, we will need to have much more information in our online catalogs.

The convenience opportunity

Everyone has heard the saying that if life gives you lemons, make lemonade. Trite but true: we now have our opportunity to take this "catastrophe" and fashion an opportunity from it. If we can meet the challenge of moving our users from "satisficing" to satisfying, from minimizing to maximizing, we will have done not only our users a favor, but ourselves as well.

Resources

Blackwell's Tables of Contents Enrichment Service
   www.blackwell.com/level2/TOC.asp
Ferguson Library Catalog
   www.futuris.net/ferg/
Ingram Library Services
   www.ingramlibrary.com
Table-of-Contents Enhancement of the Catalog
   www.library.cornell.edu/cts/martyrep.htm
UC Berkeley Library Proposal
   sunsite.berkeley.edu/PEP/

6

PUBLIC SERVICE

Human and Humane Assistance

Revisiting Digital Reference

Co-Branding and Libraries

Patriotism As If Our Constitution Matters

Human and Humane Assistance

This column was originally published Library Journal on July 15, 1999; it is reprinted here for the historical perspective it affords, but see "Revisting Digital Reference" later in this chapterfor an update.

Over the last several years we have made much progress in building digital libraries, but one major problem remains largely unsolved. The digital library is a lonely place. When we use digital libraries from afar, there are no reference librarians hovering over our shoulder as we flounder around a web search engine, or fail to find the book we seek in the web-based catalog. We lack the most basic library assistance that until now we have been able to take for granted. This does not bode well for digital libraries, nor for the users they serve.

Fortunately, this fact has not gone unnoticed. A groundswell of support for reinserting the human touch into the digital mix has begun. The Library of Congress (LC) has organized and hosted several meetings specifically on this issue that have attracted a lot of interest, and has committed to at least serving as a clearing-house for information on this topic.

All-night reference service

At the urging of many individual librarians who wish to provide personal assistance to remote users (see "Serving the Remote User: Reference Service in the Digital Environment"), LC may go much further in helping libraries provide digital reference. The most in-triguing possibility is a digital reference network comprised of an international consortium of libraries. Imagine an American uni-versity student needing reference assistance at 3 a.m. Why can't a librarian on duty in Perth, Australia, provide some essential front-line help? Meanwhile, librarians in the American university could in turn help students in Perth in the middle of the night.

The form that such online interaction might take is still under debate and will be shaped by the technologies that become avail-able and widespread. E-mail interaction is widespread, but is usu-ally hampered by a significant time delay. Real-time interactive technologies such as "chat" (conversation via keyboard), digital sound, and digital video will enhance the reference encounter, but are not yet widely available. Until most people have either a mi-crophone or digital camera attached to their computers (a minor expense, but still unusual), we may be limited to technologies like chat and to windows within which participants can share screen shots, documents, or other items.

But technology is unlikely to be the limiting factor. It's difficult to organize a global network of reference librarians who can respond appropriately to queries from around the world. Par-ticipating organizations will want to know that their staffs will not be overwhelmed by queries from outside their primary user group, and to be certain that their primary users will be served reciprocally.

Some pioneering projects

We are not completely without experience in this area, though. The Internet Public Library (IPL), a project of the University of

Michigan's School of Information, has provided e-mail-based reference service for years. Over time, IPL developed a sophisticated infrastructure for routing queries, tracking them through the answer system, and logging the results. IPL also uses volunteers—professional librarians from all over the United States. Even so, IPL must turn some queries away, and those which are answered can take anywhere from two days to a week or more to complete. Also, users are encouraged to consult answers to FAQs and pathfinders on particular topics, before asking their questions.

Several other projects offer e-mail reference service, and the book *Building and Maintaining Internet Information Services* provides a good overview of these kinds of services. Author R. David Lankes, the director of the Virtual Reference Desk (VRD), sponsored by the ERIC Clearinghouse on Information & Technology, reviews a number of e-mail-based reference services and suggests a model that describes the question-answering process used by these services. Lankes's model includes some method of question acquisition (commonly e-mail or the web), tapping into a pool of possible respondents, answer formulation by an expert, delivery of the answer to the user via E-mail, and some kind of question/answer tracking mechanism. The VRD aims to develop a national network of digital reference services for the kindergarten through high school (K-12) education community. It also sponsors conferences on virtual reference.

Going beyond e-mail

Beyond e-mail, a number of projects have experimented with the use of Internet-based video to deliver reference service. Eric Morgan of North Carolina State University led a 1996 project to "explore the feasibility of long distance, real time communication for the exchange of ideas among librarians and quite possibly between librarians and other information seekers." His basic finding was that neither librarians nor their institutions were ready yet conceptually. There are, however, early adopters of this technology.

For example, the University of Michigan Undergraduate Library experimented in 1995-96 with video conferencing to provide video-based reference service to dorm students (see "The Virtual Librarian"). The results: few students actually asked questions, but those who did were impressed with the service; the questions that were asked tended to be ready-reference rather than in-depth research questions; the technology at the time was not robust enough to be reliable; students and librarians mis-communicated because each couldn't see the other's computer screens; and, most students and some staff were self-conscious on camera.

The University of California, Irvine Science Library has experimented with videoconferencing technology since 1996 (see "Interactive Reference Service") to offer reference assistance to medical students at a computer center half a mile away. The chat and "whiteboard" (the capacity to share graphics or web pages) features of the software used were very helpful additions to the video and sound interaction.

These activities are encouraging, but we still have a long way to go. According to Steve Coffman (see "Reference as Others Do It," *American Libraries*, May, 1999, pp. 54-56), we are not even doing as well as we could with an existing, tried-and-true technology—the telephone. Coffman advocates that libraries learn from private-sector centralized call centers. Such call centers use a centralized staff, interactive voice-response systems, automated call distribution, question analysis techniques, sophisticated software, and training and monitoring to answer customer inquiries.

The flip side of this equation, as described in "Serving the Remote User," is that if we are unprepared to serve the needs of our remote users, a vacuum will be created that could be filled by those experienced with commercial call centers and related technologies. But we shouldn't require a threat to motivate us to do what we should be doing anyway—serving the needs of our users.

Resources

Before Its Time: The Internet Public Library
    www.press.umich.edu/jep/03-02/IPL.html
Building and Maintaining Internet Information Services: K-12 Digital Reference Services
    www.vrd.org/books.shtml

Building Interactive Reference Service (IRS) at UC Irvine: Expanding Reference Service Beyond the Reference Desk
www.ala.org/Content/ContentGroups/ACRL1/Nashville_1997_Papers/Lessick,_Kjaer,_and_Clancy.htm
Internet Public Library Ask a Question Service
www.ipl.org/div/askus/
Reference in a Digital Age
www.loc.gov/rr/digiref/history.htm
See You See a Librarian Final Report
sunsite.berkeley.edu/~emorgan/see-a-librarian/
Serving the Remote User: Reference Service in the Digital Environment
www.csu.edu.au/special/online99/proceedings99/200.htm
The Virtual Librarian: Using Desktop Videoconferencing to Provide Interactive Reference Assistance
www.ala.org/Content/ContentGroups/ACRL1/Nashville_1997_Papers/Folger.htm
Virtual Reference Desk
www.vrd.org
Virtual Reference Desk Conference
www.vrd.org/conf-train.shtml
Virtual Reference Desk Conferences
www.vrd.org/conf-train.shtml

Revisiting Digital Reference

In 1999, I wrote about digital reference in "Human and Humane Assistance." Clearly, we have come a long way. Back then, computer-based chat was nearly the only option for providing that service. Today, we can choose from a baker's dozen of full-featured online reference products. (For a complete rundown of the choices, see "Live Digital Reference Marketplace," *Library Journal's netConnect*, Fall 2002, pp. 16—19.)

Yet another indicator of the recent popularity of digital reference is the advent of both an annual conference (the Virtual Reference Desk meeting) and an electronic discussion (DIG_REF) devoted to the topic. Although some online reference pioneers (such as R. David Lankes) may argue that the trend to move the reference encounter to the Internet began a good while ago, most librarians were not seriously thinking about delivering reference service via this method until recently.

The beginnings

Online reference in the early days was not pretty. It mostly consisted of e-mail or chat. E-mail reference required the patron to wait up to several days before being helped, while chat was limited to what a librarian could type in immediate response. On the opposite end of the scale, a number of us thought that the future of digital reference was to be the online video encounter (see the 1996 experiment "See You See a Librarian," for example). Although the idea of a video-based encounter has mostly fallen by the wayside—who wants to be seen on a bad hair day?—modern digital reference software is now capable of much more than simply chat. (full disclosure: I am on the Advisory Board of Docutek, which offers a digital reference product.)

Features expand

Typical features of digital reference software include online chat, screen sharing (where the screen of the user can be seen by the librarian), co-browsing (where the patron will see everything the librarian sees as he or she navigates a path, or vice versa), queuing of patrons, canned answers and scripts ("I'm working on your question and will be with you in a minute," etc.), and statistics. A number of products provide methods to edit, store, and catalog reference transcripts for searching and referral. Some have the abilities to send files, share forms (e.g., patrons can watch the librarian type in a catalog search on his or her web browser), and highlight (the ability of the librarian to highlight text on the user's screen).

Pricing models for the various applications vary widely. Vendors are trying to determine appropriate pricing models at the same time libraries are trying to figure out what they can afford. But the interesting parts of digital reference are not software features and pricing but the practical and philosophical issues surrounding this kind of service.

Looking at the numbers

Many early adopters of this technology are concerned about the generally low usage levels of online reference. The problem is that it may be too early to tell whether the reason is lack of awareness on the part of the community being served, or a lack of interest. Although this question is of primary importance (no publicly funded organization wants to waste money on an underused service), we need more experience and better measures before we can determine where the problems lie.

Before drawing too many conclusions from what at first glance appears to be generally low usage patterns, we need to acknowledge two important aspects of this service. It is free from proximity (the user doesn't have to be in the library) and, in some cases, from time constraints (in the case of extended-hours service, or 'round-the-clock service). Even if only a small percentage of patrons are served via online reference, the service may be important if those patrons would be unserved without it.

The importance of transcripts

Anecdotal evidence from early adopters of digital reference indicates that the value of transcripts in a searchable database for answering subsequent questions has been highly overrated. Meanwhile, that same anecdotal evidence has pointed out important unanticipated uses of these transcripts.

One use is to alleviate the anxiety of staff about their ability to be effective online reference librarians. After reading transcripts of actual online reference transactions, librarians are more likely to believe that they can do it, too. Another is that transcripts can be useful learning tools. For the first time in our profession we have a growing body of written records of reference transactions to study.

Second thoughts

Despite the seeming stampede toward moving the reference desk onto the information superhighway, there are critics raising questions. The rather harshly written critique "Virtual Reference: Overrated, Inflated, and Not Even Real" is one such example. A more calmly written piece from a reference insider (Steve Coffman of LSSI, providers of reference software and services subsequently purchased by Tutor.com) calls the future of collaborative digital reference into question (see "What's Wrong with Collaborative Digital Reference?", *American Libraries*, December, 2002, pp. 56 and on). This is neither unsurprising nor unwelcome. Offering digital reference services is a major step for any library, and we should be very sure it is worth at least experimenting with it before investing both staff time and money.

Whither digital reference?

Digital reference is in its infancy. We are still gaining important experience and are learning a great deal with each new experiment. *Library Journal* 's "round table" on digital reference (*Library Journal*, October 1, 2002, pp. 46—50) made clear that this area of the profession is in great ferment and creativity while also being in a very early stage of implementation.

Will digital reference become an essential part of standard library service? It's clearly too early to tell. That makes it all the more disturbing to hear tales of libraries cutting back on reference desk hours as a result of offering digital reference. No matter how successful digital reference proves to be, in-person and telephone reference services will remain important. As with any new technology or potential service, the essential question must be, "Does it provide better service to our clientele?" If it doesn't, then no technology—no matter how new and shiny—will be worth our time and that of our patrons. It should come as no surprise that answering such an essential question will take time, will be accompanied by a number of false starts, and will be debated with inflated rhetoric on both sides.

Resources

DIG_REF Discussion
www.vrd.org/Dig_Ref/dig_ref.shtml
Live Digital Reference Marketplace
libraryjournal.reviewsnews.com/index.asp?layout=article&articleid=CA251679

An LJ Round Table: Live Digital Reference
   *libraryjournal.reviewsnews.com/index.asp?layout=articleArchive&articl
   eId=CA245058*
See You See a Librarian Final Report
   sunsite.berkeley.edu/~emorgan/see-a-librarian
Tutor.com Virtual Reference Toolkit
   www.vrtoolkit.net
Virtual Reference: Overrated, Inflated, and Not Even Real
   www.charlestonco.com/features.cfm?id=112&type=ed
Virtual Reference Desk Conference
   www.vrd.org

Co-Branding and Libraries

The common business practice of co-branding enables an organization to purchase content or service while making it appear as if it were its own. A typical such arrangement may involve a news feed that goes to any client that licenses that service. The content is "co-branded" with the client's look and feel, and there may be no clue as to the content's source. Such an arrangement is as old as the hills, notably with newswires. The Associated Press (AP) has provided content (first photos, then stories) to newspapers around the world since 1934—and those newspapers acknowledge the AP with different levels of clarity. But libraries are not newspapers, nor e-commerce sites, so why should librarians care about co-branding?

Guiding users?

Imagine library users who come to a local library's web site in search of some information. A typical library has licensed a number of online databases on behalf of its clientele and has put together a list of useful resources. If the user has difficulty determining which resource to choose, and the library has done its job well, the user should also find the phone number of the reference desk and a label like "Questions? Call us!" (Don't use the jargon "reference desk" unless you absolutely must.) Or the library may link to topical pathfinders that provide advice on how to use databases.

But as soon as users select a database to search, they have jumped off the cliff, in most cases. Any assistance the library wishes to provide disappears as the user's screen is entirely taken over by the database provider. There is no phone number for help. There is no link back to the library's web site. Users are left to their own devices in an interface that may be completely new. This describes the situation in almost all libraries today. Content is provided in "silos" that neither acknowledge nor accommodate the needs of the organizations purchasing it. This is simply ridiculous. It's a business practice that must change if libraries have any hope of fulfilling their responsibilities to their users.

A better example

Luckily, we already have an example of co-branding in the library world. For some time, the Librarians' Index to the Internet (LII), a searchable, annotated subject directory of more than twelve-thousand Internet resources, has provided co-branding to many libraries. To see how this works, check the co-branding page for LII.

To co-brand, the library simply provides HTML for its own design, and then that "look" is applied to the content. All the links are also altered to make sure that the localized look carries forward to all subsequent LII links. If you visit a few of these co-branded versions (all linked from the co-branding page), you will see just how dramatically the site can change and yet still retain the same content. Still, once you select a link to a particular resource you leave the controlled environment of the LII, and thus lose the co-branding. The only way to make co-branding "stick" as the user navigates around the web is to use HTML frames, which have their own problems—as I will describe below. Thus there is, unfortunately, no way to provide a button or link (to seek help from a librarian) that will never go away—users must use the back button or reenter the original URL.

Adding co-branding in the form of a top or side menu bar shrinks the available screen space, but not as much as had HTML frames been used. Frames chop the screen into two or more separate spaces that allow one portion to change while the others stay consistent. Thus framing is a popular co-branding technique and can even be used—and in some cases, is often used—to co-brand sites with which there is no relationship.

For an example of "co-branding kidnapping," see About.com; when you click on another web site to which About.com points, the About.com menu bar remains. By using HTML frames, About.com can make your browser retain its branding and menu selections.

If it isn't clear by now, this type of co-branding is unethical, at the very least (because the hapless user has very little evidence that About.com has not created the resources to which it points), and may even be illegal. For more on the legality of framing, see "Legal Issues on the Internet: Hyperlinking and Framing." Co-branding should always be a decision between the two parties involved.

Technical feasibility

It takes very little technical savvy to offer co-branding. In most systems, it's easy to co-brand content that is dynamically generated (as opposed to static web pages). If a software program is already looking for parameters to guide it to construct the requested page, an additional parameter could identify the requesting location. Based on that location, a different set of buttons and styles can be sent to the client along with the (unchanged) content. I know this is trivial because I've done it. So if a vendor tries to put you off by bemoaning the difficulty in customizing its screens, ask for specifics.

Benefits to libraries

Co-branding offers at least a few benefits to libraries. With very little effort, libraries can add apparent depth to their web offerings. If content looks like it comes from the local library, then users will assume the local library has had a hand in shaping, creating, or paying for it. Small libraries can suddenly appear to be able to offer services that only large libraries could previously provide. This capacity to mark licensed content as a service provided by the library can help preserve or expand funding support.

Co-branding allows libraries to offer support methods even as users visit off-site locations, all without using problem-causing, unethical, and possibly illegal HTML frames. As information systems increase in complexity, it's essential to offer local assistance.

Also, licensing and co-branding databases can be a major advantage that libraries (and their reference services) have over question-answering competitors such as Google Answers, which mostly relies on free web resources. Finally, co-branding may be a first step toward offering a more unified user interface to a variety of resources—e.g., how the search and results screens look, and the labels for standard functions.

Ebrary.com also provides a co-branding service for library partners. Other vendors have established co-branded services (such as Northern Light), but usually with large commercial web sites rather than libraries.

More vendors should start providing co-branding opportunities to libraries, and librarians should request such services from their vendors. Those vendors that do so will find that they have a marketing edge. If libraries cannot add that service layer, we will continue to lack the means to serve our patrons wherever their searches take them.

Resources

About.com
   www.about.com
Co-Branding the Librarians' Index
   lii.org/search/file/cobrand
ebrary.com
   www.ebrary.com
Google Answers
   answers.google.com
Legal Issues on the Internet: Hyperlinking and Framing
   www.dlib.org/dlib/april98/04orourke.html
Northern Light
   www.northernlight.com

Patriotism As If Our Constitution Matters

You have probably thought about what you will do if the FBI comes to your library and requests your circulation records for the last few months. And you've no doubt thought about your web logs that keep track of every click a user makes. It all gets down to individual action or inaction. Is it OK to relinquish a principle if you might save one, or even hundreds, of innocent people? What if by releasing the reading habits of one of the 9/11 hijackers you could have prevented the horror? If you knew what was at stake, you would have. But it is probably never that clear a decision. On July 4th, do you think about what it is about America that makes you a patriot? If you're like me, it is that in this country you can say what you think, vote for whom you want, and read whatever you please, all without the government looking over your shoulder. At least until the passage of the USA PATRIOT Act.

The PATRIOT Act

The USA PATRIOT Act (Uniting and Strengthening America by Providing Appropriate Tools Required To Intercept and Obstruct Terrorism) cannot be quickly summarized, but the American Library Association (ALA) provides useful web sites on the law. Mary Minow's article "Library Records Post-PATRIOT Act" offers a valuable table summary.

There are several crucial things the law specifically allows federal law enforcement to do to protect us from terrorists. As ALA councilor and military veteran Karen Schneider says, "Under the PATRIOT Act, entire databases of library patron records can be taken by the FBI. There is no accountability, and the proceedings are all sealed...any court order issued under Section 215 of the PATRIOT Act prevents the recipient from saying anything to anyone other than the library's own legal counsel or the handful of staff required to retrieve the files requested by the court order."

Signs of resistance

Some libraries have found innovative ways to resist. As reported in "Librarians Try To Alter PATRIOT Act," the Santa Cruz Public Library, California, posted signs stating that federal officials could seize information about book borrowing. Anyone wishing to complain is directed to U.S. Attorney General John Ashcroft. Director Anne Turner also found a subtle way around the gag order. "At each board meeting, I tell them we have not been served by any [search warrants]. "In any months that I don't tell them that, they'll know." At the 2003 Midwinter Meeting, the ALA Council passed a resolution urging "librarians everywhere to defend and support user privacy and free and open access to knowledge and information." The resolution goes on to say "that sections of the USA PATRIOT Act are a present danger to the constitutional rights and privacy rights of library users." Not a direct call for civil disobedience, but draw your own conclusions.

Digital diligence

We face particular problems with our public services delivered via web servers. Every time patrons click a link on our web site, their Internet addresses are recorded, along with what they looked at. More insidiously, our web catalog systems often record this same information as well as the search terms used. Digital libraries, in other words, can be wonderful supports for spying. Many libraries are working to either purge such files, or to "anonymize" them by replacing the numeric Internet addresses—which can be traced to a particular machine—with an arbitrary values.

The best thing would be to alter your web logging so that individual IP addresses are not recorded at all. If you need to know where your users come from, you should "wash" your logs of numeric IP addresses that could be traced to an individual. One way to do this is with a script that changes an IP address to something like "stanford.edu.user1." For more information, see the web site Web Log Washing.

Hope and despair

In March 2003, Rep. Bernie Sanders introduced the Freedom To Read Protection Act, which would reinstate the legal standards for libraries and bookstores that existed prior to the PATRIOT Act. The Senate's Library and Bookseller Protection Act has similar aims. Meanwhile, the Bush administration is preparing USA PATRIOT Act II. The fight is far from over.

If you are visited by the FBI, I hope you know exactly what you will do and why you will do it. Meanwhile, there are things you can do to decrease the exposure of your users to searches and seizures. Keep only what you're willing to give up. Destroy everything else.

Resources

ALA Office of Intellectual Freedom PATRIOT Act Site
www.ala.org/alaorg/oif/usapatriotact.html
ALA Resolution on the PATRIOT ACT
tinyurl.com/98zb
ALA Washington Office PATRIOT Act site
www.ala.org/espy
Librarians Try To Alter PATRIOT Act
www.sfgate.com/cgi-bin/article.cgi?file=/c/a/2003/03/10/
LIBRARIES.TMP
Minow, Mary: Library Records Post PATRIOT Act
www.llrx.com/features/libraryrecords.htm
USA PATRIOT Act
www.eff.org/Privacy/Surveillance/Terrorism_militias/hr3162.php
Web Log Washing
sunsite.berkeley.edu/Web4Lib/RefCenter/logwashing.html

7
ORGANIZATION AND STAFFING

The Most Important Management Decision:
Hiring Staff for the New Millennium

Building Agile Organizations

Factoring In the Only Constant

The Engines of Innovation

Skills for the New Millennium

Honoring Technical Staff

The Digital Librarian Shortage

The Most Important Management Decision: Hiring Staff for the New Millennium

The field of digital libraries is in a constant state of change. What we do today may not be what we will do tomorrow. In such a state of flux, what tends to remain the same? The staff you hire. Technologies may change, some people may come and go, but when you make a hiring decision, its consequences likely will last for decades. Here, I try to help you make these consequences good ones.

What should one seek for in a digital librarian? What skills, experience, and qualifications will best help you build a library for the new millennium? There are two main ways to approach this issue, depending upon your perspective.

Skills or traits?

Some managers may prefer to identify the specific skills they require and hire staff with those skills. For example, if Java programming experience were deemed to be important, only candidates who know Java would be considered. However, if you use this strategy you must not only determine which skills are important today, you also must predict those that will remain important in the future. Instead, it may be more productive to choose staff who can evolve as the needs of the organization change. Change, after all, is the only constant. That Java programmer you just hired may soon be programming in a new language—or an old one. The funny thing about change is that the outcome is rarely obvious before it becomes a reality.

So, what personality traits should you seek in staff? Below is my wish list, but of course no single individual will—or should—have all of these qualities. Rather, any candidate for a digital library position should clearly have several of these qualities.

The capacity to learn constantly and quickly. I cannot make this point strongly enough. *It does not matter what they know now.* Can they assess a new technology and what it may do (or not do) for your library? Can they stay up-to-date? Can they learn a new technology without formal training? If they can't, they will find it difficult to do the job.

Flexibility. The staff of your digital library most likely won't be doing the same thing for long. As technologies, protocols, and standards evolve and change, what they do must change with accordingly. Look for someone who thrives on change.

An innate skepticism. Many technologies are hyped way beyond their capacity. A healthy skepticism about such statements provides a safety net of common sense.

A propensity to take risks. If you want to invent the future, you must also be aware that sometimes you will fail, and that no failure is complete if you learn from the experience.

An abiding public service perspective. Any digital library will benefit from having staffers who understand the needs of its users, and who will strive to meet those needs. Many of those currently building digital libraries do not have a public service background, and it often shows in complicated and obtuse interfaces.

An appreciation of what others bring to the effort and an ability to work with them effectively. Building digital libraries is a team effort. Your staff will need to work well together, often across lines of seniority, rank, and office structure. You need people who can call upon the skills of others wherever they may be, and who will support their colleagues. Anything less is hubris.

Skill at enabling and fostering change. Since change is constant, organizations need staff who can guide it, using judgment and communicating well. They must be able to distinguish between whining and constructive criticism. They should sense when to advocate and when to compromise.

The capacity and desire to work independently. Most effective professionals will both want and be able to work with little or no supervision. Given a certain set of responsibilities and goals, they can work with creativity, skill and energy to achieve them. They will chafe under close scrutiny and be insulted by too much questioning. They will expect their managers to help garner needed resources, and stay out of the way. They will want managers to provide advice and guidance, but not motivation.

No specifics needed

By now you may have noticed that I've not mentioned experience with a particular technology. Believe me, that is the least of your worries. Anyone who exhibits the traits outlined above will be able to pick up whatever skill or experience is deemed necessary. Also, they will be able to work cooperatively with others under little supervision. They will learn constantly and well. They will hold every technology up to the harsh light of public service and throw out those that don't measure up. People like that will do well by you no matter what the new millennium holds for libraries—digital or otherwise.

Building Agile Organizations

It's essential to hire flexible staff to meet the challenges of building digital library collections and services. But it's also important to maintain organizational agility. New tools and technologies offer new ways we can meet the needs of our users, but only if the organization can accommodate them. Agile organizations are marked by committed staff, skilled managers, and commonly held beliefs in the organization's mission.

If we are to create the kinds of organizations that our present challenges and opportunities require, we must strive to create agility where none may now exist. Here are some ways to do so.

Communication and leadership

Good communication within the organization—both from above and below—is essential. Communication should not be stifled by over-controlling management or by resentful staff. An agile organization offers many avenues of communication. Line staff must have ways to bring issues to management's attention, and managers must promulgate decisions without delay to all staff. Nothing harms the *esprit de corps* of an organization quicker, or with worse effect, than regularly hearing about an internal decision from an external source. Similarly, management should not have to discover front-line problems from customers.

Leadership can come from anyone, at any level of an organization. In fact, those at the top are sometimes not close enough to the ground to see what's coming. For example, look at what happened at Microsoft. Bill Gates did not understand the Internet and the impact it would have on his company. Those of us who were Internet-savvy were amazed when Gates attempted to remake the Internet with a Microsoft label and call it MSN (Microsoft Network). It took an employee to make him see the light, and when he did he turned the company around on a *dime*. It was stunning. (See "How the Web Was Won: The Inside Story of How Bill Gates and His Band of Internet Idealists Transformed a Software Empire" by Paul Andrews, 1999.

Librarians are better consensus builders than leaders. That

quality makes us inclusive, cooperative, and willing to build on the work of others. However, we don't always rise to the occasion on an individual basis. In an attempt to include everyone in decision-making, we end up watering down the decision. Radical change cannot be achieved by consensus management, except perhaps in times of clear and present danger. Sometimes you need good, old-fashioned autocratic leadership.

Management and working groups

An agile organization requires agile management. Managers must use techniques such as those described above to build agile organizations. They also should make it clear to all employees that individual agility is valued and honored, and then follow through. Individuals who exhibit professional flexibility should be recognized for their efforts. Do not expect employees of an organization to value something that management does not.

Standing committees will meet forever whether or not there is anything of substance to discuss. Such committees should be avoided at all costs and tolerated only as a mechanism from which to spawn task forces and project teams that get the work done. You can appoint anyone to such a group on an ad hoc basis, give them a specific charge, and disband the group when the charge has been completed.

Staffing and budget

Agility in staffing involves whom you hire and how you hire them. Strive to bring staff on board who exhibit the flexible traits I outlined earlier in the chapter. Also, rather than thinking that every job requires a full-time, permanent staff member, consider the range of potential staffing opportunities. It's more flexible to hire part-time staff temporary staff and contractual staff if any unions involved will allow such options.) As your staffing needs change, you can adjust the mix if you are not completely committed to permanent staff. The Bureau of Labor Statistics reports that in the 1990s, use of temporary staff for jobs in the information technology sector grew dramatically. (See "The Changing Temporary Workforce.")

Truly agile organizations will set aside a portion of the budget to move quickly in new directions. Most libraries lack such money. In these cases, you might consider trimming areas of the budget to support new endeavors. Still, such exercises are time-consuming, and and lower staff morale. Also, try to seek extramural funding from foundations and government agencies.

An essential organizational trait

Libraries are experiencing rapid and unpredictable change. Only a decade ago, the Internet was hardly a blip on most library radar screens. Now it is essential.

It took years for most libraries to learn about and begin to implement what was obviously a vital technology; this demonstrates that most libraries are far from agile. But with effort, libraries can create the kind of agile organizations that we require to meet the ever-changing needs of our users in a timely and effective manner.

Resources

The Changing Temporary Workforce
   stats.bls.gov/opub/ooq/1999/Spring/art03.pdf

Factoring In the Only Constant

The only constant is change. This is surely no truer than in the process of creating and managing digital libraries. Until recently, though, change came rather slowly to libraries; one could even say that change (at least in the form of deteriorating collections) was viewed with some animosity.

Over the last few decades, libraries have weathered a series of revolutionary changes: converting our catalogs from paper to digital form; collecting a much wider range of materials (some in short-lived formats), and facing a world in which our collections and services are increasingly delivered to a remote clientele. If these changes were all there were, we might see the light at the end of the tunnel. But they are just the beginning. Meanwhile, our organizational response to these watersheds has mostly been stopgap in nature. We continue to act as if significant and rapid change is a temporary condition rather than a permanent one. Owing to that, we never address the required organizational changes.

Learning to "zoom"

In the article "Survival Is Not Enough," Seth Godin describes how a culture of stability also affects businesses. Whereas entrepreneurs welcome change because it creates new opportunities, well-established organizations tend to stultify and resist change once they occupy a successful niche. Godin advocates training employees to make small changes constantly—a process he calls zooming. By establishing an organizational culture of "zooming," he asserts, the organization itself can begin to respond quickly to change on an incremental, evolutionary basis. Such an organization will tend to go where it should much sooner than one that resists change. Those organizations that resist change until it becomes inevitable are likely to face dramatic (read: painful) changes that are probably too late to be effective. Godin describes how the culture that resists change springs from the erroneous assumption that "someone is in charge, that the world is stable, that you get to choose what happens next." Chaos, after all, is the natural state of the universe.

Our profession is not ignorant of organizational change—far from it. Our professional literature is replete with articles that talk about "managing" or "coping with" change and with its apparent evil twin, "stress." (Recently, "stress" has been updated with a prefix, of "techno-.") It's as if change could be managed, and stress were a natural and inevitable response to it. Neither is true.

Managing our response

Change defies management. The best we can do is to manage our response to change, by creating organizations that foster it and helping staff make it a part of their lives. The myth of change management is predicated on the principle that we can see exactly where we want to go, and that therefore we can manage a process to get there. The problem is that by the time we get there, we are no longer where we need to be. Change is constant, and therefore our response must be as well.

Stress is not an inevitable by-product of change. Some people thrive on it. And even those who do not thrive on it find that they must at least deal with it. The good news may be that our children, who are growing up in a world of change (e.g., "serial employment"), are more likely to adapt. Those of us who grew up in an era when our parents worked at the same job for life tend to have the most trouble.

For managers and employees

Since change is inevitable, you must strive to build organizations in which change is second nature. This means creating flexible management structures, such as task forces that are given a specific charge and then dissolved upon completion. It means communicating frequently and well, both up and down the organization's hierarchy. It means rewarding innovation and punishing loitering. It means supporting staff with training opportunities to help them use new applications. It means giving staff the power to suggest change and the responsibility to carry it out. It means taking risks and gracefully accepting the inevitable failures.

Be flexible

In a world of change, flexibility and adaptability are essential. Your job description is a starting point, not a contract. Sometimes you will stop doing something you like in order to do something you don't. Other times, it will be the opposite. If your boss gives you new duties but does not tell you to stop doing what you have been doing, it may be because he or she wants you to figure it out. Do what is most important to meet the goals of the organization, and don't feel guilty about those things you can't get done.

You are responsible for your own education, which may range from requesting training from your organization to keeping up with the professional literature. You must keep up with the changing needs of your organization, and the people it serves, and how best to meet those needs. You are responsible for telling managers what they need to know about your work and how it needs to change to serve your clientele better. You are responsible for suggesting a solution for every problem you raise. You are responsible for not whining.

Do not manage change—foster it. If change is the only constant, factor it in.

Resources

Survival Is Not Enough
    www.fastcompany.com/online/54/survival.html

The Engines of Innovation

You don't need to be a futurist or a rocket scientist to know that our profession is rapidly changing. Our clientele—and their abilities and needs—are changing demographically, and the tools we use to do our work are different. The very content that we buy and provide access to is more diverse, and often requires delivery in entirely new ways.

Such interesting times require imagination and innovation to create collections and services. Many libraries are rising to these challenges and taking advantage of new opportunities. Some are experimenting with online reference service, while others are experimenting with loaning e-books. Many more examples of library innovations (e-journals, local databases, tutorials, etc.) can be found at the web site Innovative Internet Applications in Libraries. Some of these projects may result in important, ongoing services, while others will fail. But even failures provide important lessons, and risk is an unavoidable part of innovation.

What makes innovative libraries different from their counterparts? What are the conditions that help foster innovation and creativity? How can libraries make effective decisions about resource allocation that take into account existing needs while providing opportunities for experimentation? How do you encourage staff to take the inevitable risks that accompany innovation? And what can management do to create an organizational climate and management structure that supports creativity?

Encouragement

To foster innovation within an organization, managers must make staff comfortable with sharing their ideas. For example, the web site Innovation Network (sponsored by consultants) offers a questionnaire to determine an organization's "innovation quotient." Although the site is aimed at businesses, it can be useful for libraries. Pertinent questions include "Do you encourage and stimulate interaction between departments and promote cross-functional projects?," and "Do you routinely solicit, listen to, and act on suggestions from people from every level and function of your organization?" A quick visit to the Idea Workout Gym provides inspirational quotes from the likes of Victor Hugo, Albert Einstein and Frank Capra.

Another good place to get the juices flowing is at the magazine *Fast Company*. Although focused on business, many of the articles on the "Innovation and Creativity" page are good reads on those topics.

Opportunity

Some of the most effective ideas are likely to come from those who interact most directly with the users. Staffers should feel like they have opportunities to share their ideas in an open, nonjudgmental fashion. Some libraries use the old "suggestion box" method, while others promote brainstorming opportunities. Some libraries use "retreats"—time set aside for brainstorming and planning—to solicit ideas actively. A retreat need not be an expensive affair, but it can help free up people to think creatively if they are far enough from the office that they cannot slip back to the demands of work) External facilitators can be helpful, since they lack the baggage of insiders and can offer a more objective perspective. As Richard M. Dougherty writes in "Planning for New Library Futures" (*Library Journal*, May 15, 2002, pp. 38—41), "Library staffs are much more knowledgeable than is often appreciated...I have found in my work that staff-driven answers are usually much better than answers produced by outside expert consultants." Tap into this knowledge and experience about local problems and possible solutions—encourage your staff to innovate. Front-line staff know what people are asking about, from e-books to Internet search strategies.

Also, an administrative structure that relies on standing committees may tend to stifle innovation if those who have good ideas are not included. Ad hoc task forces provide an opportunity to bring together the right mix of staff to think creatively about a problem. Ad hoc task forces can draw from all areas of library operations—for these people with the appropriate kinds of experience or skills.

Support

Once you decide to act on an idea, resources must be allocated from internal sources, or augmented from external opportunities. Resources can include money or staff or both, but at the least, something that had been getting done before will need to be put aside to create something new. Organizational buy-in by staff, especially management, to try the innovation will be essential, and in direct proportion, to the amount of resources required, and allocated.

Expect the unexpected

Be prepared for the unexpected result. Do not get so caught up in trying to make your initial idea succeed that you miss the real lesson. By beginning with a prototype, you can gain some important experience during a time when you can still easily make changes. Later, when the innovation is in "production," it will be much more difficult to respond to discoveries you may make about how people use your new service. For example, librarians at UCLA discovered during their experimentation with digital reference that some users were actually quite near to an actual reference desk. These students (the users) did not want to get up to ask a question for fear of losing their computers. Discovering this means that UCLA (and others offering similar services) may be better able to serve those in-house users of digital reference.

Providing a clean exit

It's the nature of innovation that some experiments will result in failure. Besides knowing this going in, other preparations and responses are necessary. First, those managing the innovation must clearly state that the innovative service is an *experiment*. It may or may not result in a permanent new service.

Have a public time line that includes set points for review and decision-making. Know when you will decide to end the effort officially, but make sure to allow sufficient time for the innovation to prove itself. Warn those who need to know that it may result in failure. Explain why it is nonetheless important to risk failure.

If your innovative service fails and you decide to pull the plug, take several specific steps. Perform a postmortem on the project, including all those involved, from creators to implementers. Determine what factors contributed to its demise and, more importantly, which aspects could be considered to be successes. What have you learned from the project? Failures are almost never without some productive lesson. For example, a regional cooperative experimented with offering a "MyLibrary" type of customizable portal. It soon became clear, however, that the level at which such customization should be provided was not centrally, but at the individual library, since the users identified more with their local facility. The cooperative was savvy enough to recognize this, put a cap on the project, and move on, recognizing that it had to consider more carefully the appropriate delivery method for services. If this project were to be revisited, the regional cooperative would be more likely to implement it as an easily configurable software package that the individual libraries could adopt.

In any case, if you decide not to continue with an experimental service, communicate clearly to staff and the public why you are not proceeding, and include any lessons learned or small successes.

What it takes

A library of any size can innovate. Imaginative solutions can, and sometimes do, come from individuals laboring in quiet solitude.

But there are definite actions that an organization can take to encourage imagination, spur innovation, support a demonstration or a prototype, and make the tough call to either end the experiment and learn from it, or to pull together the resources to carry it into production. How well your organization performs these tasks will define how effectively it can innovate. In interesting times, innovation separates the vital, responsive organizations from those that are merely getting by.

Resources

Fast Company Innovation & Creativity articles
    www.fastcompany.com/guides/innovation.html
Innovative Internet Applications in Libraries
    www.wiltonlibrary.org/innovate.html
Innovation Network
    www.thinksmart.com
"Planning for New Library Futures"
    libraryjournal.reviewsnews.com/?layout=article&articleid=CA216311

Skills for the New Millennium

In "The Most Important Management Decision: Hiring Staff for the New Millennium (earlier in this chapter)," I described several personal characteristics essential to digital librarians. Those who possess these traits should be able to pick up the new skills, such as the ones identified, needed to create and manage digital library collections and services. No one likely will have all of the following skills and experience, nor will most employers require all of them. Some skills may be taught in library schools, while others must be learned elsewhere, or on the job.

Imaging technologies

Digital librarians typically capture digital surrogates of physical items (for example, books, journal articles, manuscripts, or photographs). Therefore, they must be aware of the various ways in which such surrogates can be captured, and of the respective benefits and drawbacks of each technique. Digital librarians must be familiar with the typical manipulations required to edit an image and to save it in different formats. This may require proficiency with software such as Adobe Photoshop.

Optical character recognition

Scanning a printed page will capture an image of the page, but it won't render the text of the page searchable or editable. This requires optical character recognition (OCR), using specialized software, such as Abbyy FineReader or Omnipage Pro. Efficient digital librarians must know how to accomplish such things as "training" the software to better recognize the scans.

Markup languages

Almost any kind of digital library work requires knowledge of markup languages—whether HTML for web pages or XML for more complex documents—for marking up anything from a document to a database record. (If you think markup is only for documents, you should read Tim Bray's "Stretching the Document Concept" in *Web Techniques*, December 1998, pp. 43-46.)

Cataloging and metadata

As with physical objects, digital objects require organization and description—often more description. Metadata that identify the individual digital images of a book's pages can digitally stitch the pages into a navigable whole. Digital librarians must understand the various ways in which metadata can be captured, organized, and used. While digital librarians may not need the cataloger's in-depth knowledge, they should be aware of pertinent standards such as MARC, AACR2, TEI headers, and the Dublin Core.

Indexing and database technology

Digital librarians often build search systems, perhaps to create a database of digitized images, or to support a directory of Internet resources. To do this effectively, they must be familiar with a variety of tools, from simple and easy indexing or search systems to complex relational or object-oriented database systems.

User interface design

While a certain amount of useful design can be learned, most of it is creative in nature—functionally creative, but creative nonetheless. Some digital librarians may have this talent, but proficient ones will know their limits and seek help from an expert information architect or graphic designer, when needed. A good digital librarian must write the functional specifications, and work with other professionals to achieve the desired goal.

Programming

Digital librarians, by and large, do not need to be programmers, but they should know their way around a programming language, or two, or three. The specific languages will depend on various factors, but a general-purpose language, such as Perl, can serve as a digital librarian's Swiss Army knife—something that can perform a variety of tasks quickly and easily.

Web technology

To deliver digital library collections and services today, you must use the web. Thus, a digital librarian must be well versed in web technology, which may mean everything from HTML codes to CGI programming. *Among the tools of the trade, this is the hammer. You can't frame a house without a hammer and you can't deliver a digital collection without the web.*

Project management

While there's such a thing as a typical digital library project, nearly all such projects would benefit from skilled management. Clever managers can communicate effectively with a diverse range of people, often both inside and outside the organization, keep the project on time and within the budget, envision the goal, and track the project to achieve it.

Resources

Abbyy FineReader
www.abbyy.com

Adobe Photoshop
   www.adobe.com/products/photoshop/
Omnipage Pro
   www.caere.com/omnipage/
Perl
   www.perl.com

Honoring Technical Staff

Librarianship faces a pivotal and possibly disastrous problem. Our noble and essential work, for which we labor in quiet and unrecognized solitude, mostly attracts people for whom technology holds little interest. Instead, we attract people who love books and who understand that democracy rests on a foundation of open access to information. We are strengthened as a profession by this, but also weakened.

We must do better at attracting technical talent, or risk sacrificing our vital professional goals. We also must work to retain the talent we've somehow been able to lure away from dot-com stock offers and salaries higher than we can afford. Recent dot-com failures have improved our market somewhat, but most library positions are still far from approaching what private enterprise pays. We need to honor new blood, fresh ideas, and the willingness to take risks. We must do this, or lose such people. If we do not, we deserve to lose them.

Losing ground

I know this from trying to hire. I know this from talking to people about why they entered the profession and why they are leaving. I know this from personal reflection about my own career.

Money is by no means everything, so I am not merely advocating higher salaries or better compensation packages, although those are worthy goals. I am talking about recognition, a sense of worth, and support. If we are to attract and keep technically talented people who also subscribe to and back our professional precepts and goals, we must compensate for our incapacity to match competing salary offers. We must honor them for their contributions, as we honor those who build our collections and who organize our holdings. We must stop assuming that, since they bring technical skill to their jobs, they are less than professional. Today, in this digital world, professional work *is* technical.

A few years ago, I was up for promotion (at an institution where I no longer work). The process required a dossier documenting my entire professional career, three letters of recommendation from those familiar with my work, and a self-authored summary of my accomplishments and their impact. I labored on it, striving to achieve a balance between overwhelming the review committee with achievements and evidence, and succinctly stating what I had done and how it was important.

My recommendation letters included at least one from someone of international stature; all were from colleagues from outside the institution. I had published two books, authored numerous periodical articles, been an invited speaker at international conferences, and in my primary job assignment had accomplished all I had been assigned and more. But I was exclusively assigned to technical tasks.

Not getting it

During the review process the word came down that the reviewers did not quite understand my work and, therefore, my contribution. They required another letter of recommendation. In a review, this is not a good sign. I dutifully solicited another letter—this time from someone inside the institution—and asked the person to focus on how my technical work helped the institution.

The promotion, when it finally came, felt like ashes in my mouth. I had already received the answer to my request for promotion: "We don't understand what you do, therefore it is difficult for us to evaluate the importance of your contribution."

It felt as if it were somehow my failing. To me, either the benefits of my contributions as a professional should have been obvious, or they clearly were not of significance. I was wrong. My contributions were *not* obvious, as much as I thought they should have been (given the international recognition I had achieved). My contributions were too technical—there were no metrics for calculating such contributions against those more traditional jobs in, for example, collection development and reference. I had, in a sense, no colleagues against whom I could be measured, and therefore my contribution, in whole, was misunderstood and unrecognized.

Remember the techies

That incident no longer bothers me—I got over it and hold no ill will toward that anonymous review committee—but there are others similar to me out there who deserve your understanding and recognition. These techies mostly make you uncomfortable because they deal with things that either enable you to do your work, or ruin your day when they don't work. But they're people like you who need appreciation and recognition just as much (or more) than they need the paycheck. Techies should be honored for their contributions, whether they have MLS degrees or not, but those who have both an MLS and technical skill are even more valuable, since they also bring a knowledge of the librarian's profession. They are few in number, and we should do all we can to encourage and support our existing professional staff to expand their technical experience and capabilities.

Library schools are attempting to meet our changing needs with updated curricula that reflect the changing needs of libraries. Institutions such as the University of Michigan's School of Information and UCLA's Department of Information Studies are but two examples. Still, not all graduates coming out of these revised programs go into libraries; many end up in new kinds of positions in the private sector.

If we cannot attract and retain qualified technical staff, we may as well pack it in now. Without capable technical staff, we have no digital future—or at least not one under our control.

The Digital Librarian Shortage

In late 2001 and early 2002, First Lady Laura Bush and the Institute of Museum and Library Services pledged support for librarian recruitment in response to a shortage of library professionals. Nowhere is that shortage more acute than in positions that require a high degree of technical knowledge and experience. Very few librarians, for example, can explain the similarities and differences between ASP and PHP (both methods of creating dynamic web pages) and why you may want to use one or the other.

Anyone who has recently tried to recruit knowledgeable staff knows what I mean. It's difficult to find librarians who are conversant with technology and who also are willing to work at the salaries we offer. In order to fill jobs, some organizations have resorted to hiring tech-savvy librarians into a non-librarian classification—simply to offer better pay. Libraries are also driven in the other direction—to hire non-librarians into positions that may have been originated for librarians. However, tech-savvy persons hired from the corporate sector may find it difficult to adjust to the mission and organizational style of a nonprofit service organization. Also, they lack the professional training, and the instilled values, that come from librarianship training. In the end, neither of these solutions are healthy for our profession.

Reversing the trend

What we can do is take our professional responsibilities seriously. Would you want to visit a doctor who did not constantly read the medical literature to keep up-to-date? We have no valid excuse for not knowing enough about information technology to do our jobs well.

No, all librarians need not know how to code software. But they should know what software is capable of doing, when a program could be easily written to accomplish a task, and what skills someone needs to write one. This kind of knowledge is crucial to good public service. You cannot imagine practical solutions to problems if you are not aware of the universe of possibilities. You won't be able to take user needs and translate them into functional specifications for technical staff unless you understand the underlying technical infrastructure and what it can do.

New jobs, new organizations

We must recast some of our professional positions to highlight the many technical competencies that we increasingly require and see that they are reclassified to an appropriate salary scale.

Then, we should aggressively recruit technologists into the field of librarianship, as well as advance those within our ranks who have those skills.

Some library schools have begun to meet the challenge of training technically adept professionals. For example, the University of Michigan School of Information offers such courses as "Introduction to XML" and "Usability Methods in Web Site Design." The school also offers a practicum in "digital librarianship."

We must also create organizations that welcome and foster those who are technologically savvy. But, as Colin Steele and Mechthild Guha point out in "Staffing the Digital Library in the 21st Century," "many of the middle to senior staff in our libraries were brought up in the more constrained environments of the role of the librarian." They may not naturally value the contributions of tech-savvy staff as much as they value book selection and traditional reference service. This may be because we are an old profession. In "The Age Demographics of Academic Librarians," Stanley Wilder found that "librarians, particularly academic librarians, are older than professionals in all but a handful of comparable occupations."

Retooling yourself

How do you become a digital librarian? For starters, crack a book or two on technical topics. But rather than reading such books from cover to cover, skim them, and read only sections that give you a sense of what the technology can do, and what associated technology it requires. Look for books that explain concepts rather than nitty-gritty details. Again, you want enough knowledge not to implement a solution yourself, but to give guidance to someone who will.

Go to workshops and training sessions that provide a high-level view of what a particular technology has to offer, what hardware and software it requires, and its sample applications. Find a colleague who knows what you want to know, and ask for some mentoring. Get on an electronic discussion list and ask a question or two. Whatever you can do to expand your technical skills will make you more valuable in your present position, and more employable for future ones.

Resources

The Age Demographics of Academic Librarians
   www.arl.org/newsltr/185/agedemo.html
IMLS Responds to Librarian Shortage
   www.imls.gov/whatsnew/01archive/071701-1.htm
Laura Bush Addresses Nation's Critical Shortage of Librarians
   www.imls.gov/whatsnew/02archive/011002-1.htm
Library Staffing Considerations in the Age of Technology
   www.library.ucsb.edu/istl/99-fall/article5.html
Staffing the Digital Library in the 21st Century
   anulib.anu.edu.au/about/steele/digital_library.html
UM School of Information Courses
   intel.si.umich.edu/cfdocs/si/courses/

The Most Important Management Decision:
Hiring Staff for the New Millennium

Building Agile Organizations

Factoring In the Only Constant

The Engines of Innovation

Skills for the New Millennium

Honoring Technical Staff

The Digital Librarian Shortage

8

TECHNOLOGY AND INFRASTRUCTURE

8

ORGANIZATION AND STAFFING

Infrastructure

Technology Decision-Making:
A Guide for the Perplexed

Avoiding Unintended Consequences

The Role of Open Source Software

Open Source Goes Mainstream

A Database for Every Need

Beyond GIF and JPEG: New Digital Image Technologies

XML: The Digital Library Hammer

Free As a Bird: Wireless Networking Libraries

Peer-to-Peer Networks: Promise and Peril

Bringing Out the Dead (Technologies)

I Know This Much Is True

Infrastructure

Infrastructure: hardly anyone thinks about it until something goes wrong. It's the computers we rely on to provide information, news, and communication. It's the network that ties them together. You can't have a digital library without it. But it's boring. So, I'm going to do you a favor. I'm only going to give you the basics—the information you can't do without. Remember: a good infrastructure will support your activities now and will be easily extensible and upgradable to carry you into the near-term future. But don't even try to buy hardware that will last much longer than three years, because whatever you buy today will be as useful as a doorstop well before a decade is past.

If you want to think long term, think software. Selecting application and system software is rather like marriage—you make a long-term commitment, and, while you may adjust (and upgrade software), divorce is painful, at best. Therefore, select software that you believe will carry you forward as your needs grow and change.

Servers

The computers that store your information are usually called "servers," since their job is to serve up information requested by "clients" (the users' computers). Servers can range in size from normal desktop computers to large mainframes. PC-class servers may be sufficient for small digital library projects, but large projects will require minicomputer-sized or larger servers. In between you will find workstation-class servers. You may also decide to rent server infrastructure from your Internet service provider, or from another.

Software

Your goals for selecting server software should be at least twofold. You will want to choose application software that provides the services you need, which may in turn dictate the system software. On the other hand, you will want your system software base to be standard enough to support a wide range of application software, both now and in the future. For example, if the database application you wish to use requires UNIX, you may be better off with the widely implemented versions of Sun Solaris or Linux (a free UNIX) than a version that has many fewer installations.

Your software will help you specify your hardware requirements. For example, if your software requires a flavor of MS Windows it will require different hardware than if it requires Sun Solaris.

Hardware

Probably the single most important aspect of server hardware is expandability. If you have a computer that can easily accept more central processing units (CPUs, or the "brains" of the computer), more random access memory (RAM—fast but volatile memory), and hard disk storage (slower but persistent memory), then your hardware base can grow with your needs. Of course, you also will want to select hardware that works well with your desired software configuration.

Clients

While the servers are in your control, the clients mostly will be beyond your library or organization. Therefore, you must decide on your "lowest common denominator" client situation: To whom will you aim your services? Will it be a person with the latest web browser and all the latest plug-ins, someone with an old browser and no plug-ins, or someone in-between? Some cutting-edge client technologies are perfectly legitimate if you also offer a reasonable alternative for those who are not so equipped—a technique I call "failing gracefully."

In general, you should aim your services toward a mid-range user, e.g., someone with a web browser that's only a release or two behind the latest, and a basic set of plug-ins. For those client workstations in your control, you should buy and configure computers based on the user tasks you wish to support for about the next three years. Plan to replace them after that.

Networks

Servers and clients are tied together with networks. The best digital library content in the world is just a bag of bits unless people can get to it. So here are some of the aspects of networking that should concern you in trying to provide twenty-first century digital library collections and services…

Speed. Just like you can't be too rich or too thin, in the computer world it's impossible to have too much speed. Speed can allow libraries to deliver full-featured digital media to workstations in the home or office. The problem with maximizing speed is that you most often have control over only a segment of the entire connection. So, all you can do is to maximize the speed of your network connection over the segments within your control.

Range and depth. The whole point to a network is access. Networks foster communication and resource sharing. But they only do it for those who are connected. Although home computer ownership keeps rising, it remains far from one hundred percent. If a significant number of your users don't have their own computers, you may need to make sure they at least have access to one. For example, a California State Library initiative called InfoPeople (Information for People) has installed public-access computers in hundreds of public libraries throughout the state and trained library staff and community volunteers both in using the Internet and building their own web sites. Programs such as this—and, of course, the Gates Library Foundation project, a much larger nationwide project—make sure that network access is available to an entire community, regardless of its income.

The bottom line

Your infrastructure is the foundation upon which your digital services rest. Without a solid and extensible infrastructure, you're toast. So how do you make sure the decisions you make today will serve you well into the future? Look for extensibility in hardware, support for open standards in software, and the fastest network you can lay your hands on.

Resources

Gates Library Foundation
   www.gatesfoundation.org/Libraries/
InfoPeople
   www.infopeople.org

Technology Decision-Making:
A Guide for the Perplexed

Technological change is rapid and constant. Yet our organizations now depend on technology to serve our clientele as they wish to, and should, be served. But choosing the technologies that will form the foundation of our future services from among the plethora available can be difficult and nerve-racking.

Part of what makes it so difficult is that no one can predict the future with any accuracy. However, we can identify criteria and strategies for making good decisions no matter what technological wonders come down the road. In "I Know This Much is True" in this (chapter I) offer some advice (e.g. "Neither an early adopter nor a latecomer be") and other comments about the state of information technology. Here's some more...

Keep an ear to the ground and an eye on the horizon. Monitor key publications, current awareness services, and trend-spotters. Current awareness publications such as Current Cites can cut down on the number of publications you need to scan. But don't limit yourself to library publications. Take a look at MIT's Technology Review and commercial publications such as the ZDNet Anchordesk and BYTE.

Hold new technologies up to the light of your mission and priorities. Just because a new technology is "cool" doesn't make it right for your clientele. Make sure any new technology improves public service or efficiency. You can make very impressive web sites using Macromedia Flash, but your users may not have the browser plug-in. Libraries may achieve a more animated web experience only for a few patrons, while the rest may see the site as a barrier.

Watch out for eight-hundred-pound gorillas. Large corporations that dominate a market (can you say "Microsoft"?) can shape the trajectories of technologies, sometimes regardless of usefulness or merit. For example, when Netscape began developing its web browser, it created its own HTML tags. Web developers began using these proprietary tags, which partly derailed and harmed the existing HTML standards process. Microsoft's entry into the market made it even worse, adding new proprietary tags. In some ways, we're still trying to shake off these powerful, and sometimes harmful, influences.

Don't ignore the upstart with a compelling new product. Syquest dominated the removable storage market until Iomega started shipping the 100 MB Zip drive, in 1995. Far cheaper per megabyte and with more capacity than a standard floppy disk, it took the market by storm. By the time Syquest released a faster, higher-capacity product at the same price (the EZ135 MB drive), Iomega had already established an unsurpassable lead, and Syquest filed for bankruptcy not long thereafter.

Don't bet the farm on things you can't control. For example, client-side technologies should not be used when a server-side technology will do. Also, site developers who depend on web users having particular plug-ins installed with their web browsers are courting disaster.

Get good advice. To keep up to date, consult experts, such as the "LITA Leaders" (including myself) of the Library and Information Technology Association (LITA) of the American Library Association. The LITA Top Technology Trends web site cites trends to watch, and Tech Experts' Reading Habits suggests useful publications.

Watch for helpful workshops and programs. Human assistance is useful. Watch for good pre- or post-conference workshops and conference programs at technology conferences, such as Internet Librarian, and Computers in Libraries.

All things being equal, open is better than proprietary. Open-source software allows you to alter software to your needs, as well as further develop the code base for others. It can also be used as the basis for cooperative development projects with other libraries.

Know your source of support. Before adopting a technology, be certain that appropriate support is available. Don't assume that good support comes with all commercial applications. Not that free software lacks support; some of the best support can come from a network of open-source software users.

You must make the best decisions you can, given the constraints of time, information and funding. There is no magic formula or crystal ball. Do your best, and learn as you go.

Resources

BYTE
    www.byte.com
Computers in Libraries
    www.infotoday.com
Current Cites
    sunsite.berkeley.edu/CurrentCites/
Internet Librarian
    www.infotoday.com
LITA Top Technology Trends
    *www.lita.org/Content/NavigationMenu/LITA/LITA_Resources_and_
    Services/Top_Technology_Trends/Top_Technology_Trends.htm*
Tech Experts' Reading Habits
    *www.lita.org/Content/NavigationMenu/LITA/LITA_Resources_and_
    Services/Top_Technology_Trends/Experts_Recommended_Reading_by_
    Expert.htm*
Technology Review
    www.technologyreview.com
ZDNet Anchordesk
    www.zdnet.com/anchordesk

Avoiding Unintended Consequences

We digital library developers don't get up in the morning wondering how we can ruin the lives of our patrons. Nonetheless, unintended consequences of our work may damage the capacity of libraries to serve their clientele, from public library patrons looking for books to researchers searching archives. We're not the only field that may fall victim to unintended consequences. For an overview of such dangers, see the paper "The Unanticipated Consequences of Technology" by Tim Healy.

The convenience factor

Anyone who has worked on a reference desk is familiar with this: most of our clientele would rather stand in line to use a computer-based periodical index than to use a more appropriate print index (see "The Convenience Catastrophe" in Chapter 5). As more material goes online, this problem gets worse, as patrons may be tempted to do it all from home. Students already believe that they can get all the information they need to write most reports from the Internet. Sometimes—and increasingly so, often due to our own efforts—they are right. Only instructors who require the use of print materials are likely to force students to enter the library.

So how can we combat the tendency to use what is easy over what is often better? One strategy would be for libraries to make print materials much more enticing. Most library catalog records for books offer such miniscule descriptions that it is surprising that anyone enters the stacks at all.

An author, title, and a few broad subject headings are a beginning, but only that. What about the tables of contents, and indexes for nonfiction books? How about taking a cue from Amazon.com, and add jacket covers, reviews, and ratings? The more information we provide about the books we have, the more interesting they will be to those who may have otherwise ignored them. (See Steve Coffman's original idea "Building Earth's Largest Library" and the response to it.)

The 'act globally' phenomenon

Internet users not only think globally but also act that way. Some seeking library books will prefer the catalog of a large library— Harvard, Berkeley, the Library of Congress—rather than their own neighborhood branches. They search a catalog, find one or more books they want, and then request them from that library. In most cases this means they will be referred back to their local branch to request the items via interlibrary loan. But wouldn't it be great if we could create one place users could go to search the holdings of their local libraries as well as all others? This megacatalog (did someone mention OCLC?) could automatically highlight local materials via zip code. The basic idea is that we need to get proficient at using technology to allow users to think globally (as in, one place to search) but act locally (as in, checking out books). Again, see Coffman.

If we want to get really good at this kind of thing, we must get serious about providing opportunities for co-branding (see "Co-Branding and Libraries" in Chapter 6). Co-branding is much more than simply attaching your name to something. It is also a way to offer local services while a user is viewing remote resources (e.g. a zip code entry should prompt a local library link).

The keyword search hegemony

Due to the popularity of web search engines, nearly all of which offer one keyword search box to search among millions (and soon, billions) of items, users think they can find everything on a topic with a few well-chosen words. Why, they think, should they be forced to understand things like field-restricted searching and controlled vocabularies? Why, indeed? Our search systems are still too primitive to do the behind-the-scenes processing needed to handle these kinds of searches well. So instead of making some informed guesses about whether they entered a call number or a subject, we make them tell us.

We should be making computers do this. For example, imagine a library catalog in which the person must only enter a few keywords—a person's name, or a few words from a title, or the subject of a book. Names are fairly easy to detect if you compare the search words against a dictionary, limiting the search to appropriate name fields automatically. If the search is not a name, perform a combined title and subject search and determine the top five subject headings from the returned records. Present those subjects to the user as links, with the question, "Is one of these topics what you are looking for?" By clicking on one of the topics, the user would be using controlled vocabulary terms limited to a particular field in the record, all without knowing anything about the underlying complexity of it.

We must get much better at meeting users where they are or want to be—and this isn't just picking an index from a long list of title, author, or subject. To paraphrase Herb White, only librarians like to search; everyone else likes to find. Ignorance is no defense. Errors of omission can have as substantial a set of consequences as errors of commission, so we must try to understand the unintended consequences of both what we do and what we fail to do.

Resources

Building Earth's Largest Library
   www.infotoday.com/searcher/mar99/coffman.htm
The Response to "Building Earth's Largest Library"
   www.infotoday.com/searcher/jul99/coffman.htm
The Unanticipated Consequences of Technology
   www.scu.edu/ethics/publications/submitted/healy/consequences.html

The Role of Open Source Software

The open source software (OSS) movement has garnered headlines in a variety of computing journals, and Linux—an open source operating system—has even been touted as a competitor to Microsoft Windows. Also, in articles and speeches, librarians such as Yale's Daniel Chudnov have exhorted colleagues to embrace OSS. So what is all the fuss about?

To understand OSS, you must first understand how software is created. Programs are written in a "high-level" language—easy for humans to understand, but not for machines. For a computer to understand a program, it must first be translated into "machine code," which lays out the steps the computer must execute. Some programming languages, such as Perl, are interpreted into machine code the moment they are executed. Other languages must be "compiled" into binary or machine form before being executed. The compiling process also renders the program unreadable, and unchangeable. To alter a compiled program, you must return to the source, the high-level version of it. Open source software, then, is freely distributed in uncompiled form and can be easily read and altered.

Commercial software is distributed only in compiled form, thereby preventing people from understanding how it was created. Distributing the source code of programs, then, is something of a revolutionary act, or at the very least an altruistic one. For a more complete definition of open source software, see http://www.opensource.org/. For more information on the OSS movement and librarians, see Chudnov's article "Open Source Software: The Future of Library Systems?" (*Library Journal*, vol. 124, no 13, August, 1999, pp. 40-43).

OSS and digital libraries

Prototyping. Developing digital library collections and services often means creating new kinds of tools and services. Prototypes are an important part of the development process.

Open source software contributes to prototype development by being free, as well as alterable to different specifications. This enables digital library developers to prototype new systems for very little up-front cost, which can help persuade funding sources to back a project.

Production services. Open source software can also be used for producing digital library collections and services, many of which already run on open source software. The popular Apache web server is but one example. Originally beginning as the National Center for Supercomputing Applications web server (NCSA) which also produced Mosaic, the first graphical web browser the Apache project allowed programmers everywhere to embellish and enhance that free software package.

Cooperative software development. The OSS model allows digital library developers to co-develop software solutions easily and openly. Commercial companies must by necessity be secretive in their projects. Tools and techniques developed by the open source movement (such as version control software) readily support collaboration among a diverse group of developers who may be physically at far remove from one another.

Cost. Since OSS is distributed for free, if a particular application turns out not to solve your problem, you have only wasted your time. Also, since cost is not a factor, it is trivial to install and test out software before committing to use it for a particular project.

Projects. The most ambitious library-based open source software development projects are those that attempt to build an integrated library system from scratch. But most OSS projects are not nearly as ambitious.

Nonetheless, small applications can be combined to create full-featured services. For example, some services on the Berkeley Digital Library SunSITE, including popular indexes to Internet resources such as the Librarians' Index to the Internet and Kid-sClick!, are based on an open source web site indexing package (SWISH-E) and in-house Perl scripts. Also, the site uses SWISH-E together with Hypermail, an application that receives incoming mail and creates a web-accessible archive, to provide full-featured browsing and searching of the large electronic discussion lists Web4Lib and PubLib.

But unless the OSS application is a well-developed and stand-alone application, such as the Apache web server, the use of OSS will mostly occur in large libraries (of all types) that are more likely to have staff who can install and maintain the software.

Resources. The best site for library-specific OSS is a web site and listserv hosted by Chudnov, "oss4lib." More general resources are available from www.opensource.org, and from the open source site from O'Reilly & Associates, a computer book publisher.

Resources

Apache Web Server
   www.apache.org
Hypermail
   hypermail.org
Open Source Definition
   www.opensource.org/docs/definition_plain.html
O'Reilly & Associates Open Source
   opensource.oreilly.com
PubLib
   sunsite.berkeley.edu/PubLib/
SWISH-E
   sunsite.berkeley.edu/SWISH-E/
Web4Lib
   sunsite.berkeley.edu/Web4Lib/

Open Source Goes Mainstream

At the time that I originally wrote "The Role of Open Source Software" (above) there were indications that OSS would be important, but there were few library-specific applications to point to as proof. Now there are several, ranging from a complete integrated library system to a system that allows library users to tailor their own portals.

For evidence that OSS is now an important part of the software market, MSNBC reported in "Microsoft Facing a Technology Gap?" that Steve Ballmer, CEO of Microsoft, exhorted the company's employees about the competitive threat OSS represents. When Microsoft flips from ignoring an issue to running scared, you know something is up. Open source software is clearly here to stay, and it is not just for geeks anymore. The Open Source Initiative web site offers a rather lengthy definition of what constitutes "open source" software. A simple definition is: software for which the source code can be viewed and changed by anyone (unlike, for example, shrink-wrapped software such as Microsoft Word, of which the source code is a closely guarded secret). For more on open source, see Frank Cervone's "The Open Source Option " (*Library Journal netConnect*, Summer, 2003).

Open source software for libraries can be classified into two categories: complete systems that handle all of the tasks related to a service (e.g., a portal system) and tools that perform specific tasks and can be integrated with other components to create new services.

Systems

Koha. The Koha.org web site states that "Koha is the world's first free Open Source Library System." Made in New Zealand, the Koha system is meant to be a full catalog: OPAC circulation, member management, and acquisitions package. Unlikely to be robust enough for large libraries (it uses Perl and MySQL), it could be just the thing for small to medium-size libraries. Try the demos at the Koha web site.

Greenstone. Originating from the New Zealand Digital Library project at the University of Waikato, Greenstone offers searching and browsing of digitized text and images. Browse the collections of the New Zealand Digital Library to understand what Greenstone can do.

DSpace. Designed to accept digital file uploads from a large group of individuals (e.g. the faculty and staff of a university), DSpace allows management of, and access to, those files.

MyLibrary. Users can create their own windows on library collections and resources with MyLibrary. By logging in and editing the default selection of resources, library users can have the search boxes of their favorite databases easily available, as well as have links to key web pages in various categories.

Tools

jake. Managing information about journals and the databases and aggregators that provide indexing for them is possible through "jake." Designed primarily as a method for other software applications to query journal and index information, it can also be searched via a standard web form, with results formatted for humans.

Prospero. Prospero is an Internet document delivery system that helps libraries send and receive electronic documents. With Prospero, you can automatically convert TIFF format images into Adobe Acrobat files and place them on a web server for patron access. One module allows staff to scan, send and receive documents, while another module provides the services for putting documents on the web and allowing patrons to access them.

Keeping up

Two good places to learn more about library-related OSS are OSS4Lib (open software systems for libraries) and /usr/lib/info. OSS4Lib maintains a list of open source software and a bulletin board with project updates and news. If you catch the OSS bug and want to hang out with others like yourself, /usr/lib/info is the place. Anyone can sign up for an account and then post questions or comments. Here is what library software developers are working on, often long before their efforts are widely known.

Resources

Dspace
  www.dspace.org
Greenstone
  www.greenstone.org
jake
  jake-db.org
Koha
  www.koha.org
MyLibrary
  dewey.library.nd.edu/mylibrary/
New Zealand Digital Library
  nzdl.org
Open Source Initiative
  www.opensource.org
The Open Source Option
  www.libraryjournal.com/openSourceOption
OSI Open Source Definition
  www.opensource.org/docs/definition.php
OSS4Lib
  oss4lib.org
Prospero
  bones.med.ohio-state.edu/prospero/usr/lib/info

A Database for Every Need

Many digital library projects require database software—whether for a catalog of holdings, subject pathfinders, or other kinds of structured information. Database solutions are actually fairly generic; the same software can support a large variety of uses. Only one of the solutions noted below (SiteSearch) is tailored, to any degree at all, for library uses (and yet can also be used for other types of data.) Libraries are increasingly finding database software to be an essential infrastructure component whether they use it to serve their library catalog or to build web pages on the fly.

So, it's likely that your library—no matter what size or type—could make effective use of database software. The good news is that there are many solutions from which to choose. The bad news is that there are many solutions from which to choose.

Depending on the computer you have to run the software, and on the size of the database, the level of usage you expect, and on your budget, one of the following options may be right for you...

Workstation solutions

Workstation solutions are database products that run on a desktop machine, typically an MS Windows NT or Macintosh computer. The advantages include relative ease in creating and maintaining the database, low cost, a large installed user base, and good self-support options (e.g., many books that explain how to use the most popular systems). However, users may face infrequent data backup, "downtime" (time when the database is unavailable), and a lack of "scalability" (the capacity to grow larger or support more users). In general, these solutions are best for small, simple databases for which you do not expect many simultaneous users.

The premier workstation solution for computers running MS Windows is, not surprisingly, Microsoft Access. Access has been around for years, and there are a large number of users you can consult for ad hoc assistance.

For Macintosh users, FileMaker Pro clearly leads in terms of numbers of installations and integration with Macintosh web servers. However, FileMaker is also now an option for MS Windows users and thus should be considered by them as well.

Server Solutions

If a workstation solution does not offer enough power or reliability, you may need to step up to a larger, faster computer that is maintained as a network server by trained staff. Using a server, you typically gain a faster processor (or more than one), more RAM (volatile memory), larger hard-disk capacity (persistent memory), and better support. This allows you to serve more simultaneous users quickly.

Server solutions vary widely in complexity, including very

simple solutions (like Sprite), those with mid-range complexity (like Microsoft's SQL Server or the free MySQL), and "industrial-strength applications, which I discuss below as "enterprise solutions."

Sprite is a free Perl module, which means it can be installed and used on any computer that runs the Perl programming language (usually, but not exclusively, Unix computers). This solution is so simple it isn't even a database—it stores data as a flat file. However, to fully exploit this solution you must be at least passingly familiar with Perl. For those who can write simple Perl scripts, this is a fine solution for small databases of a few thousand records which do not require frequent updates.

MySQL is compliant with the Structured Query Language (SQL) syntax and thus can be queried with the same syntax used to query large commercial databases like Oracle and Sybase (see below). However, unlike those solutions, MySQL is free. It nonetheless can handle thousands of records with aplomb, and with decent hardware support can easily handle many simultaneous users. This is the industrial solution for those who don't have industrial dollars.

These solutions tend to be best when you have more time than money on your hands. Since they're free, you don't need much cash, but you will need time to program web front-ends to them so users can easily interact with these database "shells."

Enterprise solutions

If your needs surpass the solutions listed above, or if you wish to create a robust and scalable infrastructure, consider an enterprise solution. They do not come inexpensively—in terms of both money, and staff time and level of expertise. These are big and complex solutions for big and complex databases. However, depending on the hardware you have, they may run fine on the same machine that runs what I call "server solutions." The difference is neither in the hardware nor the operating sytem environment, but in the complexity, robustness, and commercial nature (and therefore in the availability of support) of the enterprise solutions.

An enterprise database created specifically with library needs in mind is SiteSearch from OCLC. SiteSearch is both MARC and Z39.50 compliant, but it also can manage many other kinds of data. SiteSearch has also been released into open source by OCLC.

General-purpose enterprise database solutions like Oracle and Sybase are primarily aimed at the business market—they may work for libraries, though they're less consistent in supporting such library standards as MARC and Z39.50. On the plus side, they are widely implemented in the commercial sector, which means experienced people and good support books should be easy to find.

Making your choice

To decide on the appropriate database software for a specific need, you must carefully consider a number of variables: the ease and effectiveness with which you can create a usable and effective database for your users; how easy or difficult it is to set up and maintain; the hardware that you have available or can purchase to run it; the number of simultaneous users you expect to serve; the amount and quality of technical support and service upon which you can rely (either in-house or commercial); and the overall cost (including any server purchase or upgrade, technical support, the cost of the software, etc.).

Although generalizations do not always apply, small libraries of any type will often be just fine with a workstation solution like Filemaker Pro, while larger libraries may require the power and scalability of server and enterprise solutions.

When it comes time to decide, take some solace, because nearly any solution will allow you to export your data, should you make the wrong decision, or to change the decision variables cited above.

Resources

FileMaker Pro
    www.filemaker.com
Microsoft Access
    www.microsoft.com/office/access/

Microsoft SQL Server
   www.microsoft.com/sql/
MySQL
   www.mysql.org
Oracle
   www.oracle.com
SiteSearch
   www.sitesearch.oclc.org
Sprite
   www.perl.com/CPAN-local/modules/by-module/Sprite/
Sybase
   www.sybase.com

Beyond GIF and JPEG:
New Digital Image Technologies

When you surf the web and an image pops up on your screen, it is most often one of only two types: GIF or JPEG. The GIF format, created by CompuServe in 1987, is limited to 256 colors or shades. JPEG images, developed by the Joint Photographic Experts Group in 1992, can store millions of colors, but at the cost of a larger file size. To create these images, you need some kind of image editing program such as Paintshop Pro (for the PC only) or Adobe Photoshop (for both PC and Mac). These programs allow you to create, edit, or manipulate images and save them in different file formats, including GIF and JPEG.

But technology continues to offer new image file formats that offer advanced capabilities while still being usable for the average web user. The Fine Arts Museums of San Francisco (FAMSF) uses an experimental image file format for their eighty-two thousand online users that allows them to zoom in so close they can almost see the brush strokes. The Library of Congress (LC) provides similar options for those viewing its online collection of panoramic maps. Although neither technology requires anything special of the client (all processing is performed on the server, and JPEG images are served to the user), each differs completely from the other.

These are but two examples of emerging digital image formats and technologies that promise to revolutionize how we use and interact with images on the Internet. For example, while presently it's impractical to make available a high-resolution version of a large image (due to the time it would take to download the file), these new image formats allow users to specify and retrieve only a segment of the image. Other capabilities of various technologies all promise, at the very least, to overcome the bandwidth challenges of serving images online.

GridPix

The image file format used by FAMSF was developed by the Computer Science Department of the University of California, Berkeley. It stores the image in three different resolutions or "layers," with each layer broken up into a grid of tiles. As the user requests a higher resolution or pans around the image, only the appropriate tiles are sent to the web browser. No browser plug-ins are required to view these images. FAMSF appears to be the only institution using this format, which has so far been a research project untested in the marketplace.

MrSID

LC uses a proprietary solution from LizardTech, Inc. (a spinoff from Los Alamos National Laboratory) called MrSID (an acronym for Multi-resolution Seamless Image Database). MrSID uses advanced image compression techniques to reduce file size with relatively little loss in image quality. While LizardTech provides free viewers to anyone who wishes to download and manipulate MrSID images, LC and others use LizardTech technology to deliver the portion of the image requested as a standard JPEG image, with no special viewer required.

The quality that makes MrSID stand out from the crowd, however, is the fact that it is the only image file format discussed here that can be "geospatially" referenced. This means you can know the "footprint" of a MrSID image on the planet—its exact longitude and latitude. This quality makes MrSID the image file format of choice for many applications for which knowing the exact position and coverage of an image is important.

Flashpix

The digital image format Flashpix has been developed and promoted by industry heavyweights including Adobe, Canon, Kodak, Hewlett Packard (HP), IBM, Intel, and Microsoft. Flashpix (FPX) stores multiple resolutions of an image in one file. Each resolution is then also tiled into 64x64 pixel squares. Thus, the system can serve only the required segment at the required resolution rather than the entire file.Unlike the similar GridPix, Flashpix has the backing of a broad-based industry group, but nonetheless it doesn't seem to have gone very far over the last few years in terms of industry use and consumer adoption.

PNG

Portable Network Graphics (PNG) is an image format designed to replace GIF. It offers smaller file sizes than GIF but doesn't lose any image information due to compression. Information about the image can also be embedded within it rather than in a separate file. Since the images can then be self-describing, if image creators use this feature web users will find it much easier to locate images using web search engines. This format is presently the only one beyond GIF and JPEG supported natively by web browsers. But support for all the capabilities of this format is still spotty.

And the winner is...

So which of these formats will unseat GIF and JPEG? It's still too early to make a reliable prediction, but Flashpix has the broadest industry support, and PNG has the backing of those who prefer technologies built on open standards. GridPix remains a research project, while MrSID is used by a number of large institutions, and is particularly good for images that can be geospatially referenced. MrSID delivers some remarkable capabilities while keeping the complexity on the server (in fact, users may never know that they're interacting with a different kind of image). My best guess is that PNG images may find limited use as GIF or JPEG images, while MrSID will be used to deliver very large, high-resolution images to provide the sharpest detail possible via network delivery.

Resources

Fine Arts Museums of San Francisco ImageBase
 www.thinker.org/fam/about/imagebase/
Flashpix
 www.kodak.com/US/en/digital/dlc/book2/chapter4/flashp1.shtml
Digital Imaging for Libraries and Archives
 www.library.cornell.edu/preservation/workshop/
GridPix
 now.cs.berkeley.edu/Td/GridPix/
Library of Congress Panoramic Maps Collection
 memory.loc.gov/ammem/pmhtml/
MrSID
 www.lizardtech.com
PNG
 www.libpng.org/pub/png/
PNG at W3
 www.w3.org/Graphics/PNG/
"The Promise of the FlashPix Image File Format"
 www.rlg.org/preserv/diginews/diginews22.html#FlashPix

XML: The Digital Library Hammer

Abraham Maslow once said, "When the only tool you own is a hammer, every problem begins to resemble a nail." Once you understand XML and the opportunities it offers for creating and managing digital library services and collections, you will begin seeing nails everywhere. It is not the only tool you have, but it is by far the most useful.

XML (Extensible Markup Language) is born of a marriage of SGML (Standard Generalized Markup Language) and the web. HTML can't do much more than describe the look of a web page, whereas SGML is too complicated and unwieldy for most applications. XML achieves much of the power of SGML, without the complexity, and adds web capabilities beyond HTML. XML provides a method by which you can mark (or 'tag') the structure of an object—a document, a database entry, or just about anything made up of definable components. XML tags define the beginning of a structure, such as a section title, and the end. Whether you know it or not, you use a similar kind of technology frequently. Whatever word processing software you use tags the text you write with style information, such as the font used.

How it works

XML differs from word processing software in several essential ways. First, it is open and transparent—the specifications can be freely read and adapted by anyone, and the markup (the tags themselves) can be seen as well as the text. Also, it is capable of describing the structure of a virtually infinite variety of objects, not just a text document. Finally, it is being built for the web—with a robust set of linking, transformation, and rendering capabilities.

To understand the XML applications described below, it will help to know the various required pieces and how they interact.

First, there is the information that has been tagged either by hand or by using an editor similar to an HTML editor. Unlike an HTML document, an XML document must be tagged according to three basic rules: 1) all tags must be in lowercase, 2) all beginning tags must have an ending tag, and 3) no tag can span another tag (that is, all tags must properly nest).

Second, you must have an XML style sheet called Extensible Stylesheet Language Transformations, or XSLT. While a style sheet usually specifies how the information that references it (typically an HTML file) should be displayed within a browser, XSLT offers more powerful, transformative features. For example, you can choose to display text or not. In some ways, XSLT resembles a simple programming language that has been optimized for transforming XML files into other forms.

Third, there should be an HTML style sheet (Cascading Style Sheet or CSS) that tells the web browser how to display the page. All three elements reside on the server, usually (but not necessarily) close to each other.

XML and software

If you use software such as Cocoon or AxKit, when a user requests an XML document from your web server, the request is passed to special software. The software then applies the XML style sheet transformations to produce the HTML version that is sent to the client along with the HTML style sheet.

If you don't use special software on the server for these operations, the client software (typically a web browser) must attempt to process the XML file. The latest versions of Microsoft Internet Explorer will attempt to process the file, but you're unlikely to be pleased with the result. Don't even try with Netscape.

Few people know this, but any library with an integrated library system from Innovative Interfaces (with Update D) can view XML versions of catalog records. Kyle Banerjee of Oregon State University has used this capability to provide information essential to relocating fifty thousand items to a storage facility. Banerjee also uses it to solve problems that many other libraries face, as with his program ILL ASAP (Interlibrary Loan Automatic Search and Print). Banerjee says that "XML and XSLT are the most significant developments in information management since relational databases and SQL."

XML and structured information

Bibliographies are commonplace in libraries, whether as lists of books by a particular author or pathfinders by subject. What are bibliographic citations but a structured set of textual elements? XML is made for this. Imagine a list of historical novels. Marked up in XML (which is almost as easy as an HTML markup), this same list could be used to create several different web pages: one that lists items by author, another by title, and another by time period. All you'd need is an XSLT style sheet that produces a different view of the document, depending on the user request. You need only maintain one XML document. This is not yet a trivial task, but employing XML gets steadily easier, as tools improve.

XML and digital publishing

XML seems made to order for publishing. A book, for instance, is a highly structured object, with basic bibliographic information, front matter, chapters, headings, paragraphs, and back matter. A book marked up in XML can be displayed in various ways—

chapter by chapter, as a table of contents (by extracting section headings from the file), and more. XML-encoded books will soon be viewed both on the web and on personal devices such as e-book readers and personal digital assistants. The Open eBook Forum has promulgated a standard method of encoding e-books in XML specifically to provide an easy method for interchanging books across reading devices.

To see this in action on the web, see "Tobacco War: Inside the California Battles," which only exists in a single XML file but is delivered in chunks of HTML to the user upon request. This one example will soon be joined by several dozen books on topics in international and area studies, all provided to the client in HTML from XML source files.

An essential precondition for interoperability is the capacity to share information effectively with other systems. XML supports that capability by providing information in a structured way. For example, the Open Archives Initiative is using XML as the carrier syntax for bibliographic information about e-prints (see "Open Archives: A Key Convergence" in Chapter 9).

XML toolbox

To learn more, the XML.com site offers a good start, while Robin Cover's XML Cover Pages is nearly exhaustive. Also see Norman Desmarais's The ABCs of XML: The Librarian's Guide to the eXtensible Markup Language. To discuss XML and its use in libraries, join the XML4Lib discussion and take a look at the book "XML in Libraries." If you are running an Apache web server and want to jump in with both feet, download and install Cocoon or AxKit. This will provide a platform to transform your XML documents to HTML on the fly. For information on using XSLT, an essential part of the process, see Chapter 14 of the *XML Bible* as well as Michael Kay's excellent book "XSLT Programmer's Reference."

MARC then, XML now

MARC was the data encoding standard upon which librarians built modern librarianship. It enabled us to create automated library systems, shared cataloging, resource networks, and many things that we today take for granted. Now libraries are becoming publishers. We must provide access to a wider array of information resources, and resource sharing is more essential than before. XML likely will provide the carrier syntax for all of this, thereby becoming the MARC equivalent of the twenty-first century.

Resources

The ABCs of XML
  www.newtechnologypress.com/ntp/inprint.html
Apache XML Project
  xml.apache.org
AxKit
  axkit.org
Cocoon
  cocoon.apache.org
ILL Automatic Search and Print
  oregonstate.edu/~reeset/illasap/
Open eBook Forum
  www.openebook.org
Tobacco War: Inside the California Battles
  ark.cdlib.org/ark:/13030/ft167nb0vq/
XML Bible, Chapter 14
  www.ibiblio.org/xml/books/bible2/chapters/ch17.html
XML.com
  www.xml.com
XML Cover Pages
  xml.coverpages.org
XML in Libraries
  www.neal-schuman.com/db/0/290.html
XML4Lib
  sunsite.berkeley.edu/XML4Lib/
XSLT Programmer's Reference
  www.wrox.com/books/0764543814.shtml

Free As a Bird:
Wireless Networking Libraries

My first time was on a Gale bus. It was during the 2002 annual conference of the American Library Association, while traveling between the Georgia World Congress Center and my hotel. I was nervous and uncertain, but it turned out to be both easier than I thought and incredibly fulfilling. While the bus rolled through downtown Atlanta, I opened my laptop, connected to a wireless network, and sent and received e-mail. To this day, I do not know who owned the wireless access point I connected to. It is unlikely they were ever aware that, for a minute or two, I borrowed a small portion of their network bandwidth. The result was that I was able to communicate when I needed to. I call this my "wireless epiphany." One definition of epiphany is "a sudden intuitive leap of understanding, especially through an ordinary but striking occurrence."

Now I understand the power and freedom that wireless makes possible. Wireless, however, is far from new to me; since early 2000 I have used it at home. I have a Macintosh PowerBook with a wireless card and an Apple Airport base station connected to my DSL service. I can roam just about anywhere on my quarter-acre lot while happily surfing the net. But what I never had experienced until Atlanta was the freedom of connecting out in the wide world, without paying a dime. "Aha!" you say, "he's trying to make a virtue out of stealing." In that specific situation you may be right. But there are movements afoot to provide free and open wireless networks in a number of communities, including the San Francisco Bay area where I live. As I was enjoying the afterglow of my wireless epiphany in Atlanta, I wondered why libraries shouldn't be a part of this.

The library potential

What are libraries about if not open access to information? With the web and the Internet playing such large roles in how we access and use information today, providing open access to a major information resource would seem a logical step. Just think—whenever people with a wireless card are on the road, they could go to the local public library and jack in. The library wouldn't even have to be open) they could just sit outside in the sun and connect.

But while the idea of providing free bandwidth may still be a bit radical—especially for libraries struggling to pay for basic services—there are a number of libraries using this technology to serve their primary clientele better. It is no surprise, given the prevalence of portable computers among college students, that the early adopters are largely academic libraries. (For more information on libraries and wireless services, see "The Pros and Cons of Wireless Networks" in the Summer, 2002 issue of *Library Journal, netConnect.*)

Early adopters

It would be hard to find a more wireless-ready library than the University of California at San Diego. All its libraries offer wireless access, and some even circulate wireless network cards and/or laptops. Users of the wireless network are required to sign in, but frequent wireless users can register their wireless device so they never need to enter a user names and passwords. At the University of Texas Health Science Center Library, San Antonio, users must also register their wireless cards to access the network. Once that is completed, they can go anywhere in the library and be connected. With additional software, they can also send print jobs to a central printing facility for (10¢ per page).

The help pages at the University of South Florida, Tampa, explain in great detail (complete with screen shots), how to configure computers to access the campus wireless network. The maps of wireless coverage are particularly instructive for those new to this technology, as they show the approximate boundary of coverage from the wireless access point on each floor. These maps basically tell wireless users where to sit to get the best signal, or even any signal at all.

Academic libraries, in a number of cases, are simply following their universitys' plans to roll out wireless access across campuses, and the libraries are the obvious place to start. EDUCAUSE, the higher education computing association, highlights a number of campus wireless initiatives in its Current Issues page on the Wireless Campus. Wireless service makes great sense for these libraries, given the generally large number of laptop users on campuses.

The list of libraries that offer wireless connections at the Wireless Librarian web site contains few public libraries. Since a wireless access point can be had for around $100, it seems like a cheap service for public libraries to provide.

Security concerns

Libraries of any type that want to offer this service need to address security issues, including those to people getting on the network who don't belong there, and people listening in on those who are on the network. In the former instance, if you choose to offer an open service, you won't need to block the unauthorized user. If you do not want an open service, you will need to require authorization, as most academic libraries do. Security breaches of the latter type, however, affect us all. New standards are in the pipeline that will address these security issues.

Wireless standards

The standard that defines the wireless technology in wide use today is 802.11b, part of a family of 802.11 protocols. It is generically called "Wi-Fi" in the popular press. The 802.11b standard offers indoor communication speeds of up to 11 Mbps (megabits per second) for several hundred feet from an access point; outdoor connectivity can extend to several miles. Factors such as barriers and certain kinds of materials can affect the signal distance and strength. The 802.11g standard offers faster speeds (up to 54 Mbps), and there are already products on the market supporting it (e.g., Apple Airport Extreme equipped computers and base stations).

For more information on the standards, see the IEEE site (for the official documents) and Wi-Fi Networking News (for the talk on the street).

Not global, only local

At one time, there was a common vision of wireless Internet access being provided by satellites—thus ensuring a constantly available connection from just about anywhere on the planet. That vision has yet to come to fruition, and may never happen. But the current situation of pools of connectivity provided by wireless access points is a good start. Libraries, as organizations focused on free and open access to information, have every reason to be at the forefront of this technology.

Resources

EDUCAUSE The Wireless Campus
  www.educause.edu/issues/issue.asp?issue=wireless
IEEE 802.11 Wireless Standard
  standards.ieee.org/getieee802/802.11.html
UCSD Wireless Connectivity
  libraries.ucsd.edu/services/wireless.html
University of South Florida Map of Wireless Access
  help.acomp.usf.edu/wireless/map.html
University of South Florida Wireless
  help.acomp.usf.edu/wireless
University of Texas Health Science Center Library Wireless
  www.library.uthscsa.edu/basics/FAQ.cfm?type=WirelessLAN
Wi-Fi Networking News
  wifinetnews.com
Wireless Librarian
  people.morrisville.edu/~drewwe/wireless

Peer-to-Peer Networks: Promise and Peril

Napster was shutdown by legal action brought by the music industry to prevent users from swapping pirated music files. But the genie's out of the bottle, and no one—no person, industry, or government—can put it back. Napster was just the tip of the iceberg. To understand this, you should know how Napster works, how something called Gnutella works, and what this may mean for libraries.

Napster under the hood

Napster was invented in January, 1999 by Shawn Fanning, then a freshman at Northeastern University. He combined the capacity to find and download music files stored in the MPEG 3 (MP3) format with the capacity of chat. He soon quit school to pursue its development full time. His once booming company, Napster, Inc., at one time had at least 45 employees at its Redwood City, California, location, and claimed twenty million users. At the same time, it was being sued by the Recording Industry Association of America (RIAA) for copyright infringement.

Napster was comprised of a client application and a set of servers. The client application could be downloaded easily, for free, and installed on any Windows or Macintosh computer. (Mac users would use alternative clients, like Macster). Users could then download files from other users of the Napster software, and perhaps share their own files. Napster was optimized for sharing music files using MP3. When you started up your Napster (or Macster) software, you were logged into one of several servers run by Napster, Inc., and any MP3 files you had open to share became available for others to search and download. (Since MP3 files are decoded, not executed, there is no virus danger.) Conversely, if you wanted to find a particular song or sound file, you could search the servers' entries for files available from currently logged-on users. If you found something you wanted, the server connected you to the other person's computer for the download. No central server stored the files; they came from the computers of individual network users.

In my experience, Napster was an effective way to share and download sound files. Still, a download could take a frustratingly long time to finish, or fail entirely. Also, the availability and quality of the descriptive information about the files was spotty. That said, for those who have no qualms about violating copyright, the music world was basically laid at your feet.

Although Napster was described as peer-to-peer networking (in which one node on the network can directly communicate with another without using a central server of some kind), in reality it was only partly peer-to-peer, since it relied on central servers for indexing and searching. This made it vulnerable to being shut down, completely, through legal action.

A true peer-to-peer network, however, is almost completely invulnerable, due to the far and wide distribution of both capability and responsibility. Napster, then, was but a pale shadow of what is to come. Welcome to Gnutella.

A publisher's worst nightmare?

Gnutella was originally developed by America Online's Nullsoft as a competing application for downloading MP3 files. It was then adopted by a loose association of developers, who pursued further development.

Gnutella is both a protocol and a software program that implements the protocol. It provides true peer-to-peer networking. When you start up your Gnutella client (see Gnutelliums for a list of clients for the major platforms), it announces your presence to all other Gnutella users on your "horizon." As much as you might like access to all the millions of computers on the Internet, that clearly won't scale. So your horizon is limited to about ten thousand other users. However, that group roster changes over time, so if you are logged on overnight you may "see" as many as forty thousand other users.

When you want to find something, whether it is an MP3 file, a recipe, an article, or just about anything someone wants to share, you send out a query. That query is passed to a few of the closest computers. They in turn each pass it to more computers, and so on, until thousands of computers have received your query. If a computer has a match, it sends back the answer via the same route it traveled to begin with. During the query stage, neither the querying computer nor the responding computer knows the identity of the other—important for those wishing to retain their privacy. When you go to download the file, however, a direct connection is established between the requesting and providing computers. Since no logs or profiles are being kept, privacy is maintained.

Gnutella rising?

My own use of an early Gnutella client for the Macintosh revealed both its usefulness and the room for needed improvement.

As an MP3 downloader, Napster clients were more responsive and easier to use. But since Napster was limited to MP3 files, and was shutdown by the courts, Gnutella is really the only option. The Gnutella response time is slow enough to encourage you to run a search in the background while doing something else, and the searching itself is primitive at best. Nonetheless, given the underlying power of the model, and because this technology is at an early stage of development, there is potential here.

Are you starting to get the picture? Anyone on the Internet can share anything they want, anonymously. There is no company or set of central servers to shut down, and no way to track those who are breaking copyright law. To quote an early description of Gnutella, "It's reliable, it's sharing terabytes of data, and it is absolutely unstoppable." We may, in fact, be seeing the death of enforceable digital copyright.

Implications for libraries

So what might this mean to libraries? First of all, as individuals begin using Gnutella to serve copies of articles, papers, and even books, users may increasingly find it easier to bypass the library entirely to locate information on their own. As we know, they will likely be missing much that we could provide, even within the Gnutella universe, given its nearly brain-dead method of searching (by file name, and no metadata is associated with the files). "The folks who developed Gnutella are very sophisticated in their knowledge of networking, but they don't know squat about information retrieval," says Karen Coyle of the California Digital Library. "They need us, even if they don't know it."

Also, there is likely to be another growing universe of information that may not (at least initially) be available through web search engines. To add another wrinkle, individual users join and leave the Gnutella network at will, which suggests a randomly pulsing (i.e., growing and shrinking) universe of information. What is there now may not be there in a few minutes, and vice versa.

One way in which libraries may be able to use Gnutella is to write our own clients, perhaps to perform digital interlibrary loan tasks for us. Daniel Chudnov, an advocate of open source software (see "Open Source Software: The Future of Library Systems?" *Library Journal*, vol, 124, no. 13, August 1999, pp. 40-43), has posited just such a use with his paper "docster: instant document delivery." It isn't too difficult to imagine other kinds of "virtual private networks" of trusted library servers to share resources legally—such as files out of copyright, (public domain) or those for which copyright payment is managed—among libraries. Sure, it might slow down network speed, but that's why libraries should consider networking among themselves before installing Gnutella clients for patrons.

Whatever happens, Gnutella represents a powerful new paradigm for network use that bypasses servers and connects individual users in new ways. If we ignore it, we do so at our own peril. If we embrace it, and bend it to our collective will, we have the potential to develop new services, or improve existing ones, in ways in which we may not have imagined until now.

Resources

docster: instant document delivery
  oss4lib.org/readings/docster.php
Gnutella
  www.gnutella.com
Gnutelliums
  gnutella.wego.com
Gnutella FAQ
  www.rixsoft.com/Knowbuddy/gnutellafaq.html

Bringing Out the Dead (Technologies)

Some of us are old enough to remember owning and playing vinyl music records. Now, if you don't have an MP3 player, you're ancient history. And between LPs and MP3s can be found several other dead or near-dead technologies—reel-to-reel, 8-tracks, audiocassettes, and CDs—all of which are relatively recent.

Sooner or later almost every technology dies (although I admit it's hard to imagine toilet paper going away anytime soon). But the life cycles of information technologies seem to be getting shorter, even though they were not long to begin with. So here's my best guess at a few technologies that I think are dead, dying, or DOA.

SGML

Structured Generalized Markup Language (SGML) was a good idea with a bad implementation. The basic idea is great—a mechanism by which people can mark text with structural and semantic meaning, providing a foundation for all kinds of sophisticated processing. For example, searches could be limited to parts of the text, or a table of contents could be extracted from the full-length work. But what you had to do to use it was as painful as pulling teeth with pliers. A decade after SGML became an International Standards Organization-approved standard in 1985, there were only about three communities of adopters: defense contractors (who were forced to by government edict), linguists, and librarians. It did, however, give birth, in 1998, to XML, which is much simpler to use and was made for the web—and by so doing sealed SGML's fate. SGML died a well-deserved death shortly thereafter.

RDF

The codification of the Resource Description Framework (RDF) in 1999 was eagerly awaited by those interested in describing electronic resources. Targeted to solve the problem of encoding metadata for digital objects using XML so that software could retrieve, parse, and index this information, it seemed like the weapon that would slay the jumbled mess that the web had become. One possible use for RDF was as a method to embed cataloging information in web sites, which could then be retrieved by RDF-aware robots. Other uses included coding rating information, providing content maps for web sites, and classifying digital library content independent of a library catalog system.

The weapon turned out to be a space-age laser. It could slay the monster if you could just understand it well enough to use it. Instead of holding to the rule of simplicity that is a hallmark of XML, as I had hoped, a group of experts in database design and information retrieval (as part of the World Wide Web Consortium's standards process) decided to build a structure based on directed labeled graphs.

If you don't understand the last three words of the previous sentence, neither will you understand RDF. Unfortunately, this will kill it dead. If no one can understand how to properly use it, or if different individuals encode the same information differently (something that is already happening, even among RDF aficionados), then it will never fill the role it was designed to play. In the end, this was much too important an effort to be left to experts.

Device-dependent e-books

E-books that require a particular device to read them hit the market with a dull "thud," which means they can be called dead on arrival (DOA). The Rocket eBook, Softbook, and other book display devices had been touted as print book replacements because of their increased functionality over ink-on-paper and their capacity to store many titles.

But these devices were pricey ($200 and up) and are unlikely to fall much lower anytime soon (a prediction borne out by reality), due to the need to offer the latest in liquid crystal display design. Meanwhile, Microsoft and Adobe have both entered the fray with software that makes virtually any Windows computer, laptop, or palm-sized device an e-book reader. Let's see: spend $200 for a device that I can use only for e-books, or just use the portable computer I already have? Do the math.

Client-side Java

When Java came on the scene a few years ago it was hailed as the perfect solution for the problem of having to write separate versions of software for each operating system (Windows, Mac, etc.). "Write once, run anywhere" was the claim. It would have been more than a claim if multiple versions of Java did not crop up.

Also, most developers writing Java programs expected users to download their applications ("applets") and run them locally. It turned out that this process could be deadly slow and would frequently crash the user's web browser. Now the latest thing is to write "servlets" that run on servers instead of on an individual user's computer. This strategy is much more successful.

Technology slayers

Technologies can be killed off by a variety of causes, but here are a few of the most important:

Abrasive complexity. A technology that has complexity that cannot be ignored is an open invitation to find some other solution to your problem. Both SGML and RDF suffer from this.

Market share. Better technologies have time and again gone down to defeat in the face of a poorer technology that was better marketed—and distributed. In a consumerist world, it isn't enough to have a better mousetrap, you must also market and distribute it well. Device-dependent e-books may be an example, facing Microsoft or Adobe.

Competition. A better technology solving the same problem: see XML.

Inefficiency. You may not think that a technology that requires more time or money than it saves would even get to market. If you believe that, you should watch more TV "infomercials." Java as a whole does not fit this bill, but client-side Java does.

The dead and the undead

I'm not the only one obsessed with technology death. Karen Schneider, in an American Libraries column titled "1,001 Uses for a Dead Gopher" (April, 2000, p. 78) covered dead technologies, technologies that wouldn't die, and some that have even come back from the dead. (If you thought you were through with typewriter correction fluid, think again.)

The Library and Information Technology Association Top Tech Trends identified in January 1999 by ten LITA technology experts includes the admonition, "Don't run aground on submerging technologies!" There isn't much advice on the web site for how to stay afloat, but stay tuned. The group gets together at every American Library Association conference and is known for being fast and loose with advice and opinion.

Obsessed or not, we all have to watch out for technologies going the way of the 8-track tape, just as we need to spot those taking their place.

Resources

LITA Top Tech Trends
*www.lita.org/Content/NavigationMenu/LITA/LITA_Resources_and_*
Services/Top_Technology_Trends/Top_Technology_Trends.htm
Microsoft Reader
www.microsoft.com/reader/
"1,001 Uses for a Dead Gopher"
archive.ala.org/alonline/netlib/il400.html
RDF
www.w3.org/RDF
SGML
xml.coverpages.org/sgml.html

I Know This Much Is True

In this crazy, mixed-up world it can be tough to distinguish fact from fancy, hype from honesty, and the next "killer" application from vaporware. As information bombards us, we must employ all of our skills as librarians to filter out the noise and find the signal. Sometimes we must rely on our own experience and intuition. So here I go out on a limb to say what I believe to be true about information technology today.

Neither an early adopter nor a latecomer be. If you adopt a technology in the early stages of development, you're asking for it. That technology may go nowhere, or be beat out by another (often worse) technology with greater market share (see below). Even if the nascent technology succeeds, you'll have to tinker with it constantly as it matures.

On the other hand, if you wait too long to adopt a new technology, your organization falls behind. So monitor technologies that you believe hold promise. Periodically assess the stage of development (e.g., "Has it been standardized?" and "Who has adopted it?"), and if it holds promise, start developing internal knowledge and expertise.

Technology with market share beats better technology. History is replete with examples of superior technologies that lost out—often because they were late to market. What this means to you is that it isn't enough to adopt good technologies—they must also be popular.

It's the customer, stupid! Beware of boys and their toys. Those who love technology can sometimes be seduced by its power and capabilities. When such decisions become a barrier to the user's needs, you're in trouble (e.g., requiring users to have the latest multimedia plug-ins to use your site). Keep your priorities straight.

Never underestimate the power of a prototype. You can explain a new system until you're blue in the face, but comprehension may escape your listeners until you demonstrate it. Prototype systems, even simple mock-up screen displays, can make your vision real. If the prototype is functional, all the better.

Back it up or kiss it goodbye. There are only two kinds of computer users—those who have lost data and those who will. Enough said.

Buy hardware at the last possible moment. Moore's law (from the founder of Intel), which states that the number of transistors that can be packed on a chip will double every eighteen months, means that computers get more powerful while getting cheaper. The same goes for peripheral equipment. So the wise hardware buyer will put off buying anything until the last possible moment, thus maximizing purchasing power.

Don't buy software with a zero at the end of the release number. If you buy newly released software, again you're asking for it. The first release of a program, or a major revision of one, is almost certain to pack its fair share of bugs—ranging from minor to catastrophic. Let others stumble over the first release.

If you can't be with the operating system you love, love the one you're with. Religious wars are for zealots—you have work to do. Become proficient in the MS Windows, Macintosh, and Unix operating systems. Know their strengths and limitations. Attain a level of comfort working with each, so you can hit the ground running in any situation.

Burn, baby, burn: the only good CPU cycle is a used one. Computers are here to do work for us. If you're not running them into the ground, you're probably not trying hard enough. Don't worry about the load on the machine; an unused CPU cycle (when the computer sits idle, awaiting the next instruction) is a lost opportunity. Worry about convincing the bean counters that you need more of them.

You can never have too much RAM, disk space, or CPU speed. Like love or money, the concept of "too much" does not apply here. Probably the single cheapest thing you can do to improve your efficiency and effectiveness is to spend money on RAM. It can be amazing what a little extra volatile memory can do for your computer. I can think of no reason why a computer for a library staff person running a modern operating system and standard applications should not have twice as much RAM as comes standard with most PCs. Your time is expensive, but RAM isn't. Have your financial officer or accountant do the math.

If you've learned a technology thoroughly, it's on its way out. The only constant is change, and, with technology, change happens fast. We have no choice but to get used to it. Do you remember Gopher? Archie? WAIS? These are all tools that came and went inside of five years, or less— mere footnotes on the time line of libraries. So learn constantly, and make strategic decisions about what deserves your attention.

For any given project, there are several ways it can succeed, and countless ways it can fail. Your job is to distinguish between them. But at least it's comforting to know that you have some latitude in your decision-making. Your choice to use one particular database, for example, likely won't decide the success or failure of your project. Other, perhaps more insidious factors like internal politics), are more likely to be your downfall.

As digital librarians, we must make decisions about technologies—which to learn and which not, which to use and which to ignore—all day, every day. But then, isn't that what librarians should be good at? We make similar decisions whenever we decide what books or journals to buy. Sure, there are some differences, but our goals remain constant. Whether we buy a book or a network hub, we must always keep the needs of our customers foremost.

9

STANDARDS AND INTEROPERABILITY

The $64,000 Question

Interoperability: The Holy Grail

What to Know About Web Services

Open Archives: A Key Convergence

Digital Libraries: Different Paths to Interoperability

The $64,000 Question

"What digital library software application should I buy?" asks the typical harried library staff member. It usually means that his or her boss decided that, to be modern, they must go digital. The librarian or library assistant then bravely surfs the Internet to find the appropriate software.

It's not that simple.

What is a digital library, after all? Is it a pile of licensed content or databases? Is it having your archival finding aids digitized and online? Is it having the content that those finding aids describe digitized and online? Is it accepting and providing online access to preprints? Is it publishing books online?

It is all that, and more. But there's no single software application to deal with the variety and complexity of digital library collections and services.

Finding the tools

Unfortunately, we're still not even close to finding the right tools. Except for online databases, we are mostly dealing with objects, at various levels of granularity. An archival finding aid describes a collection of objects. The objects described by a finding aid, such as individual historical photographs or a book, are discrete objects that may also be part of a logical collection. They can be described individually and placed within the context of a collection, when appropriate. They are the "atoms" of librarianship—an irreducible component.

However, these atoms vary greatly. The description and structure of objects as diverse as photographs, journal articles, books, manuscripts, and data sets can vary significantly. How can we create one software application to manage and provide access to such a diverse group? One solution is to "encapsulate" all objects in a standardized descriptive structure so that software written to that specification will understand each type of object.

Consider trying to make a handwritten diary available online in a complete and usable manner. This requires individual page images (to see the actual handwriting), a transcription of each page (so the diary is readable and perhaps searchable), and a way to navigate the diary. Any given item might comprise hundreds of individual files, and each image file would have to be matched up with its associated transcription. Also, these would all have to be appropriately slotted within the whole so that a reader can page through the manuscript.

Metadata (information that describes an object) is needed—and lots of it! More specifically, structural metadata is needed to specify which image file corresponds with "page one" and which text represents the transcription of that page. If we can agree on a standard method for encoding this structural metadata, and make this specification open and public, then anyone who wishes to can write software to interact with these objects. This is the goal of the University of California at Berkeley's Making of America II Project (MOA II).

Back to the future

To see this in action, go to their web site and select the link for "The HTML-based MOA II Document Viewer." This leads to an application (a Java servlet) that lists a number of objects that have been encoded using the MOA II XML document type definition (DTD), which defines a method for encoding structural metadata. To see the system capabilities, select, for example, the "Patrick Breen Diary" (Breen was a member of the ill-fated Donner Party). If you click on a day in the left frame, the associated diary page appears in the right window. Drop-down menus above the right window allow different resolutions of the page image, including even the transcribed text. Buttons allow browsing forward or back. The lower left corner shows the XML source document.

The MOA II web site offers more information about the MOA II DTD and how the project is producing objects encoded to that specification. The Digital Library Federation publication "The Making of America II Testbed Project: A Digital Library Service Model" provides some essential background.

The latest work is moving the specification from a DTD model to an XML schema, called the "Metadata Encoding and Transmission Standard" (METS). This not only brings the MOA II work into an XML framework that allows more software flexibility, it also adds the ability to either embed metadata (e.g., author and title) into the object description itself, or to point to it in an outside source, such as a separate database.

Other questions remain, such as how the objects are discovered by users in the first place, since some of these objects are not represented in library catalog records. But by encapsulating digital objects in standardized ways, we can create new modes of discovery. For example, a library might write an application to crawl remote collections of MOA II objects, extract descriptive metadata from them, and index them for searching. When an item of interest is discovered, the record link would enable a user to retrieve it from the library holding it.

We likely won't have a single "digital library application" for every library. But with projects like MOA II, we can avoid the problems caused when each library makes up its own rules for encapsulating and describing digital objects. This may not be the answer to the $64,000 question, but it is close.

Resources

The Making of America II Project
    sunsite.berkeley.edu/moa2/
The Making of America II Testbed Project: A Digital Library Service Model
    www.clir.org/pubs/reports/pub87/pub87.pdf
Metadata Encoding and Transmission Standard (METS)
    www.loc.gov/standards/mets/

Interoperability: The Holy Grail

As fast as digital libraries are being built, they still remain islands of order in a sea of chaos. Locating them by using web search engines or subject directories is just the first step in a long process. Users must then go to each one, searching or browsing it before moving on to the next. This laborious method for locating digital library objects (from full-length books to individual photographs) is obviously anachronistic.

What digital librarians envision instead is an infrastructure that supports simultaneous searching of multiple and geographically distant collections. Anyone who discovers any individual digital library should be able to search easily (and perhaps transparently) across a wide variety of collections from other libraries worldwide. That, at least, is the vision.

So what will make this vision a reality? There are different models for achieving this level of interoperability between libraries in support of resource discovery and retrieval. In the end, it probably isn't so important what model we use as long as we get the result we seek.

Whereas in "Twenty-first Century Cataloging" (see Chapter 4) I focused on metadata standards and draft standards for cataloging digital objects, here I look at how to provide cross-collection searching of these records. Because digital libraries are still largely in the experimentation and research stages, diversity is more prevalent than standardization.

The union catalog model

One way to achieve seamless access to a variety of physically distant collections is to contribute bibliographic records or access aids to a central database. Librarians are, of course, experienced at this, having built OCLC, the largest union catalog of bibliographic records in the world. For digital library objects, however, we do not have an equivalent union catalog.

Probably the best example of this model is the American Memory project of the Library of Congress (LC). As part of its National Digital Library Competition (jointly sponsored with Ameritech), LC proposed serving as a central repository for "coherent access aids" (e.g., MARC records, Dublin Core records, or archival finding aids encoded in SGML), while the actual digital objects themselves would remain at their individual host institutions. Caroline Arms's 1997 paper "Access Aids and Interoperability" describes this model.

A quite different way to approach interoperability is to establish standards to which all digital libraries would adhere, and then provide an interface to search all the collections simultaneously. This exists to some degree now, as the Networked Computer Science Technical Reports Library (NCSTRL).

NCSTRL provides one-stop shopping for CS tech reports from hundreds of institutions around the world by requiring that each site install the same software package (Dienst) and create bibliographic records using the same format (RFC 1807). At any of the NCSTRL sites, the search is sent simultaneously to all other sites; then those sites search their local indexes and return their finding, which are received and collated by the initiating site, and then are displayed to the user. When a particular record or report is requested, the remote server that has the report responds to the request.

That, at least, is the model. However, due to poor response times, the bibliographic records are gathered from NCSTRL sites and indexed centrally at two or three index servers. In a sense, this model has retreated to that of a union catalog.

The "intelligent agent" model

Yet another method may be to create an "intelligent agent" (a special kind of software program) that can roam the network searching digital libraries for objects of interest. The agent would report back periodically with any results. Requirements for success include, at minimum, that the agent know where to find digital libraries, have the capacity to query these libraries appropriately, and possess methods to process search results into a common format for merging and browsing. One benefit: as long as the agent knows how to perform queries, the underlying architecture of each digital library can be different. Intelligent agents are unlikely to do well with an uncategorized, all-inclusive database like the web. But digital library catalogs are, if anything, the exact opposite. They are organized collections of selected objects of a similar nature. They usually support highly specific queries and will frequently return useful results. These factors make intelligent agents a real possibility for providing an appearance of interoperability when none may exist by design. However intriguing, I don't know of a working example of such an agent.

Whither interoperability?

Of these models, only the union catalog model is fully functional with present technology. Although the distributed searching model is interesting, slow server and network response times makes it presently impractical. The lack of prototype systems makes it difficult to assess the intelligent agent model.

Differing levels of bibliographic description create a barrier to interoperability with all of these models. Some items are described only at the collection level (in the case of archival finding aids), while others are described at the item level (MARC and Dublin Core records). Thus, a user may be required to search different systems or else navigate results that mix individual items with collection descriptions. This watershed divide in how digital objects are described probably presents the biggest barrier to seamless interoperability.

We seem to be, at least, on the right path. Most digital library projects describe their objects using some type of standard, or developing standard, thus making it possible to migrate their records to whichever becomes the clear winner. A number of cooperative projects are underway in which libraries work together to provide easy access to their combined collections. And organizations like the Digital Library Federation and LC work toward the goal of interoperability. So, although we are still in the early stages of achieving the kind of vision that many digital librarians have of easy access to digital collections around the world, we are close enough to have gained some experience along the way.

Resources

"Access Aids and Interoperability"
    memory.loc.gov/ammem/award/docs/interop.html
Digital Library Federation
    www.diglib.org
Dublin Core
    dublincore.org
Encoded Archival Description (EAD)
    www.loc.gov/ead/
Intelligent Agents
    agents.umbc.edu
National Digital Library Competition
    memory.loc.gov/ammem/award/
NCSTRL
    www.ncstrl.org
Request for Comments (RFC) 1807
    ftp://ftp.isi.edu/in-notes/rfc1807.txt

What To Know About Web Services

As amazing as technological progress in libraries has been in the last decade, more dramatic opportunities await. One such opportunity, under the prosaic name "Web Services," would knit together software applications to construct powerful new services. Just imagine being able to pull patron information—transparently and quickly—from one system to complete an ILL transaction in a completely different system. Not only that, but those transactions would not need to be written in the same language, or executed on the same platform, or even be dependent on more than basic, publicly available information. In other words, we are talking about interoperability of a high order.

Web Services defined

In a nutshell, Web Services are a suite of protocols that define how requests and responses between software applications should be encoded (using XML) and transferred (e.g., over the web using HTTP or e-mail) and how such services should be described and registered for discovery and use. Tracy Gardner, in an *Ariadne* article, called Web Services "interoperable building blocks for constructing applications." If you know of CORBA and Remote Procedure Calls (RPC), then you are halfway there, since those are similar technologies. Still, examples should make the concept easier to comprehend.

The Portuguese National Library

The Portuguese National Library is developing Web Services (in association with its catalog vendor BookMARC) using the Portuguese National Catalog, a database of one million UNIMARC records. By sending a properly formatted message to the catalog (using SOAP, see below), a UNIMARC record can be retrieved in response to an ISBN.

Another service allows for retrieving sets of records by searching various record fields. These examples are part of a larger set being implemented by the library, says Joaquim Carvalho of BookMARC. Additional services promised include searching, inserting, updating, and validating records.

Such an infrastructure offers robust interoperability with disparate systems. This project is one of the best documented, including step-by-step instructions and source code in "How To Consume Sirius Web Services."

WRL Consortium

The digital library system of the Washington Research Library Consortium (WRLC), called ALADIN, provides subscription databases, digital collections and library catalogs for seven medium-sized academic research libraries. Recently, ALADIN has begun using Web Services to provide simple, network-based interfaces to its services. By providing a Web Services interface to patron information (e.g., items checked out), individual campus libraries can easily provide this information as part of their own services. Thorny issues such as user authentication can become part of the infrastructure supporting these functions. As Don Gourley of the WRLC says, "With Web Services we can use our existing infrastructure and knowledge of web applications to link together different systems." This project is described in much greater detail in my book *XML in Libraries*.

A rebirth for Z39.50?

Web Services may also give Z39.50 a new lease on life. Z39.50 International—The Next Generation (ZING) is Z39.50 using Web Services protocols. The Koninklijke Bibliotheek in the Netherlands is using the ZING Search/Retrieve Web (SRW) service to make its catalog accessible via SOAP. For more information, see *XML in Libraries*.

Web Services protocols

The web is based on a collection of protocols (conventions for communication), ranging from defining how the bits get from place to place (TCP/IP) to those that define the web itself (HTTP and HTML). Web Services add extra protocols to the mix—including SOAP, WSDL, and UDDI—which help define a new set of opportunities for communication.

SOAP. Of all the Web Services protocols, the Simple Object Access Protocol (SOAP) is the most essential. SOAP allows disparate software on a variety of platforms to communicate by specifying a standard XML encoding for messages between systems. See "Overview of SOAP" for a good start.

Once you understand how SOAP works, it can be more powerful than simply sending a message from one application to another. SOAP provides for three parts to a message: an optional header, a mandatory body, and optional attachments. The body, plus any optional attachments, is intended for the final destination. The header, however, can support in-transit processing. For example, an authentication server could process only the header of a SOAP message, passing the body of authenticated messages on to the final destination.

For those who want to get a quick start on using SOAP to create Web Services, the Apache project has software that can help. Apache SOAP takes care of reading and writing the XML and sending and receiving it over the network. See also the Apache SOAP follow-up project, Apache Axis.

WSDL and UDDI. Pronounced "wiz-dull," the Web Service Description Language (WSDL) is the method by which a specific Web Service is described. A WSDL definition for a specific Web Service will specify the format of the messages that can be passed from requester to responder, the address (URL) of a service, and the protocol to use (e.g., the web, secure web or HTTPS, or e-mail). These descriptions are then deposited in a UDDI repository. The repository holds these descriptions for discovery by those wishing to use Web Services. (See the "Overview of WSDL.") Universal Description, Discovery, and Integration (UDDI) is the part of Web Services that enables potential users to discover the existence of individual Web Services. Potential users search a UDDI repository, or are pointed to a particular WSDL description that they can retrieve from a UDDI repository.

Limitations of Web Services

As interesting and encouraging as these emerging services are, Web Services are not the be-all and end-all of library web opportunities. Art Rhyno of the University of Windsor, Ontario, cautions that Web Services "may not be enough to wire together a busy circulation system and a patron database." However, he says, Web Services can be "a way to bring together systems that don't have to talk together for their primary function but can take advantage of each other for extended services." Some examples he cites are linking the online catalog to Google (which is Web Services-enabled, see "Google APIs" in the Link List); or allowing item due date information to populate a personal calendar.

As with most technologies, we will likely discover that Web

Services can be very useful for solving particular problems, but not so great for others. Since the protocols upon which Web Services are based are still new, we are still discovering the best applications for them.

Resources

Apache Axis Project
    ws.apache.org/axis/
Apache SOAP
    ws.apache.org/soap/
Google APIs
    www.google.com/apis/
How To Consume Sirius Web Services
    ptolemy.bookmarc.pt:8001/kb/kb000002.html
IBM developerWorks
    www-106.ibm.com/developerworks
An Introduction to Web Services
    www.ariadne.ac.uk/issue29/gardner/
Overview of SOAP
    developers.sun.com/sw/building/tech_articles/overview_soap.html
Overview of WSDL
    developers.sun.com/sw/building/tech_articles/overview_wsdl.html
Simple Object Access Protocol
    www.w3.org/TR/SOAP
UDDI Registry
    www.uddi.org
Web Services Description Language
    www.w3.org/TR/wsdl
XML in Libraries
    www.neal-schuman.com/db/0/290.html
ZING SRW
    www.loc.gov/z3950/agency/zing/srw/background.html

Open Archives: A Key Convergence

In "The Grand Challenges," one of the first "Digital Libraries" columns I ever wrote (see Chapter 1), I identified interoperability—the capacity of a user to treat multiple digital library collections as one—as a key digital library challenge.

Unfortunately, progress has been slow since then—except for a few significant developments. One such development started in October, 1999, when several organizations—including the Digital Library Federation, Association of Research Libraries, and Los Alamos National Laboratory—recruited a group of experts "to work towards achieving a universal service for author self-archived scholarly literature." Self-archiving denotes the process of authors depositing their own papers into an archive. A common practice among scientists is to make preliminary drafts of their papers (or "preprints") available to colleagues prior to publication. Preprints can subsequently undergo peer review and then be published in a professional journal.

One outcome of the meeting (which took place in Santa Fe, New Mexico) was the establishment of the Open Archives Initiative (formerly known as the Universal Preprint Service initiative). The initiative aims to develop an open architecture that supports simultaneous searching and retrieval of papers from disparate archives. This is the logical next step after several separate projects have successfully archived papers of various kinds (such as technical reports, theses, dissertations, preprints, working papers, and conference papers). There are lessons to learn from each of the projects.

Successful repository projects

arXiv e-Print Archive. Although ten years is not long for a print-based archive, it's very long for a digital one. The e-Print Archive at the Los Alamos National Laboratory has been around for almost a decade and has developed into a large and busy collection (of over 100,000 papers). It accepts and provides access to preprints in physics and, to a lesser degree, in other scientific disciplines. Authors self-submit their papers to the archive, and can also replace or remove them. Submissions are not reviewed, but authors must register before contributing papers. This service is free (which may be readily apparent from the spare and sometimes obtuse user interface). Since scientists are accustomed to sharing their work in preprint form, this archive model works well. It is unlikely, however, to work as well for humanities scholars, who don't tend to work this way.

NCSTRL. Networked Computer Science Technical Reports provides access to computer science technical reports, from over one hundred institutions worldwide through a single interface. Originally supported as a research project by a grant from the Defense Advanced Research Projects Agency (DARPA), NCSTRL is no longer merely a research project, but is now a production service for archiving these reports.

A search initiated at any NCSTRL site queries a central database of metadata. When the user selects a particular paper to view, it is fetched from its remote repository. The underlying NCSTRL infrastructure consists of Dienst, a protocol and software suite overlying a standard web server. See the article "The NCSTRL Approach to Open Architecture" for more information on the underlying architecture.

NDLTD. The Networked Digital Library of Theses and Dissertations (NDLTD), based at Virginia Tech, archives digital theses and dissertations. According to the project, more than seventy institutions (mostly universities) have joined the effort, but so far only a relatively small number of digital works are available. Nonetheless, this effort brings to the initiative a useful and unique area of grey "literature" that otherwise would be available only through a commercial service or directly from each university.

NASA Technical Reports Server. NASA Technical Reports Server (NTRS) is a gateway to twenty different U.S. government-based technical report servers that contain three to four million abstracts and more than one hundred-thousand full-text reports. NTRS uses wide area information servers (WAIS) technology developed by Thinking Machines, Inc., which was popular in the early 1990s, but which has now largely disappeared from the Internet. Although the technical infrastructure is nearly ancient history in Internet terms, the system nonetheless works.

Tying it all together

The Open Archives Initiative aims to specify the methods by which these various individual archives can interoperate. Such interoperability will largely be achieved by specifying three things: first, a protocol for "harvesting" (gathering) metadata from participating archives; second criteria that can be used to selectively harvest metadata; and third, a common metadata format for archives to use in responding to harvesting requests.

At first, the initiative will use a modified version of the Dienst protocol that comes out of the NCSTRL effort as the harvesting protocol. Dienst is well established for this kind of activity, having supported the same kind of work on behalf of computer science technical reports for some years. Accession date was thought by the Santa Fe meeting attendees to be the most important criteria for selective harvesting, with author affiliation, subject, and publication type also being deemed important. For the metadata component, a minimal set of the Dublin Core elements will be used.

Additional participants in the Open Archives effort include the California Digital Library of the University of California, through its eScholarship initiative, CogPrints (Cognitive Sciences archive), and RePEc (Research Papers in Economics).

Why this is important

In today's world, the hapless user who simply wants to discover what unpublished literature exists on a particular topic is faced with a dilemma: trying to find all the individual servers that might possibly have such information by searching web search engines, and then searching each archive individually. This is a "solution" that will neither scale nor suffice. "Digital libraries have historically been islands of information," says Michael Nelson, the manager of the NASA Technical Reports Server, "and there has been no way to bind them together into one collection." That's why he and others are excited about the possibilities of achieving some measure of interoperability among archives of scholarly and scientific papers and preprints.

The Open Archives Initiative may be just what's required, while leading the way for binding together other kinds of digital library collections. If this initiative can specify an appropriate architecture for treating multiple, disparate collections as one, then those who are planning projects with other kinds of material may be able to learn from the Open Archives experience, or use some of the same infrastructure.

Resources

arXiv.org
  arxiv.org
CogPrints
  cogprints.ecs.soton.ac.uk
Dublin Core
  dublincore.org
eScholarship
  www.cdlib.org/programs/escholarship.html
NASA Technical Reports Server
  ntrs.nasa.gov
NCSTRL
  www.ncstrl.org
The NCSTRL Approach to Open Architecture
  www.dlib.org/dlib/december98/leiner/12leiner.html
NDLTD
  www.ndltd.org
Open Archives Initiative
  www.openarchives.org
RePEc
  repec.org
Santa Fe Convention of the Open Archives Initiative
  www.openarchives.org/sfc/sfc_entry.htm

Different Paths to Interoperability

In "'Interoperability: The Holy Grail" (earlier in this chapter), I discussed the importance of interoperability between digital library projects. Users should be able to discover through one search exactly what digital objects are freely available from a variety of collections, rather than having to search each collection individually. In "Open Archives: A Key Convergence" (also earlier in this chapter), I highlighted a project that is achieving interoperability among e-print servers, or simply among various repositories of digital content. For digitized materials specific to libraries, there are at least two good examples of projects that are achieving the same goal through similar but intriguingly different means.

The LC model

For three years (1996–99) the Library of Congress (LC) and Ameritech teamed up to offer digitization grants (of up to $75,000 each) to libraries in the United States. LC required successful grantees to provide suitable access aids for the items digitized with award money. These access aids could be in one or more formats: 1) U.S. MARC records, 2) Dublin Core records (following LC guidelines for usage), 3) structured headers (encoded in Text Encoding Initiative format) for searchable text reproductions, and/or 4) Encoded Archival Description finding aids.

Awardees were required to supply LC with the records for the items digitized. These records were added to the LC American Memory collection, thereby providing one place to search the digital collections of LC as well as those of all libraries receiving LC/Ameritech awards. The digitized items themselves remain at the individual institutions, as do copies of the item records.

This highly centralized model for creating a union catalog was possible because LC and Ameritech controlled the funding, and thus could establish record-creation guidelines before digitization occurred, providing for a high level of interoperability among different institutions. It required a high level of commitment and pre-coordination among participating institutions, and a willingness from all participants to follow set guidelines. These collections have been incorporated so seamlessly into the existing American Memory collections that users can easily be unaware that they are searching non-LC collections.

Taking the work a step further, LC is developing a "core set of metadata elements to be used in the development, testing, and implementation of multiple repositories." This work should be particularly helpful for digital library projects that are looking to contribute records to a union catalog—either now or in the future.

The Picture Australia model

In contrast to the LC model, the Picture Australia project came about after a good deal of library content—nearly five hundred thousand items—had been digitized and cataloged. Picture Australia aims to bring together access to digitized images relating to Australia from several institutions (currently dozens, including libraries, the National Archives, and the National Gallery). The particular challenges dictated a more flexible solution than that chosen by LC.

Since records had already been created for digitized materials, Picture Australia needed a method to collect the records, massage them into a common record format, index them, and make them available for web searching. Rather than requiring participating institutions to ship data periodically to a central location (the National Library of Australia serves as the lead institution), project developers decided to collect the records monthly by using a software spider. This allows institutions simply to put their records in a specific location on their servers, to be collected automatically.

The collected records must then be translated into a common record format (fields are based on the Dublin Core, and the storage format is XML), and indexed. Most of the issues remaining for Picture Australia relate to this translation of heterogeneous metadata into a common set of elements. One problem is the loss of context. As Debbie Campell, the first Picture Australia project manager, put it, "A collection of images may have a collective title such as 'Images of Paul Revere.' But the image title may be reduced to 'On a horse.' So the loss of context becomes a discovery issue."

Mounting challenges

There is also the problem of differing subject vocabularies, particularly between libraries and museums. The use of geographic names without qualification (such as the name of, say, the state in which such is found) can also be problematic for those not familiar with Australian geography.

The cataloging problems can go deeper, depending on how the participating institutions have cataloged their materials. A key issue is granularity. Whereas one institution may keep track of first and last names, for example, another may not (for more on this, see "The Importance of Being Granular" in Chapter 4). Differing formats can be another issue. One library may keep track of dates as month-date-year, while another spells out the month and year only. These are issues that must be rectified when translating contributed records into a common format. To see examples that illustrate some of these record variations, see the Picture Australia Metadata Guidelines.

Despite these challenges, Picture Australia is clearly successful in its effort to provide access to a wide range of pictorial material in one, easy-to-use location. Its success rests on several factors. According to former project manager Campbell, one factor was a forgiving time frame. Although each project task was estimated and delivered according to a schedule, there was no overall deadline for release. This allowed some flexibility in reacting to unforeseen problems. Another factor was the low threshold for participation. Institutions contributing records were required to do very little to make their records available to Picture Australia. "Picture Australia is quickly able to "repurpose" the investment already made in digitization and description," Campbell said.

The Picture Australia model has another advantage. It has its own brand identity, independent of any single institution. This encourages contributors to participate more equally than is possible when assigning records to a single institution, as with the LC model.

Pick a model, any model

Union catalogs are a good thing. They make accessible from one location what was formerly only accessible by visiting multiple locations, and often only by learning different search interfaces. Our users need more union catalogs.

There is no "best" model. Use what is appropriate. If you are beginning a project that provides you with the opportunity to set down guidelines ahead of time, by all means do so—it will save time and trouble later. But many great chances for creating union catalogs will come after records have been created. The best thing about Picture Australia is that the project has proved that not only can union catalogs be created after the fact, but that they can be done well.

Resources

American Memory
   memory.loc.gov
Dublin Core
   dublincore.org
LC/Ameritech Collections Online
   memory.loc.gov/ammem/award/online.html
LC Core Metadata Elements
   www.loc.gov/standards/metadata.html
Picture Australia
   www.pictureaustralia.org
Picture Australia Metadata Guidelines
   www.pictureaustralia.org/metadata.html

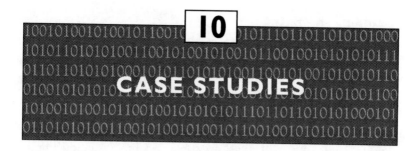

10

CASE STUDIES

Reality Check: Shanghai Surprise

Science Portals

Reality Check: Shanghai Surprise

As I write this (in 1998), Shanghai lies beneath me, covered in a warm blanket of humidity that appears to be half rain and half fog. Even from the twenty-second floor of my hotel, the incessant honking of car horns can be heard, as drivers warn pedestrians, bicyclists, and motorcyclists who share the street that they are about to be run over. Like most major cities, Shanghai is a city of contrasts. But here, disparity seems even more shocking. Five-star hotels are only minutes away from narrow, dark alleys where people live in miserable conditions. But that is changing, and quickly. Shanghai is an explosion masquerading as a city. Everywhere you turn a new high-rise goes up. Tall cranes line the skyline. Bamboo scaffolding covers the outsides of buildings under construction or renovation. Arc welding creates a light of unnatural brightness long after the sun has set. China is awakening as an economic superpower, and Shanghai leads the way. Nonetheless, it faces some serious challenges. The city's infrastructure, from its streets to telecommunications, needs work.

Scanning the past

Amid all this growth, decay, and turmoil lies a shining gem called the Shanghai Library. The building is less than a year old (in 1998) and the promise made by its gleaming facade is largely kept by the collections and services made available. The facility is huge, with 83,000 square meters of floor space and a tower twenty-four stories tall off to one side. No wonder we feel lost as the group I am with (here to attend a Chinese digital library conference) is led down long, nondescript hallways until we reach a small room. Inside are three flatbed black-and-white scanners and one color scanner, all attached to computers. As we enter, white-gloved workers scan old Chinese printed books, page by page. This operation, our guide informs us, involves materials up to six hundred years old. Other materials, not yet processed, have been proven to be more than one thousand years old. The materials are being scanned at a resolution of 300 dots per inch (dpi) in black-and-white mode. Later we learn that others are scanned in color. The retrieval system allows manuscripts to be retrieved not by full-text searching (optical character recognition of Chinese texts is very difficult) but by opting for certain browsing criteria until a particular manuscript can be selected. Once one is chosen, the full bibliographic record is displayed, and the user can then choose which scanned page to view.

Liu Wei of the Shanghai Library and Institute of Scientific and Technical Information of Shanghai later explains that this is but one of four digital library projects they have planned. In addition to digitizing ancient and rare Chinese books, they plan to digitize audio materials of Chinese traditional drama and opera, the Philosophy and Social Science volume of the National Newspaper and Periodical Index, and photographs relating to Sino-foreign interaction in the early twentieth century.

The library is blessed with a modern computer facility, complete with climate control and enough space to segregate the IBM and Sun Microsystems servers in spaces separated by glass walls. In 1998, the library's Dynix automation system boasted 40 GB of disk storage and ran on four IBM RS6000 servers. The fast intranet, over which the library serves the scanned manuscripts, employed a series of Sun Microsystems workstations with another 56 GB of disk storage. The scanned manuscripts, however, are saved on CD-ROMs that were served through two robotic cabinets where twenty-one hundred CD-ROMs can be stored and delivered to twenty drives for access.

Infrastructure imbalance

Unfortunately, this strong internal infrastructure is unmatched by an equally strong external one. While drinking tea in a stylish room reserved for entertaining guests, the library's deputy director, Miao Qihao, explains that external network connectivity is presently quite slow. It's difficult to access the Internet, particularly for resources outside of China. The Shanghai Library has only five public access Internet stations for a city of thirteen million inhabitants. (These add to the workstations from which the digitized collections can be viewed.) And the Shanghai Library has no branches (although there are roughly twenty unaffiliated public libraries that serve particular areas of the city). Each day, people queue up to get on the waiting list to use these few stations. Once they get their turn, they must share a 64 KB line—a little more than double the speed of most home modems—to the outside world. As quickly as China is modernizing within Shanghai, infrastructure underdevelopment prevents faster network access.

The importance of having a robust infrastructure over which digitized content can be reliably and speedily delivered is hard to overestimate. While the Shanghai Library may have a very healthy internal infrastructure, what it has to deliver can only be viewed inside its walls.

But in the end, what is important is that everyday Chinese manuscripts are being scanned and preserved. One day, when the infrastructure can sustain it, scholars from around the world may be able to view a remarkable collection of Chinese books and manuscripts that they would find difficult to access any other way. And that, after all, is what digital libraries are all about.

Resources
Shanghai Library
  www.library.sh.cn/new-eng/

Science Portals

The Internet offers a wide range of materials to help teachers and students with science education. The problem is finding them. Anyone seeking science information must either search an index such as Google, or browse a large number of individual web sites. Both strategies are problematic, as Google can return false drops or links to non-authoritative sites, while browsing is extremely inefficient.

Luckily, two science portals, both released in December, 2002, are likely to change how people find scientific data. One is a central search service constructed through harvesting metadata, while the other offers a handcrafted subject directory and cross-database searching.

The National Science Digital Library

The National Science Digital Library (NSDL), supported by the National Science Foundation, consists of two programs–one supports a portal to science information and the other funds online science collections, services, and targeted research. The NSDL was first funded in fiscal year 2000 and has supported 119 projects since then.

For most of us it is the portal that will be the most useful. The database of science materials currently (in early 2003) held about 250,000 records. To build the portal database, NSDL has brought in content from other sites, such as records for video clips from the Informedia project at Carnegie Mellon, web site records from the Internet Scout Project, and bibliographic records for scientific papers from the arxiv.org physics repository. Whenever possible, it uses the Open Archives Initiative protocol for metadata harvesting. It is no surprise that the Dublin Core with extensions is employed as the metadata standard.

"We're in the roads and sewers phase," said Carol Terrizzi, communications director for the project, "which means we're still building our infrastructure." The portal is powered by uPortal, open-source portal software developed by and for universities. The underlying technologies include Java, XML, and XSLT. The plan is to create specialized portals that will help bring to the surface information for primary school teachers and other communities. Cornell University, where Terrizzi and other portal staff are located, is providing core integration support, along with Columbia University's Electronic Publishing Initiative (EPIC), and the University Corporation for Atmospheric Research, Boulder, Colorado.

For librarians who wish to see the roads and sewers in construction, visit the NSDL Communication Portal. Here you can see more about the technical underpinnings of the NSDL, as well as work to help build it yourself, such as entering metadata for digital science collections.

Science.gov

Similar to the useful FirstGov portal to government information, Science.gov is a portal that provides one-stop shopping for scientific material from government agencies. Launched by an alliance of fourteen scientific and technical information organizations from ten major government science sections, Science.gov receives key administrative support and coordination from CENDI, an interagency working group of senior scientific and technical information managers.

Science.gov is both a subject directory to key science web sites and a cross-database search engine. The subject directory is maintained by the National Technical Information Service and identifies approximately seventeen hundred government-based or -supported scientific web sites. Users can both search and browse its records. In addition, users can simultaneously search dozens of scientific databases with one query. The application providing this capability is Explorit from Deep Web Technologies.

In contrast to the NSDL, which has received a great deal of funding, Science.gov has been created with little monetary sup-

port. What it has received has been in the form of "in kind" donations: staff time and infrastructure from the participating government units. As Eleanor Frierson, the co-chair says, "Science.gov
is a prime example of the power of cooperation. By working
together we have accomplished something none of us would have
been able to do alone." Frierson invites input from librarians on
what they would like to see at Science.gov and says that, given the
far-flung nature of the project, representatives should be able to
speak at library conferences, wherever they might be held.

Sustainability

What does the future hold for these portals? The NSDL is well
funded, and if that funding holds (funds for the next four years
are believed to be secure), it should be around for a long time.
Ironically, the shoestring nature of Science.gov may also support
longevity. With costs low and public benefits likely to be great,
there is no reason why it should go away. But even if these portals
do not become long-term services, they will serve our public while
we will learn more about large-scale record harvesting and cross-
database searching.

Resources

NSDL
    nsdl.org
NSDL Communication Portal
    comm.nsdlib.org
Science.gov
    science.gov
Uportal
    mis105.mis.udel.edu/ja-sig/uportal

COPYRIGHT AND INTELLECTUAL PROPERTY RIGHTS

Before Digitizing

The Copyright War

Before Digitizing

Before beginning any project to digitize material (either published or unpublished), you shouldn't just assume that you have the legal right to do so. It's an act of publication to digitize something and to make it available on the Internet. Unless you own the copyright to that material, or if it is in the public domain, or if you have received permission from the rights holder, you should not do it. For purchasing or leasing already digitized material, the license or purchase agreement should clearly spell out your rights and responsibilities, as well as those of the information provider.

Copyright law in the United States tries to strike a balance between the rights of a work's creator to receive adequate compensation, and the benefit to society as a whole by limiting those rights in specific ways. For example, the First Sale Doctrine allows persons (or libraries) to dispose of books as they see fit, without further compensating the author. (Think of all the library book sales that would be illegal without this provision!)

Another limitation on the rights of a copyright holder allows

237

users to copy small parts of a copyrighted work for particular purposes, such as teaching or interlibrary loan. This is called "fair use."

Carol Henderson, former Executive Director of the American Library Association's (ALA) Washington office, titles her useful article "Libraries as Creatures of Copyright." Creators of intellectual property, the publishers that market those works, and libraries that collect and make those works more widely available, are all players that copyright law should consider in balancing societal good. Historically, the balance has worked fairly well. It is not yet clear, however, that it will work as well in the future.

Copyright in the digital world

The Digital Millennium Copyright Act (DMCA) was signed into law on October 28, 1998. It updates the Copyright Act for digital material and brings U.S. law into compliance with the requirements of the World Intellectual Property Organization (WIPO) treaties negotiated in December, 1996. The library community struggled to shape the DMCA, largely through the participation of ALA in the Digital Future Coalition (DFC). The DFC is a coalition of mostly professional associations that are "committed to preserving the time-tested balance between the rights of owners of intellectual property and the traditional use privileges of the public."

Regarding digital preservation, the DMCA has specific provisions that permit "authorized institutions to make up to three digital preservation copies of an eligible copyrighted work; electronically 'loan' those copies to other qualifying institutions; permit preservation, including digital means, when the existing format in which the work has been stored becomes obsolete." (For more information, see links below from ALA and the U.S. Copyright Office.)

A different but related measure signed into law the day before the DMCA, the Copyright Term Extension Act, extends the term of copyright for some materials. For more information on its relationship to libraries, see "Primer on the Digital Millennium."

Fair use

The principle of fair use generally does not apply to digital library projects that convert a body of material to digital form for long-term access on the Internet. These projects typically require permission from the rights holder. Fair use may, however, apply for specific, limited uses—for example, academic digital course reserves. The material would be removed at the end of the courses. This type of situation would likely be protected under the principle of fair use, but I am not qualified to provide legal advice, and an attorney should be consulted for interpretations of the law.

Determining copyright status

Unfortunately, it can be an involved process to determine the copyright status of a work, depending on the item. First, you must determine whether or not the item is in the public domain. Some material—e.g., U.S. government information—is created in the public domain while other material can pass into this status after a specified period (see "When Works Pass into the Public Domain"). Material in the public domain may be republished (including selling it for profit) without obtaining permission, or paying a use fee, to the creator.

If a work has been published, the U.S. Copyright Office Circular "Duration of Copyright" is the authoritative source to consult to determine if an item has passed into the public domain, but "When Works Pass into the Public Domain" is much easier to use for this purpose. If the item in question is in the public domain, you're home free. For published works not in the public domain, it's best to contact the publisher. You can also consult the U.S. Copyright Office Circular "How To Investigate the Copyright Status of a Work." Unpublished materials can be more difficult, and searching the WATCH database is your best bet.

The essential first step

It's usually not difficult or onerous to abide by copyright laws when digitizing collections. It does, however, take care and forethought. Determining copyright status is an essential first step, long before paper hits scanner.

Resources

Copyright, ALA
   www.ala.org/Content/NavigationMenu/Our_Association/Offices/ALA_Washington/Issues2/Copyright1/Copyright.htm
Copyright and Fair Use
   fairuse.stanford.edu
"Copyright Basics," U.S. Copyright Office Circular 1
   www.loc.gov/copyright/circs/circ01.pdf
Digital Future Coalition
   www.dfc.org
DMCA: The Digital Millennium Copyright Act, ALA
   www.ala.org/Content/NavigationMenu/Our_Association/Offices/ALA_Washington/Issues2/Copyright1/DMCA__The_Digital_Millennium_Copyright_Act/Default2515.htm
Digital Millennium Copyright Act Summary, U.S. Copyright Office
   www.loc.gov/copyright/legislation/dmca.pdf
"Duration of Copyright," U.S. Copyright Office Circular
   www.loc.gov/copyright/circs/circ15a.pdf
"How To Investigate the Copyright Status of a Work," U.S. Copyright Office Circular 22
   www.loc.gov/copyright/circs/circ22.pdf
"Libraries as Creatures of Copyright: Why Librarians Care About Intellectual Property Law and Policy"
   archive.ala.org/washoff/copylib.html
Primer on the Digital Millennium
   www.arl.org/info/frn/copy/primer.html
U.S. Copyright Office (USCO)
   www.loc.gov/copyright/
WATCH
   tyler.hrc.utexas.edu
"When Works Pass into the Public Domain"
   www.unc.edu/~unclng/public-d.htm

The Copyright War

Copyright as we presently know it is dead. To be specific, copyright law as it currently stands is not only unenforceable, it is widely perceived by the general public as overly protective of publishers and, to a lesser extent, creators. Thus, even as copyright law is strengthened in the legislatures and the courts, it is dead to many in our society. Check the newspaper. Millions of music-loving people have violated existing copyright law not only with seeming impunity but also with no sense of wrongdoing (see "The Heavenly Jukebox" for some history). But this isn't just about Napster and MP3 files anymore; it's about any digital content—and since nearly all content can be digitized, that's just about everything. Copyright law is supposed to seek a balance between protecting the right of creators to be compensated for their work—thereby encouraging more creations—and the rights of the public to gain access to it. The public right of "fair use" counterbalances the rights of the author and/or publisher to receive recompense. (See "Libraries and the Fate of Digital Content" *Library Journal*, vol. 126, no. 11, June 15, 2001, pp. 44–47.)

Publishers don't get it

Copyright law has seen several major revisions just in the last twenty-five years. New technologies, such as audiocassette recorders and VCRs, have sent the "content industries" into the courts and legislatures to retain—or enhance—the rights they thought these technologies would destroy. In fact, those technologies have enhanced the capacity of the content industries to make money from intellectual property. The Internet doesn't appear to be different. Still, the content industries have followed historical precedent by trying to lobby and sue to protect their rights. Publishers are almost uniformly afraid that their revenue stream will dry up when their content is available for free on the Internet. Those who actually create the content (authors, artists, etc.) are more divided. More than twenty-five thousand musical groups—generally newer ones shut out of the big-label bottleneck—were happy to have their music available via Napster. Meanwhile, publishers such as National Academy Press have offered many full-text titles available online for free. Such access actually increases sales of the print counterpart, according to the NAP.

Now, scientists and scholars are increasingly demanding that research and scholarship be made available for free online. For example, the Public Library of Science, which began as a movement to force publishers to open up journal content for free online access after six months, soon grew into a publisher of scientific journals in its own right.

Few publishers seem to understand that simply because a certain journal article, book, or song can be freely downloaded doesn't mean that the very same people won't ever want to buy it. They may have already bought it, or they may want to sample it before buying it. Or they may want it in the particular format in which it is published (in a nicely printed volume, or with liner notes, etc.). People will pay for convenience, service, and quality guarantees. In apparent acknowledgment of this, the Public Library of Science offers a print subscription even though the online version is free.

New technologies equals more money

David Boies, the lawyer who took on Microsoft on behalf of the Department of Justice, cites both cable television and VCRs as technologies that increased revenues for the very industries that feared that such technologies would destroy their business (see "David Boies: The Wired Interview"). But perhaps no one has argued this point more forcefully than John Perry Barlow in his *Wired* article "The Next Economy of Ideas." "When you're selling [products], there is an undeniable relationship between scarcity and value," he wrote. "But in an economy of [ideas], the inverse applies. There is a relationship between familiarity and value. For ideas, fame is fortune." Starving authors and artists know this only too well. You need exposure to create value, and the more exposure the better. You should be so lucky that people distribute your work far and wide for free.

Indeed, people now have the technical capability to share content easily and anonymously with others—or access the content that others provide. I explained this in "Peer-to-Peer Networks: Promise & Peril" (in chapter 8). With Gnutella, or Free-Net, or other true peer-to-peer technologies, it's possible to share whatever you happen to have with anyone within range of your computer—and to do so anonymously, without fear of reprisal. Is this morally bankrupt? Perhaps, but consider this: the simple right to loan a book that you bought is now gone in the digital world, thanks to new legal protections sought by content providers. The National Research Council report entitled "The Digital Dilemma: Intellectual Property in the Information Age" puts it this way: "The information infrastructure has...the potential to demolish a careful balancing of public good and private interest that has emerged from the evolution of U.S. intellectual property law over the past two hundred years."

Let's recap. Publishers think that widespread digital distribution of their content for free will destroy their economic base. Meanwhile, evidence suggests the opposite. Creators benefit greatly from increased exposure, and they will see no revenue decline unless their publishers do. The only factor left in the equation is the public at large. Would they be any worse off if intellectual property were easier to locate, review, and buy?

Publishers fight back

But that isn't our problem. Our problem is that publishers will fight hard to deny others the right to distribute their content for free. In a sidebar to the "Heavenly Jukebox," international copyright expert P. Bernt Hugenholtz puts it this way:

> "In the old days of analog media (say, five years ago) the copyright monopoly was limited to acts of exploitation. In the digital environment, because acts of usage necessarily involve some sort of digital copying, the monopoly has expanded to include every conceivable act of transmitting, viewing, receiving, or simply using a copyrighted work."

We see this in the Digital Millennium Copyright Act (DMCA) and in the Uniform Computer Information Transactions Act

(UCITA). Libraries, the world's best protectors of copyright, will continue to uphold the letter and the spirit of the law even as it becomes more and more restrictive, and even as our professional associations protest.

As Rich Wiggins, senior information technologist in the Computer Laboratory at Michigan State University, wrote in a Web4Lib posting, "What worries me is a world in which millions ignore copyright, so it's dead for them, but libraries and librarians honor copyright judiciously."

Some disagree. Walt Crawford, commentator and information architect at the Research Libraries Group, Inc. (RLG), argued on Web4Lib that my position "overstates and oversimplifies the case considerably." However, he basically agrees that copyright law must be changed, mostly to regain the lost balance regarding digital information: "Copyright isn't dead—but (as law) it isn't a set of stone tablets either." Other Web4Lib contributors acknowledge that laws regarding digital copyright are too restrictive, and that many of the public at large get away with ignoring copyright.

Will we be irrelevant?

Meanwhile, the general public will increasingly consider us not only irrelevant (since they can download so much from the Internet) but also as a barrier to information access. To fight that, we will need to fight for the digital equivalents of the doctrines of "first sale" and "fair use" as if our lives depended on it. (See "Before Digitizing," in Chapter 11, for an explanation of these doctrines, and check the Web4Lib discussion.)

To some degree, our professional lives depend on copyright. If we allow publishers to restrict our rights to the information we have purchased so completely that we are unable to provide basic library services, we will have failed in our ability to fulfill our mission. Widespread civil disobedience may be our only ethical option.

Resources

"David Boies: The Wired Interview"
   www.wired.com/wired/archive/8.10/boies.html
 "The Digital Dilemma: Intellectual Property in the Digital Age"
   www.nap.edu/books/0309064996/html/
DMCA: The Digital Millennium Copyright Act, ALA
   www.ala.org/Content/NavigationMenu/Our_Association/Offices/
   ALA_Washington/Issues2/Copyright1/DMCA__The_Digital_Mille-
   nium_Copyright_Act/Default2515.htm
"The Heavenly Jukebox"
   www.theatlantic.com/issues/2000/09/mann.htm
"Libraries and the Fate of Digital Content," *Library Journal*, vol. 126, no
   11, June 15, 2001, pp.44-47.
National Academy Press
   www.nap.edu
"The Next Economy of Ideas"
   www.wired.com/wired/archive/8.10/download.html
Public Library of Science Core Principles
   plos.org/about/principles.html
Web4Lib (discussion of the topic)
   sunsite.berkeley.edu/Web4Lib/search/web4lib/index.cgi?query=copyright
   +death+computers &sort=swishrank

12

PRESERVATION

Time Is Not On Our Side:
The Challenge of Preserving Digital Materials

Coping With Disasters

Time Is Not On Our Side: The Challenge of Preserving Digital Materials

Digital libraries are sitting on a time bomb. Yes, libraries are already familiar with deteriorating materials, but digital libraries face an even graver threat. While digital library materials do not decay like old paper, they nonetheless may become unusable. And digital librarians have learned that solutions must be different as well.

The nature of the problem

"Preservation," Yale's Paul Conway writes in the report "Preservation in the Digital World," "is the acquisition, organization, and distribution of resources to prevent further deterioration or renew the usability of selected groups of materials." The currently accepted preservation formats are acid-free paper, microfilm, and photographic reproduction. None of these are digital. In fact, there is no accepted format for preserving digital information. Rather, Conway and others discuss preservation strategies, rather than formats. Preservation in the digital world, it turns out, has much more to do with long-term institutional commitment than with short-term fixes. Why? Because preserving digital information is not simply a matter of determining which format will resist physical deterioration the longest—although that is still one aspect of the problem. The more serious threat is technological obsolescence. Remember 8-track tapes? Technology marches on and leaves previous, outmoded technologies in the dust.

The key publication that outlines the dilemmas of digital preservation and the need for a strategy to deal with the problems is "Preserving Digital Information: Final Report and Recommendations," from the Research Libraries Group (RLG). This seminal report identifies the need for a migration strategy, so that as each technology reaches the end of its life, any information stored in that system or format can be brought forward into a new format or system. Migration therefore differs from the concept of refreshment, in which data from one deteriorating hard disk, CD-ROM, or tape, are copied to another.

As outlined in the RLG report, migration strategies can take several forms. One strategy is to change the storage medium, with the most extreme solution being to print the item on acid-free paper, thus losing its digital nature altogether. An alternative: change format, i.e., move documents in proprietary word processing formats such as WordPerfect to ASCII or SGML-encoded text.

Central repositories needed

Standards for document formats, data storage, and information interchange are needed to help libraries and archives build effective data migration strategies. Given the specialized nature of this kind of work, as well as the costs of migrating information from one format to another, we may need to cooperate in funding central repositories to take on these tasks. We already have models of similar kinds of cooperative efforts in organizations like the Center for Research Libraries (CRL), which collects rare items on behalf of a coalition of research libraries, and efforts such as JS-

TOR, which archives scholarly journals. A central digital archive could be supported by dues or fees from participating libraries and be reponsible for migrating the information it holds to prevent its loss through media decay or technological obsolescence.

The more complex the material...

So far I've allowed you to assume that we are talking mainly about relatively straightforward materials—digital books, journals, and word processing files. Such mainly textual materials can typically be migrated from one technology to another without a great deal of information loss. For example, many of us can move files from one word processing program to another without much loss of content or context.

But what about much more complex materials that were born digital, such as multimedia presentations? What happens when the hardware and software environment required to run such items is no longer available? What are the best preservation options for such complex items? We are just beginning to consider how these problems can be solved.

As may be apparent at this point, a viable digital preservation strategy requires institutional commitment and a structure of policies and procedures. "A Strategic Policy Framework for Creating and Preserving Digital Collections," produced for higher education institutions in the U.K., is a useful discussion of some of these issues. This framework identifies three main stages in the life of a digital resource (creation, management/preservation, and use) and appropriate roles and functions of different stakeholders (funding agencies, libraries and archives, etc.) in preserving the resource. For an example of a specific digital preservation policy statement, see the National Library of Australia's "Statement of Principles for the Preservation of and Long-Term Access to Australian Digital Objects."

Doing the job once

An essential aspect of any preservation program is quality, or the importance of doing the job once, and doing it right. This is particularly urgent for digital librarians, since standards for digital preservation are still being formulated. For example, what if you wish to digitize a deteriorating print item? Several years ago you would have probably scanned the item at 300 dots per inch (dpi). Since technology has both improved since then and dropped in price, you would now likely scan it at twice that resolution.

If there is this much difference in how an archival master is produced over just a few years, what does this bode for the long-term? What compromises in quality are we making now that we may regret later? It is just such issues that keep digital preservationists awake at night. While they are unable to get any sleep, one thing digital preservationists can ponder is how things have changed. With print materials, preservation is an endgame. Typically, you don't have to think much about preservation until the book begins to crumble, or the binding starts coming apart. With digital material, everyone wants a commitment up front that you will keep this material around for the foreseeable future.

Within minutes of announcing the opening of the Berkeley Digital Library SunSITE February 1, 1996, I had a return message from a colleague wondering what commitment we had to preserving the material we were making available. What is it about digital information that turns the preservation process on its head?

Perhaps we need to cultivate an open market for digital information: when a library or archive no longer wants to maintain a particular collection, it announces this fact widely. If no person or organization steps forward to rescue it from extinction, then it probably is not worth saving anyway. After all, although individual libraries should check to see if they have the only copy of a print item before throwing it away, there is no formal mechanism for doing so, nor any requirement to do so.

Digital preservation resources

Besides the publications mentioned above, a number of resources can help you explore these issues further. "Preserving Access to Digital Information" (PADI), hosted by the National Library of Australia, points to a number of bibliographies, discussion lists, journals, web sites, and more; the "What's New" section is a good way to keep current. The "Conservation Online" (CoOL) web site is also an important resource, although it covers the preservation of non-digital material as well. "RLG DigiNews" and the occasional "Conserve O Gram" from the National Park Service are also useful publications. Organizations active in this issue include the Commission on Preservation and Access (CPA) and the Digital Library Federation (DLF), both of which are under the umbrella of the Council on Library Information and Resources (CLIR).

Resources

Center for Research Libraries
  www.crl.uchicago.edu
Conservation Online
  palimpsest.stanford.edu
Conserve O Grams
  www.cr.nps.gov/museum/publications/conserveogram/conserv.html
Council on Library Information and Resources (CLIR)
  www.clir.org
Digital Library Federation
  www.diglib.org
JSTOR
  www.jstor.org
Preservation in the Digital World
  www.clir.org/pubs/abstract/pub62.html
Preserving Access to Digital Information (PADI)
  www.nla.gov.au/padi/
Preserving Digital Information: Final Report and Recommendations
  www.rlg.org/ArchTF/
RGL DigiNews
  www.rlg.org/preserv/diginews/
Statement of Principles for the Preservation of and Long-Term Access to-
  Australian Digital Objects
  www.nla.gov.au/preserve/digital/princ.html
A Strategic Policy Framework for Creating and Preserving Digital Collections
  ahds.ac.uk/strategic.htm

Coping With Disasters

Now that we've all witnessed a disaster that beggars the imagination (the terrorist acts of September 11, 2001), preventing disaster seems not only an appropriate topic, but an imperative one. As Mike Handy, acting director of information technology services for the Library of Congress, said after September 11, "Until recently, our planning efforts have assumed the most significant threats to be from accidental disruptions such as natural calamity, fire, power failure, etc. Obviously, now our assumptions include previously unimaginable possibilities." Although clearly the most unthinkable disaster would involve the loss of life or injury to library users and staff, that type of disaster planning is outside the scope of this column. Rather, I will consider what can be done to protect your digital library services and collections from the many disasters—whether they be outrageous or minor—that may befall those who do not prepare. Through planning and preparation, we can help prevent disasters from happening, or to minimize the damage if they do.

Prevention

"An ounce of prevention is worth a pound of cure" remains a valuable aphorism for disaster prevention. Everything that you can reasonably do to avoid or lessen the impact of disasters by planning ahead of time will be well worth your time, effort, and resources. For digital systems, the classic prevention technique is an effective protection system. Effective computer protection systems are constructed in layers.

The first layer is the disk itself—or, more accurately, the way in which data are stored on the disk. The most secure way to store data on hard disks is by using RAID technology. RAID, an acronym for Redundant Array of Inexpensive (or Independent) Disks, specifies various methods of storing data that are optimized for different requirements. For example, if you want to provide a reasonable level of performance while achieving a moderate level of protection, you may choose a less-protective level of RAID (for example, RAID Level 1, which is simply "mirroring"—creating—another complete copy of the data). If, on the other hand, protection is more important than response time, then a more protective level of RAID may be selected. For example, Level 5 distributes both the data and information required to recover it across several physical disks, which can protect you from the failure of multiple drives.

Other layers of protection

The second layer of protection includes such strategies as uninterruptable power supplies (which can prevent disk drive damage in power failures), fire extinguisher systems, alarm systems, and other methods for securing the computer disks (or the area where they are kept).

The third layer entails making copies of the data—backing it up. The typical computer backup system copies the data you want to secure to another disk, tape, or other digital medium. This backup can be incremental (wherein only changed files are backed up), or complete. For better protection, the second copy should be stored at a location distant from the first (and I mean really distant—the farther the better, considering the impact of disasters like earthquakes and hurricanes). A common technique for locating data close to where it is needed can also serve as a default backup system. Called "mirroring," this technique was developed primarily in response to slow or costly Internet connections. For example, those in Australia must pay a per-byte charge for overseas Internet traffic. Therefore, it's helpful for them to copy, or mirror, popular sites locally. Not only can this serve as a default backup, but it can also be essential in emergencies such that users can be shunted from the main site to the mirror location.

What might be considered the logical endpoint of this technique is represented by a preservation scheme advanced by Stanford University. Called Lots of Copies Keep Stuff Safe (LOCKSS), the strategy employs a large pool of interconnected and physically distant computers that constantly share copies of each computer's data. If any single computer crashes, the data it contained could be recovered from other computers still online. The system is designed to use standard-issue PCs, even those that would be too underpowered to run standard office applications (a typical LOCKSS installation would only require something like a PC with a 100Mhz Pentium chip with 32MB of RAM, and one or two large disks).

Whether LOCKSS is used or not, since the price of hard disk storage is so cheap (you can find disk drives for pennies to the gigabyte, and prices continue to drop), there is no logical reason for not creating multiple redundant copies of critical data. This can (and should) be as simple as setting up a script to copy all of your data to additional hard drives each night. If those drives are physically distant—which the Internet enables easily—it is even better.

Emergency response & recovery

Good preparation includes knowing what you will do in the middle of an emergency. One of the quickest and easiest ways to solve an emergency situation is to route users to a mirror (see above). If, for example, www.whatever.org goes down, that domain name can quickly be assigned to a host computer that has a mirror. Once this change propagates to the Internet routing system (which can take from a few hours to a few days), users will be none the wiser that they are going to a different physical location, since the domain name remains unchanged.

If you're not lucky enough to have a mirror, you will need to do something else. What you do will depend on how essential your operation is to those who matter. If your data are important but not essential, then hang tight until the emergency passes, and then you can move on to the "recovery" stage. If your systems must be constantly responsive, then, one hopes, you will have determined ahead of time how you will cope. Again, planning is everything.

Once the emergency has passed, you should know what steps must be taken to get everything back up and functioning. Specifically, you should know in advance how to install new hardware and software, retrieve data from a backup system, and get everything back online. Here you will discover just how well (or poorly) you have prepared. Those who have planned well will find this process to be quick and smooth, while those who haven't will find it time-consuming and difficult.

Run with the big boys

If you have data you can't afford to lose, you can't afford to be without a disaster plan. The plan should include aspects dealing with prevention, emergencies, and recovery. Luckily, there is little to prevent small libraries from having a disaster plan similar to that of the Library of Congress, which uses many of the techniques outlined here. If you don't know where to begin, start with the Federal Emergency Management Administration's *"Emergency Management* Guide for Business & Industry," which will guide you through the process of making a plan that will get you through just about anything—except perhaps the unimaginable.

Resources

Disaster Recovery Journal's Glossary
    www.drj.com/glossary/drjglossary.html
Emergency Management Guide for Business & Industry
    www.fema.gov/library/bizindex.shtm
Keeping Memory Alive: Practices for Preserving Content at the National
    Digital Library Program of the Library of Congress
    www.rlg.org/preserv/diginews/diginews4-3.html
LOCKSS
    lockss.stanford.edu
Public Library Association Tech Note: Disaster Planning for Computers
    and Networks
    www.ala.org/Content/NavigationMenu/PLA/Publications_and_Reports/
    Tech_Notes/Disaster_Planning.htm

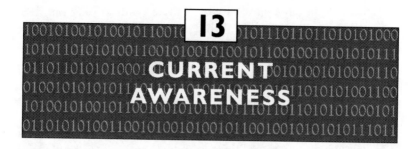

13

CURRENT AWARENESS

Feed Your Head: Keeping Up By Using RSS

Learning and Retooling

Strategies for Keeping Current

Feed Your Head: Keeping Up By Using RSS

Keeping up has never been easy, although we can probably be forgiven if we think it is harder today. From print magazines to journals, from electronic discussion lists to web logs, there seems to be more sources of information than ever. Wouldn't it be nice if you could filter all this stuff and receive brief notes for what interests you?

The idea of a current awareness service is nothing new. What is new is that recent web-based technologies have made it easier to discover and subscribe to these services, and to create and manage them. But the potential for these technologies is not limited to individual notification. They are increasingly used for other functions, such as automatically updating web sites.

How it works

The linchpin technology is RSS, variously described as "RDF Site Summary" (referring to the Resource Description Framework),

"Rich Site Summary," and "Really Simple Syndication." But RSS, as used on most sites, has nothing to do with RDF. It is a very simple XML syntax for describing a "channel," or "feed," of information that consists of "items" (e.g., news items) with titles and URLs.

In fact, that's just about the whole thing. Each channel is required to have a "title," a "link" (URL), and a "description." Other tags are optional (for the complete spec, see RSS 2.0). Each channel has one or more items, of which only a title or description is mandatory, although most items typically have a title, link, and description (which is often a commentary rather than true description). There are optional fields for each item, but simplicity in production and use is one of its strong points.

Feeds are typically read through an "aggregator," which allows the information to be presented in a variety of ways. Feeds can be either web-based or special client software. Client software is available for all platforms, and Peter Scott's web page "RSS Readers" lists the options. With client software you can subscribe to feeds and have them automatically updated when starting up the client. Steven Cohen's article "RSS for Non-Techie Librarians" is a good introduction to readers and their uses. Web-based aggregators do not require the downloading of special client software, but options for interacting with the feeds are fewer.

Finding and searching

So how do you find feeds that interest you? One way is by serendipity, which may happen when visiting a web site and seeing an orange "XML" or "RSS" button placed on the page—an indication that an RSS feed is available. But a more systematic way is to visit one or more web-based aggregators—no client software required—that bring together a variety of feeds. A web-based aggregator useful for librarians is LIS Feeds, which offers a simple-to-use web-based interface for reading feeds from library-related sources. General purpose aggregators include sites like Newsisfree.com and syndic8.com. One good way to find feeds is to use feed searching sites to search your favorite topics, then look for sites with information of interest.

You can search feeds at Newsisfree.com and Feedster.com, which act in a similar way to Google. Apparently, Feedster.com also indexes Newsisfree.com, since hits from that site appear as well. The search results include a link to the feed that provides the news item, and options to see all items from that feed, or just the links and titles, or the raw RSS.

Roll your own

Where it gets really interesting is in using RSS to update web sites automatically. Jonathan Eisenzopf, in "Making Headlines with RSS," offers a Perl module for both maintaining and using (as in a web site) RSS feeds (XML::RSS, dependent upon XML::Parser). Imagine creating an RSS feed of new books arriving at your library. You could allow users to subscribe to this feed and use it to highlight new books on the front page of your web site. Once the basic Perl (or PHP, or other scripting language) is in place, you sit back and do nothing. Now that's my kind of assignment!

Of course, creating your own RSS has potential problems. But that is what validators are for. These software programs—often available through web submission—check your syntax for errors. RSS is no different; there is a web site to make sure your RSS is valid according to the specification (see the "RSS Validator"). RSS is a low-overhead way to provide current awareness services within a digital library environment. The XML syntax is brain-dead easy, while the software is freely available. We are just beginning to explore how to integrate it into library services.

Resources

Introduction to RSS
   www.webreference.com/authoring/languages/xml/rss/intro/
LIS Feeds
   www.lisfeeds.com
Making Headlines with RSS
   www.newarchitectmag.com/archives/2000/02/eisenzopf/
RSS 2.0
   blogs.law.harvard.edu/tech/rss/
RSS for Non-Techie Librarians
   www.llrx.com/features/rssforlibrarians.htm

RSS Readers
   www.lights.com/weblogs/rss.html
RSS Validator
   aggregator.userland.com/validator

Learning and Retooling

Digital librarianship differs from any previous type of librarianship. Sure, you still select, acquire, organize, provide access, and preserve, but these basic library activities are completely different in the digital realm. The acts of selecting, acquiring, and organizing digital collections bear almost no resemblance to the same activities for print. Providing access to these materials is also completely different. There are no doors to keep open, only servers to "keep up." And it hardly requires mentioning that preservation of digital collections presents some particular and new problems.

If everything is so different, what if you must manage a digital library project and you left library school more than two years ago? You learn. You retool. You ask for guidance from others who are doing it. You visit libraries where they are doing similar projects. You take courses, or attend workshops or institutes.

Following are some resources that may get you started. Learning styles vary considerably. Some people learn best in a formal classroom situation, while others enjoy trial and error, referring to books as needed, and pursuing the topic on their own. Your own learning style will indicate the appropriate instructional technique.

Online Resources

As you might imagine, several online resources can be used to learn more about digital library activities. Online tutorials or instructional resources can take the place of, or enhance, classroom learning. Project documentation can provide real-world examples of how others plan and manage their projects. Online discussions can be particularly helpful when you have a question that hasn't been addressed in print or online.

DIGLIB. DIGLIB is the electronic discussion list of digital library issues and the emerging specialty of digital librarianship. Though a low-volume list, it is an important source of conference announcements, new digital library projects, and digital library issues.

Moving Theory Into Practice: Digital Imaging Tutorial. This online tutorial by the Cornell Department of Preservation and Conservation is exceptional in both its easy-to-understand presentation style and its authoritative and professional perspective. Here you are learning from the best, but in a way that is so easy you'll hardly realize how much you are picking up. A very good site, by those who know.

Project documentation. There is probably no collection of publicly accessible digital objects larger than the Library of Congress' site "Building Digital Collections: Technical Information and Background Papers." The sheer size of the Library's digital collections would be significant in itself, but the collections have also been organized and digitized with careful thought and planning. Luckily, much of the best thinking from those involved with these projects is available online in the form of white papers and technical descriptions.

Courses or workshops

You may prefer to take a formal course rather than use self-paced tutorials. There are many resources for such classes, from professional organizations or commercial training companies to community colleges and university extension programs. It may be hard to find a course that focuses on digital library issues per se, though some library schools offer them. If you can't find such a course, instead you may need to study specific software programs (such as Adobe Photoshop), programming languages (like Java or Perl), or technologies (for example, the Internet). Check your local community college or university. Commercial training companies may often be found in the Yellow Pages under "Computer Training." Local professional organizations may also offer one-day workshops, which maybe either practical, hands-on affairs, or theoretical lectures.

Digital Imaging for Libraries and Archives. This occasional week-long workshop by Cornell University Library Department of Preservation and Conservation aims to provide librarians, archivists, curators, and others with the means to develop a baseline knowledge about the use of digital image technology, from conversion to presentation to preservation. The training focuses on the reformatting of paper and film-based library and archival materials, and on the use of digital images in a networked environment. Cornell is presently working on a new workshop, *Digital Preservation Management: Implementing Short-Term Strategies for Long-Term Problems.*

LITA Regional Institutes. The Library Information and Technology Association sponsors a variety of institutes around the U.S. on issues related to digital librarianship.

The School for Scanning. Organized by the NorthEast Document Conservation Center, this occasionally held workshop brings together top people in the fields of digital libraries, museums, and archives. Over three days, the three hundred or more attendees listen to lectures, see demonstrations, and interact with faculty and fellow participants. For information on when and where the next School for Scanning will be held, see the NEDCC web site.

UK Office of Library Networking. UKOLN has offered workshops on such hot digital library topics as metadata, Z39.50, managing web systems, and other topics.

Site visits

Sometimes there is no substitute for visiting a digital library project in person. By talking with staff, you can discover issues, problems, and solutions before they make it into the published literature. You also may get your particular questions addressed, perhaps more candidly than in a formal presentation. For ideas on where to visit, see IFLA's Digital Libraries: Resources and Projects.

Internships

Internships can be a valuable way to gain experience. In the summer of 1996, the UC Berkeley Library accepted an intern (Kirk

Hastings) from the School of Library and Information Studies at San Jose State. His project was to digitize, organize, and make web-accessible a collection of material by and about Jack London. The result is the Jack London Collection, one of the most popular sites on the Berkeley Digital Library SunSITE. Kirk went on to make significant contributions to digital projects at the University of Virginia and the California Digital Library.

Resources

Building Digital Collections: Background Papers and Technical Information
    memory.loc.gov/ammem/ftpfiles.html
Digital Imaging for Libraries and Archives
    www.library.cornell.edu/preservation/workshop/
Digital Libraries: Resources and Projects
    www.ifla.org/II/diglib.htm
Digital Preservation Management: Implementing Short-Term Strategies for
    Long-Term Problems
    www.library.cornell.edu/iris/dpworkshop/
DIGLIB Electronic Discussion
    www.ifla.org/II/lists/diglib.htm
The Jack London Collection
    sunsite.berkeley.edu/London/
LITA Regional Institutes
    www.lita.org/institut/
Moving Theory Into Practice: Digital Imaging Tutorial
    www.library.cornell.edu/preservation/tutorial/
NorthEast Document Conservation Center
    www.nedcc.org
UK Office of Library Networking Events
    www.ukoln.ac.uk/events/

Strategies for Keeping Current

Even as technology makes it easier for us to gather information, the explosion of technology makes it harder than ever to keep up. Ten years ago, most libraries weren't on the web. XML was born only five years ago. Yet both technologies are now key pieces of the foundational infrastructure of nearly every major library. But do the math: if you exited library school prior to 1993, you're toast—unless you've kept up. Awareness of new technologies and what they have to offer is one thing, but taking that awareness to the level of knowledge—and eventually experience—is an even greater challenge. How do we maximize the little time we have for professional development?

Before I share some strategies, let's acknowledge that it takes time, effort, and commitment to keep current. Depending on your "tech" comfort level, it may involve a good deal of tolerance as well. But if you want to use current information technologies to address the problems and opportunities that your library faces, then you must quit complaining, and lock and load.

Learn as you breathe

Learn all the time without even thinking about it. We are born to learn, but somewhere along the way many of us pick up the idea that we must be taught in order to learn. We think that if someone doesn't stand up in front of us and talk to us using either a chalkboard or PowerPoint slides, we cannot learn. We must regain our sense of wonder, and thus, our desire to learn.

Make strategic learning decisions

Even if you are learning all the time, you can't learn everything. Luckily, there are many things that you can safely ignore. We do this all the time without thinking much about it, but professionally, it can be dangerous to blow things off without first doing some investigation. When you hear about a new technology or issue, take a quick look and categorize it. My categories are "trash" (not worth my time), "monitor" (still in distant early warning phase, can be safely ignored for now), "dabble" (what's this about?), and "need to know" (I can use it in my job, now). Revisit such categories as conditions dictate.

Use professional filters

Consider the old-fashioned, pre-web kind of filters: people who make decisions about what is important. Today these include current awareness services, such as Current Cites, the Research Libraries Group's ShelfLife, and portals like Steven Bell's Keeping Up, and LIS Feeds (which provides access to a variety of library-related, RSS-syndicated, current awareness services—also known as web logs). They are all produced by professional colleagues who select items of interest and provide context and commentary.

Quiz trusted colleagues

As hard as you try, it's unlikely that you'll ever know as much about most technical topics as some of your colleagues. If you have passing (or better) acquaintance with your local technology experts, ask them key questions. What is essential to know about this technology? Is it important now, in the near-term, further into the future, or possibly never? What are the, say, three things this technology does or enables that I should know?

Learn by doing

Build prototypes and make mistakes. Prototypes can provide a better way to elicit feedback than a description ever could. Simply creating a "smoke and mirrors" prototype of HTML pages that mimics the system you're after can be much better than trying to explain how it should work. It is trite but true that you can learn a lot from your own mistakes.

Be responsible

You are accountable for your own learning. No one is more responsible for your professional development than you. Don't expect the organization that hired you to make sure you are developing as a professional.

Take the necessary time

Your place of employment owes you the time and training to do the tasks at hand, unless you were hired explicitly for specific knowledge and skills. Beyond the requirements of the job, you must heed your calling as a librarian and information professional. To be effective in our profession you must constantly learn and retool. Accept that change is constant, and constant learning is the only reasonable response. Gone are the days (if they ever existed) when everything you need to know about being a librarian could be learned in library school. Learn to thrive on change. Anticipate it, smell it out, and chase after it. If you do this well enough, instead of being the victim of change, you will be its agent.

And you will be able to mold change to serve your public better.

Resources

Current Cites
    sunsite.Berkeley.edu/CurrentCites/
Keeping Up Web Site
    staff.philau.edu/bells/keepup/
LIS Feeds
    www.lisfeeds.com
ShelfLife
    www.rlg.org/shelflife/

A
DIGITAL LIBRARIES
(by Date)

DATE	TITLE	CHAPTER
11/15/97	Digital Potential and Pitfalls	Chapter 1. Introduction
12/1/97	The Grand Challenges	Chapter 1. Introduction
1/1/98	The Banal Barriers	Chapter 1. Introduction
2/15/98	The Most Important Management Decision: Hiring Staff for the New Millennium	Chapter 7. Organization & Staffing
3/15/98	Learning and Retooling	Chapter 13. Current Awareness
4/15/98	Twenty-first Century Cataloging	Chapter 4. Cataloging and Classification
5/15/98	Reality Check: Shanghai Surprise	Chapter 10. Case Studies
6/15/98	Infrastructure	Chapter 8. Technology and Infrastructure
7/1/98	Interoperability: The Holy Grail	Chapter 9. Standards and Interoperability
8/1/98	So Much to Digitize, So Little Time (and Money)	Chapter 2. Acquisition and Digitization
9/15/98	In-House Digitizing Options	Chapter 2. Acquisition and Digitization
10/15/98	The Art and Science of Digital Bibliography	Chapter 4. Cataloging and Classification
11/15/98	The Print Perplex: Building the Future Catalog	Chapter 4. Cataloging and Classification
12/1/98	Everything You Always Wanted to Know About Digital Imaging But Were Afraid to Ask	Chapter 2. Acquisition and Digitization
1/1/99	Skills for the New Millennium	Chapter 7. Organization and Staffing

DATE	TITLE	CHAPTER
2/15/99	Beyond GIF and JPEG: New Digital Image Technologies	Chapter 8. Technology and Infrastructure
3/15/99	Time Is Not On Our Side: The Challenge of Preserving Digital Materials	Chapter 12. Preservation
4/15/99	Where the Rubber Meets the Road	Chapter 5. Access
5/15/99	The Purpose of Digital Capture: Artifact or Intellectual Content?	Chapter 2. Acquisition & Digitization
6/15/99	Human and Humane Assistance	Chapter 6. Public Service
7/1/99	Personalizing the Digital Library	Chapter 5. Access
8/1/99	Before Digitizing	Chapter 11. Copyright and Intellectual Property Rights
9/15/99	Outsourcing Digitization	Chapter 2. Acquisition and Digitization
10/15/99	User Interface Design: Some Guiding Principles	Chapter 5. Access
11/15/99	I Know This Much Is True	Chapter 8. Technology and Infrastructure
12/1/99	A Database for Every Need	Chapter 8. Technology and Infrastructure
1/1/00	The Role of Open Source Software	Chapter 8. Technology and Infrastructure
2/15/00	Open Archives: A Key Convergence	Chapter 9. Standards and Interoperability
3/15/00	The Digital Library Federation	Chapter 1. Introduction
4/15/00	Technology Decision-Making: A Guide for the Perplexed	Chapter 8. Technology and Infrastructure
5/15/00	Electronic Theses and Dissertations: Progress?	Chapter 3. Building Collections
6/15/00	Beg, Buy, Borrow, License, or Steal	Chapter 2. Acquisition & Digitization
8/1/00	The Emerging Role of E-Books	Chapter 3. Building Collections
9/15/00	Peer-to-Peer Networks: Promise and Peril	Chapter 8. Technology and Infrastructure
10/15/00	Bringing Out the Dead (Technologies)	Chapter 8. Technology and Infrastructure
11/15/00	Selecting Collections to Digitize	Chapter 2. Acquisition and Digitization

DATE	TITLE	CHAPTER
12/1/00	Co-Branding and Libraries	Chapter 6. Public Service
1/1/01	Avoiding Unintended Consequences	Chapter 8. Technology and Infrastructure
2/15/01	Different Paths to Interoperability	Chapter 9. Standards and Interoperability
3/15/01	XML: The Digital Library Hammer	Chapter 8. Technology and Infrastructure
4/15/01	Building Agile Organizations	Chapter 7. Organization and Staffing
5/15/01	Honoring Technical Staff	Chapter 7. Organization and Staffing
6/15/01	The Copyright War	Chapter 11. Copyright and Intellectual Property
7/1/01	The $64,000 Question	Chapter 9. Standards and Interoperability
8/15/01	The Digital Library Divide	Chapter 1. Introduction
9/15/01	The Other E-Books	Chapter 3. Building Collections
10/15/01	Cross-Database Search: One-Stop Shopping	Chapter 5. Access
11/15/01	Coping With Disasters	Chapter 12. Preservation
12/15/01	The Convenience Catastrophe	Chapter 5. Access
1/15/02	The Consequences of Cataloging	Chapter 4. Cataloging and Classification
2/15/02	Factoring In the Only Constant	Chapter 7. Organization and Staffing
3/15/02	The Digital Librarian Shortage	Chapter 7. Organization and Staffing
4/15/02	Metadata As If Libraries Depended On It	Chapter 4. Cataloging and Classification
5/15/02	The Importance of Being Granular	Chapter 4. Cataloging & Classification
6/15/02	The Engines of Innovation	Chapter 7. Organization & Staffing
7/15/02	What To Know About Web Services	Chapter 9. Standards and Interoperability
8/15/02	Free As a Bird: Wireless Networking Libraries	Chapter 8. Technology and Infrastructure

DATE	TITLE	CHAPTER
9/15/02	Institutional Repositories	Chapter 3. Building Collections
10/15/02	MARC Must Die	Chapter 4. Cataloging and Classification
11/15/02	MARC Exit Strategies	Chapter 4. Cataloging and Classification
1/15/03	Revisiting Digital Reference	Chapter 6. Public Service
2/15/03	Library Catalogs: The Wrong Solution	Chapter 5. Access
3/15/03	Science Portals	Chapter 10. Case Studies
4/15/03	Not Your Mother's Union Catalog	Chapter 5. Access
5/15/03	Feed Your Head: Keeping Up By Using RSS	Chapter 13. Current Awareness
6/15/03	The Right Solution: Federated Search Tools	Chapter 5. Access
7/15/03	Patriotism As If Our Constitution Matters	Chapter 6. Public Service
8/15/03	Open Source Goes Mainstream	Chapter 8. Technology and Infrastructure
9/15/03	Strategies for Keeping Current	Chapter 13. Current Awareness
9/15/03	Open Access Journals	Chapter 3. Building Collections

B

DIGITAL LIBRARIES (by Title)

DATE	TITLE	CHAPTER
7/1/01	The $64,000 Question	Chapter 9. Standards and Interoperability
4/15/98	Twenty-first Century Cataloging	Chapter 4. Cataloging and Classification
4/15/99	Where the Rubber Meets the Road	Chapter 5. Access
5/15/00	Electronic Theses and Dissertations: Progress?	Chapter 3. Building Collections
10/15/98	The Art and Science of Digital Bibliography	Chapter 4. Cataloging and Classification
1/1/01	Avoiding Unintended Consequences	Chapter 8. Technology and Infrastructure
1/1/98	The Banal Barriers	Chapter 1. Introduction
8/1/99	Before Digitizing	Chapter 11. Copyright and Intellectual Property Rights
6/15/00	Beg, Buy, Borrow, License, or Steal	Chapter 2. Acquisition and Digitization
2/15/99	Beyond GIF and JPEG: New Digital Image Technologies	Chapter 8. Technology and Infrastructure
10/15/00	Bringing Out the Dead (Technologies)	Chapter 8. Technology and Infrastructure
4/15/01	Building Agile Organizations	Chapter 7. Organization and Staffing
12/1/00	Co-Branding and Libraries	Chapter 6. Public Service
1/15/02	The Consequences of Cataloging	Chapter 4. Cataloging and Classification
12/15/01	The Convenience Catastrophe	Chapter 5. Access
11/15/01	Coping With Disasters	Chapter 12. Preservation

DATE	TITLE	CHAPTER
6/15/01	The Copyright War	Chapter 11. Copyright and Intellectual Property Rights
10/15/01	Cross-Database Search: One-Stop Shopping	Chapter 5. Access
12/1/99	A Database for Every Need	Chapter 8. Technology and Infrastructure
2/15/01	Different Paths to Interoperability	Chapter 9. Standards and Interoperability
3/15/02	The Digital Librarian Shortage	Chapter 7. Organization and Staffing
8/15/01	The Digital Library Divide	Chapter 1. Introduction
3/15/00	The Digital Library Federation	Chapter 1. Introduction
11/15/97	Digital Potential and Pitfalls	Chapter 1. Introduction
8/1/00	The Emerging Role of E-Books	Chapter 3. Building Collections
6/15/02	The Engines of Innovation	Chapter 7. Organization and Staffing
12/1/98	Everything You Always Wanted to Know About Digital Imaging But Were Afraid to Ask	Chapter 2. Acquisition and Digitization
2/15/02	Factoring In the Only Constant	Chapter 7. Organization and Staffing
5/15/03	Feed Your Head: Keeping Up By Using RSS	Chapter 13. Current Awareness
8/15/02	Free As a Bird: Wireless Networking Libraries	Chapter 8. Technology and Infrastructure
12/1/97	The Grand Challenges	Chapter 1. Introduction
5/15/01	Honoring Technical Staff	Chapter 7. Organization and Staffing
6/15/99	Human and Humane Assistance	Chapter 6. Public Service
11/15/99	I Know This Much Is True	Chapter 8. Technology and Infrastructure
5/15/02	The Importance of Being Granular	Chapter 4. Cataloging and Classification
6/15/98	Infrastructure	Chapter 8. Technology and Infrastructure

INDEX

Index to come